WHEN
MONEY
IS THE
DRUG

WHEN MONEY IS THE DRUG

THE COMPULSION FOR CREDIT, CASH, AND CHRONIC DEBT

DONNA BOUNDY

HarperSanFrancisco
A Division of HarperCollinsPublishers

FIRST EDITION

Library of Congress Cataloging-in-Publication Data
Boundy, Donna
When money is the drug : the compulsion for credit, cash,
and chronic debt / Donna Boundy. — 1st ed.
p. cm.
Includes bibliographical references (p.   )
ISBN 0-06-250212-3 (acid-free paper)
1. Money—Psychological aspects.   2. Compulsive shopping.
I. Title.
RC569.5.M66B68   1993
616.85'227—dc20   92-56426
                                                            CIP

93 94 95 96 97 ❖ HAD 10 9 8 7 6 5 4 3 2 1

This edition is printed on acid-free paper that meets the American National Standards Institute Z39.48 Standard.

For LEONA
because good friends are
so much a part of
true wealth

CONTENTS

ACKNOWLEDGMENTS

I AM GRATEFUL to the many people who shared with me their private struggles with the alchemical substance of money. Their experiences and insights greatly enriched the text.

A heartfelt thanks goes also to Harris Breiman, Erica Lindsay, and Francesca Tanksley for reading early drafts and providing me with invaluable feedback and ideas, many of which helped to shape both the letter and spirit of this material.

In addition, I would like to acknowledge Laura Kaplan, Carlos Marsero, Ann Marie Amodeo, Judy Fischetti, The Woodstock Library, Tom Colello, Bart Friedman, K. J. McIntyre, Susan Ray, Cary Bayer, Collette Dowling, Marcia Shepard, Marilyn Griffith, Marijo Mallon, Christina Stack, Elena Zang, Terry Tomlinson, and my healing circle of friends. Each of you has played an important role in helping me to complete this book. I especially want to recognize my mother, Esther Boundy, for her unflagging support, courage, and willingness to grow.

Finally, I wish to thank my agent, Meredith Bernstein, for believing in this project from the beginning and my editor, Barbara Moulton, for helping to shape the manuscript in important ways.

NOTES TO THE READER

GIVEN THE GENDER limitations of the English language, it is a challenge to write without a gender bias. Every time we refer to an indefinite person (such as "the compulsive spender") we are forced to choose between using the masculine pronoun *he*, the feminine pronoun *she*, the awkward and cumbersome combination *he or she*, or the distracting *s/he*. The course taken in this book is to alternate pronouns. With this approach, it is hoped that both male and female readers will benefit from the material presented—because money addiction knows no gender bias.

You will notice that the word *debt* is often used in this book as a verb, *to debt*. For example, there are frequent references to "compulsive debting." This is intentional, as it is the author's belief that money disorders involving the compulsive use of credit go beyond the scope of the grammatically correct term *to borrow*. Author Jerrold Mundis first coined the use of *debt* as a verb in his landmark book on recovery in 1988. As he noted, such usage helps distinguish the compulsive use of credit from more innocuous forms of borrowing.

The personal stories included in this book are largely composites of various individuals. In all cases, names and identifying details have been changed to protect anonymity.

WHEN MONEY IS THE DRUG

INTRODUCTION

I FIRST BEGAN TO SUSPECT there was something self-defeating in the way I handled money when, in my early thirties, I began to take inventory of where I'd been and where I was going. The evidence that I had some kind of "money problem" had been accumulating for some time, and I could no longer ignore it. The way I handled money just seemed to be *different* from the way most other people I knew did. Even others who worked in low-paying fields like mine didn't seem to struggle the same way, and certain routines I went through were growing suspiciously repetitive:

- Writing checks against insufficient funds, then suffering fear and anxiety while I tried to cover them in the next few days.
- Seeing the bounced check notices come in the mail and not even opening them.
- Wondering when I returned home at night whether the electricity would be off because I hadn't responded to the final, *final* notice before the cutoff date.
- Avoiding calls from creditors, or making arrangements for repayment I knew I'd never be able to keep, feeling that I couldn't say no to them.
- Depositing my tax refund in a new savings account each year, determined to finally have a cushion, only to draw it out within a few weeks to buy something—anything.

- Getting money from the automated teller machine even when I knew I'd written checks against the balance shown that hadn't cleared yet.
- Managing to lose anything I had of value, or setting myself up to have it stolen.
- Rummaging through my purse for spare change to put gas in my car, always running on empty.
- Sending off minimum payments on my credit cards, fully believing I was keeping "current." (Paying only the fifteen-dollar minimum each month, a five-hundred-dollar couch wound up costing me nearly a thousand dollars.)
- "Having to" shop on the way home from my stressful job, even though I could ill afford to buy anything; winding my way through the stores so that all the uncomfortable feelings inside of me were temporarily suspended.
- Always thinking ahead to how I could get out of my present squeeze, feeling inordinate relief when the finance company approved another loan, never even asking what the interest rate was.
- Having little to show for it all. Driving an old wreck of a car that I felt embarrassed about and that overheated in traffic jams; working at a job I found totally draining; needing dental and medical care and not getting it, because somehow there was never money for that.

It may be true that some of my money problems were related to the fact that the social services field in which I worked was notoriously underpaid, that social work is considered a "woman's field" and women are typically paid less than men. But that didn't explain the self-destructive patterns. I knew in my heart that to blame my money habits solely on society was to miss both a painful truth and a chance to change. Other people with little money didn't do some of the things I did, so I had to question what was going on. It occurred to me that just as some people develop dysfunctional ways of eating and are said to have eating disorders, I seemed to have developed a dysfunctional pattern with money. I wondered, "Could there be such a thing as *money disorders?*"

By this time in my life, I'd already completed a five-year stint of psychotherapy, which was enormously helpful to me in gaining self-esteem, recovering from a depression, and avoiding unhealthy relationships. Yet oddly enough, my therapist and I had never once discussed money. I'd managed to bounce only one or two checks to him in the five years, pretending I'd made an error in my math. I didn't want to alert him to this secret of mine, and he didn't pursue the subject. Until recently, few therapists had much awareness of money disorders. Besides, we live in a culture that—in the 1970s and 1980s at least—accepted compulsive spending and borrowing as normal.

One night around this time, I was out to dinner with a friend (I would never say "I can't afford it," even when I couldn't). After dinner, the conversation turned to money. We were trying to decide which one of us would put it on her credit card, when somehow it came out that neither one of us had any cash, and we were both over the limits on our cards. Both of us had planned to charge it and take our chances that the restaurant wouldn't phone the credit card company for approval.

My friend, a bright, respected administrator for a national philanthropic organization, earned an excellent salary, lived in a charming home, and dressed in style. But, she confided to me that night, not only was she broke, but her checking account had just been attached by the state for nonpayment of income taxes. She described how humiliated she had been when the teller told her she couldn't draw any money out of her own account, how she had nearly passed out in the bank. Here we were, two seemingly competent, professional women who led a double life—the one others saw, and the one only we and our creditors knew about. Cautiously at first, then with the intensity of a dam bursting, we shared our secret for the first time, without covering up. So relieved were we to find someone else who understood how painful money madness can be, the words tumbled out.

I have forgotten now whose card we put the dinner on that night, but that conversation proved to be the starting point of my money recovery. It was the first time I admitted to myself and to someone else that things were out of control, that there really were some negative consequences, that it hurt and I deserved better. That night I knew I had a money disorder; I just didn't have a name for it.

In the months that followed that breakthrough, both my friend and I sought out a support group for people with debt problems. I didn't always think I needed it, and I didn't always attend. I hated everyone else I met at those meetings and convinced myself they were either much worse off than I was or the opposite—they didn't know money problems the way *I* did. The clarity of that night in the restaurant was often lost as old, familiar patterns reasserted themselves and comfortable rationalizations settled back in. Still, I inched my way along a recovery path—on one day, off the next.

What motivated me to keep pursuing the possibility that I had a money disorder were two things: First, I suspected that my money problems weren't just about money, but that the way I handled money was a reflection of some core psychic conflict that related to how I dealt with *all* resources, and with life itself. If I was right, then healing my money issues would likely have ramifications far beyond my checkbook balance. Second, I had a nagging sense of hope, a suspicion that life could be *really good,* and I truly desired that. What "that" was, I couldn't quite say, but it had to do with culture, creativity, and community. It had to do with music, money, and good work. It had to do with beauty, health, and ideas. In hindsight I realize that what I was longing for is what I now call "true wealth," a state of personal en-richment that has little to do with actual cash flow but every-thing to do with one's relationship to money. I suspected that money disorders interfered with the achievement of this sense of enrichment.

What I discovered as I talked and read and meditated was that my particular money pattern involved compulsive spending, compulsive debting, and something else—what I came to call addiction to deprivation. The core dynamic of my problem with money seemed to be my fear of having any; I was committed to struggle.

A year after starting down my recovery path, I quit the job that drained me and began developing the career I really wanted—as a writer and video producer. I also moved to the area where I most wanted to live and took up the hobby of playing percussion as I'd always longed to do. It had honestly never occurred to me before that I could *choose* my career, choose where I wanted to live, and choose to play music if I wanted to, that I could really have the things that gratified me. To someone who doesn't have this particular self-defeating pattern with resources, all of this is probably self-evident, but to me it was a profound revelation. Other aspects of my re-covery work included halting the credit binge by paying for everything with cash and addressing the inner feelings of de-privation and codependency that fed my spending, debting, and deprivation pattern. Step-by-step, I began moving toward greater emotional and fiscal solvency.

My healing journey continues, and writing this book has been a part of it. Because I found virtually nothing that helped me understand my money pattern as an actual disor-der, similar to an eating disorder or codependency, I deter-mined several years ago to write something for people like myself who are wandering around in the dark trying to get a grasp on what's happening to them.

Of course, not everyone with money problems has a pat-tern similar to mine. Some people have just the opposite problem: they're hung up on acquiring wealth rather than depriving themselves of it, to the point where their lives revolve around money too. Others are driven by an intense fear of spending money, irrationally convinced that there won't be enough. Still others can be successful up to a point, then always do something to sabotage themselves. The other money disorders that are explored in this book include compulsive spending, compulsive debting, money codependency, fear of spending, and money hunger or greed.

Compulsive gambling is missing from this list because it has already been recognized as an addiction, researched, and widely written about in the last twenty years. By not including it directly in my discussion, however, I do not intend to imply that it is not a money disorder. Certainly it involves money. Many who gamble seem to be addicted to deprivation, if one takes the end result—net loss—to be the desired result. Certainly, there are elements of money lust involved, as well as compulsive spending and borrowing. Compulsive gamblers will probably identify with quite a bit in this book, in fact, and may well find it of benefit.

But the primary audience I am addressing is the millions of people who suffer from other vague, ill-defined, easily rationalized patterns of behavior with money that *cause them pain and distress:* the humiliation of bounced checks, bitter fights with a spouse over spending, worry about debts, the codependent's shame at giving until it hurts, the exhaustion of the burned-out wealth addict, and the constricted life of the person terrified to spend money at all.

This book is also for people who live with and/or love someone with a compulsive money pattern. Just as alcoholism affects everyone with whom the alcoholic comes in regular contact, so too does money dysfunction have negative effects on others: spouses, children, friends, co-workers, and creditors.

If you have "money problems," you will probably find as you read that you won't fit neatly into one single category but will see yourself in several different chapters. Each area of money madness is discussed separately here purely for the purposes of furthering our understanding, not to suggest that one is either a debtor *or* a spender, a wealth addict *or* a hoarder. Often, of course, there is overlap. To derive the greatest benefit, read about all of them, not just the ones you most identify with. Then take what applies, and leave the rest.

This book is a synthesis of my own experience in money recovery, the insights of those I interviewed, the work of other writers on the subject of money, and my training as a specialist and writer in the area of addiction. It is not intended as the definitive volume on money disorders but as one contribution to what is likely to be an area for growing exploration. I hope what you discover here will enhance your understanding, inform your quest for personal recovery, and perhaps provide you with some ideas for enriching your life.

Readers who are already involved in a recovery program for some other addiction are likely to find much about my approach to money disorders familiar, because I use the paradigm of addiction. You will be able to extrapolate from your experience with other addictive behaviors to your use of money as a mood-changer.

People who are new to any kind of recovery work may find it unsettling to contemplate the similarities between their money habits and full-fledged addictions. It may help to consult a book that I coauthored, *Willpower's Not Enough*, which focuses on the generic dis-ease of addiction. The ideas put forth there provided the framework for me to expand the addictive model to include money disorders. It is my belief that all compulsive habits are more alike than they are different, and that they are all different expressions of the same addictive dis-ease.

Further, I believe that our growing vulnerability to addictive behaviors of all kinds—from chemical addiction to eating and money disorders, codependency, and workaholism—is the result of living in a culture that is failing to meet legitimate human needs, needs for self-esteem, empowerment, community, creativity, and meaning; that our craving for various mood-changers is the natural result of chronic negative mood states arising from these unmet needs. We are becoming more vulnerable to using *anything* as a mood-changer, including money.

As a society, we can go on groping for more magical solutions to our collective and individual money problems, or we can use this "sobering" time of the 1990s to transform our relationship with money. As more and more of us begin rejecting addictive solutions to our money problems, we can begin to create a healthier, more solvent, and truly prosperous society.

PART I

Money Madness

CHAPTER 1

MONEY MADNESS

Never in the history of the world have so many people been so rich; never in the history of the world have so many of those same people felt themselves so poor.

LEWIS LAPHAM
MONEY AND CLASS IN AMERICA

Most Americans today are frantically engaged in fighting for first-class cabin space on the Titanic.

HAZEL HENDERSON
QUOTED IN PHILIP SLATER, *WEALTH ADDICTION*

THE SIGN OF A HEALTHY relationship with money, according to many psychotherapists, is that it doesn't interfere with one's satisfaction in life. The noncompulsive person will make money as best she can and will use it constructively to support her life, but will not sacrifice health, family life, leisure, or freedom for it. Yet for more and more of us, getting money, protecting money, getting rid of money, worrying about money, lusting after money, and holding onto money have become an almost constant focus, overshadowing our other life goals, such as the pursuit of satisfying relationships, peace of mind, and creative interests. Has money become the drug of choice for our time? Are we a society of money addicts? Consider these facts:

- American couples—including wealthy couples—fight more about money than anything else.
- Consumer debt tripled during the 1980s—even though average real wages were stagnant or declining.
- The rate of personal bankruptcy is rising 23 percent a year. Nearly one million Americans went bankrupt in 1991.
- Americans save only 6 percent of their income, compared to the British, who save 12 percent, and the Japanese, who save 17 percent.[1]

Whether someone is compulsive with money or not has little to do with the actual amount involved. A person can be broke and still be driven by greed, can have lots of money and be a compulsive debtor, and can spend one dollar or a million dollars compulsively. It's not the amount of money you earn, spend, or borrow that makes it compulsive, but *the way you use it* and the *effect* it has on your life. Your use of money is compulsive if it's causing problems in your life, yet you keep repeating the pattern. Here are some examples:

Compulsive shopping. The compulsive shopper uses the distraction and stimulation of shopping as a drug to escape negative moods.

> Thirty-eight-year-old Ruth is the grandchild of a wealthy textile tycoon. As a child, she got everything she wanted—except love and affection. As an adult, she treats herself the same way—spending money on clothes and externals but ignoring her own inner needs for love, security, and stability. In the past five years, Ruth has squandered her entire inheritance and has little to show for it but closets full of clothes—and lots of shame and guilt.

Image spending. This person spends money in highly visible ways—even when the money's not there.

Forty-seven-year-old Will *always* picks up the tab in restaurants and bars, drives a Mercedes (on the verge of being repossessed), and lives in a half-million-dollar house in a posh suburb. Behind the scenes, though, he's bouncing checks and scheming to outwit creditors. Will is driven by an insatiable need to be admired and to appear important and powerful.

Compulsive debting. The compulsive debtor escapes the pressure of today's debts with the quick fix of another loan or another bad check—only to dig in deeper each time.

At thirty-two, Joyce, an administrative assistant, is $30,000 in debt from credit cards, loans, and store credit. Joyce operates under the illusion that as long as she still has credit, or can punch her card into the magic money machine (ATM) and get a fix, she's not broke. She pays only the minimum on each account but soon will be unable to do even that. At this point, she's exhausted all credit lines and is starting to be harassed by her creditors.

Codependent with money. The codependent spender uses money to try and win love and avoid abandonment.

Thirty-three-year-old Judy is the child of a compulsive gambler. As an adult, Judy developed a pattern of bailing men out financially and at twenty-five moved in with Frank, himself a compulsive gambler. Judy stayed with him for eight years, paying all the bills for both of them, even though it meant going without dental care, new clothes, and other things for herself. She tried several times to move out, but always felt guilty. Judy is a classic codependent, acting out her self-rejection through this money pattern.

Fear of spending. The person with a fear of spending is driven by an intense fear that there's not going to be enough.

14

He judges everything by how much it costs, hoards money, and worries about every expenditure.

At fifty, Clifford is only now beginning to see that he has a problem with money, now that his wife has left him and he's become estranged from his children. To him, keeping a tight grip on his money always seemed necessary to keep others from squandering it. In reality, he was acting out unresolved feelings of not getting enough as a child. And now he's paying a price.

Money lust. When a person is driven by a hunger for money at any cost, acquiring wealth takes priority over all else—and no amount of money is ever enough.

Thomas, at fifty years old, was president of a major northeastern university—until recently, when he was sentenced to eight years in prison for defrauding the school of more than three million dollars. Thomas was driven to acquire more and more money, even though he was jeopardizing his career, his reputation, and his family's well-being. Ironically, he never really enjoyed the money he had.

Money self-sabotage. The self-saboteur lets himself become successful *up to a point,* then does something to undermine it. Often, he makes a bundle again and blows it again.

Forty-year-old Dean acquired half a million in assets in just a few years, buying and selling real estate. But, he says, it "didn't feel right." Then Dean made a series of bad decisions—selling precipitously and lending large sums to a friend who was a compulsive gambler. Dean is now back to zero, but he says it feels comfortable. His father always told him he'd never amount to anything.

Addiction to deprivation. Despite her talents and ability to earn, the deprivation addict keeps herself broke, maintaining strict allegiance to an identity as "one who is deprived," an underdog.

Thirty-one-year-old Anita grew up with an alcoholic father who sexually molested her. Because he also gave her whatever she wanted materially, Anita came to associate having money with being abused and having no control. As an adult, she kept herself broke—working at low-paying jobs despite her abilities. She even stole toilet paper and paper towels from public places and searched under vending machines for dropped coins. Anita has what is called a "poverty mentality." To her, having no money feels safe, though the toll on her health and career is finally compelling her to seek help.

As you can imagine, people rarely fit neatly into just one category but often have symptoms of two or more self-defeating patterns at the same time. The compulsive spender is often a compulsive debtor as well, the wealth addict may periodically sabotage himself, and the person who is codependent with money is often also addicted to deprivation.

Money disorders affect nearly all of us in some way. Either we experience the negative consequences of such a pattern ourselves, or we are close to someone who does. Money disorders, like alcoholism, affect not only the person suffering directly, but anyone closely involved with him: a spouse or partner, children, friends, co-workers, creditors.

It's important not to see a money disorder as something to be ashamed of. It's a mirror that helps you to learn about yourself. If the crisis is used as an opportunity to learn and grow, it can lead to greater financial and emotional health. By confronting money disorders—as individuals, as families, and as a nation—we can transform our use of *resources* in general, because money problems aren't just about money but our behavior with anything that can be possessed, saved, spent, lost, or taken away—including love, security, and power.

16

In many cases, our dysfunctional money patterns are "inherited," passed along from one generation to the next. If your father was a compulsive debtor, chances are good you'll either become a compulsive debtor yourself or (like your mother) become involved with one. It's natural to take on our parents' attitudes, belief systems, and behaviors—either by imitation or by making ourselves the "opposite" of our parents. In either case, who we are with money is a direct result of what we learned at home.

If money was used to control people or lavished as a substitute for love, that is how we learned to use it. If money was a taboo topic, whispered about in hushed tones and loaded with hidden meaning, we probably have lots of uncomfortable associations with it. If the money in our family was gained through unethical or illegal means, we may have inherited some guilt and ambivalence toward the "dirty" substance. And if our family had little money, we probably picked up a sense of shame and unworthiness as a result. Many people with serious money disorders come from dysfunctional families in which there was some ongoing trauma such as an addicted parent, sexual abuse, domestic violence, or emotional abuse or from a family in which one or more role models had money disorders.

It is also impossible to separate our individual money patterns from the money dysfunction on the national level. Many of those in leadership positions over the past two decades—both in government and in the business world—have exhibited the symptoms of money disorders and have conducted the affairs of our nation and our corporations accordingly. Many features of compulsive, addictlike behavior have become standard operating procedure in our nation, including denial, short-term thinking, a drive for immediate gratification, blame, and deceit.

The most familiar example of dysfunctional money behavior at the governmental level is our handling of the federal deficit. Throughout the 1980s, we—both leaders and public—were largely a nation in denial. President Reagan campaigned on a promise to balance the budget—then doubled the deficit in six years.[2] Short-term thinking informed both government and corporate financial decisions during that decade, putting reelection votes and quick profits before balanced budgets and other features of sound money management. The public was deceived into going along with policies that were against their best interests.

The national ramifications of our collective dysfunctional money behaviors are profound: crushing personal, corporate, and government debt burdens; the selling off of our assets to keep up with debt payments; Third World–like gaps developing between rich and poor; and the "monetization" of our relationships. But because of their pervasiveness on every level of government, business, and family, we have been blind to money disorders. Until recently, we accepted compulsive spending, money lust, and burdensome debt as normal, even good. We have been living in what amounts to a money-addicted culture, in which democracy and consumerism have become synonymous and compulsive spending and borrowing are the rule at almost every level of government and business.

We tend to assume that the lives of people all over the world revolve around money as ours do, but Jacob Needleman, writing in *Money and the Meaning of Life*, brings a cross-cultural perspective to bear: "In other times and places, not everyone has wanted *money* above all else; people have desired salvation, beauty, power, strength, pleasure, propriety . . . adventure, conquest, comfort. But now and here, money—not necessarily even the things money can buy, but *money*—is what everyone wants."[3]

When money is valued above all else, every decision in our lives is weighed in financial terms. Whether we enjoy our work, get some sense of accomplishment, or contribute to the greater good becomes less important than how much it pays. Whether we love our partner and our children becomes less important than how well we provide for them. Whether we are moved by a work of art becomes less important than how much it will earn as an investment. I know of a little girl who, when she told her mother she wanted to help people when she grew up, was treated to a lecture about choosing a profession that paid well. Our noblest dreams and desires are ridiculed if they aren't likely to produce enough money.

For many of us, money has replaced church, community, and family as the entity around which we organize our lives. Much of our talent and energy—creative, physical, mental, and emotional—goes into getting, thinking about, protecting, and otherwise dealing obsessively with money. The mall is our place of worship, and shopping our ritual. Without question, our tax laws are pored over, studied, and quoted more than any sacred text. And we willingly endure many hardships in our worship of the Almighty Dollar, including fourteen-hour workdays, long-distance commutes, loss of leisure, sometimes even the risk of illness or arrest. Perhaps we are willing to do all this because, in the secular worship of money, poverty is considered a cardinal sin.

The compelling urge to organize ourselves around money is all the greater when other forms of currency are lacking in our lives: meaningful work, a sense of community, love, creative play, to name a few. In the absence of anything greater, we devote ourselves to money. Not that money can't be a central, and even sacred, part of an otherwise full and meaningful life; the problem arises when we use money to *take the place* of other nourishment in our lives and consider it the source of our fulfillment.

People often assume that only the poor have money problems, but it's not that simple. True, people without money are always trying to get more, but people with money often spend more time than anyone else focusing on it: protecting it, hiding it, spending it, avoiding taxes on it, getting *more* of it. And a great number of money crimes are committed by people who don't, objectively speaking, need money.

To cite only one of a multitude of examples, Michael Milken, the high-flying bond trader jailed in a 1980s insider trading scandal, made $550 million—legally—around the same time he was committing securities law violations.[4] As Aristotle wrote in *Politics,* "The greatest crimes are caused by excess and not by necessity. Men do not become tyrants in order that they may not suffer cold."[5] It's not actual poverty that drives the money addict but *inner poverty*—a condition of emotional, spiritual, creative, and social impoverishment.

One reason money has become a vehicle for compulsive behavior is that money, no less than food and sex, is a powerful symbol in our psyches, loaded with unconscious meaning. To some people, money represents the security they can't find in intimate relations; to others, money is bad, to be avoided at all costs; still others associate money with sex and go through it as quickly as they do sex partners. In a society in which more and more people feel powerless over conditions in their lives, money represents a source of control or power. People who were sexually abused as children, who had their most precious possession of self-determination and boundaries taken away from them, are overrepresented among both compulsive spenders and those addicted to deprivation. They seem driven to keep themselves broke, feel most secure when they have little that can be taken away.

Because of the intense charge that money carries, there has been a powerful injunction against talking about money in any direct or revealing way. In many families, it's considered vulgar or indelicate to discuss money matters. We prefer to use euphemisms, like "comfortable" or "of limited means" rather than more loaded terms like *rich* and *poor.* Bring up the subject of money, and people cough, clear their throats, hold their breath, change the subject, leave the room, glaze over—or become passionately inflamed. Couples often avoid talking about money in any depth before getting married or moving in together. Later on, it's common for their different money patterns and priorities to clash.

Our reluctance to discuss money reflects some deep-rooted ambivalence and confusion about it. All our lives, we've received double messages about money. We've been taught to want many things and to strive for financial rewards, yet we have also been given powerful injunctions against excess, against being showy, against appearing to have it too easy. The rich are at once loved and hated, worshiped and resented. This reflects in part, perhaps, the conflict between the Puritan ethics of thrift, conservation, hard work, struggle, and sacrifice and those of our modern marketplace, which is built on the reverse: entitlement, excess, consumerism, image, and a compulsive search for *more*.

There are other reasons we're so reluctant to talk about money. Those of us who don't feel we're measuring up financially find that talking about money makes us feel awkward, ignorant, vulnerable, and ashamed. If we don't speak the language of money, we'd just as soon keep quiet. People *with* money may avoid talking about it so as not to seem greedy or preoccupied with it. And for people with compulsive money patterns, the subject of money is fraught with strain and stress. Talking about money is just plain too upsetting. To talk about money is to reveal so much about ourselves that we feel exposed. Perhaps that's because, as Russell Lockhart points out in his essay in *Soul and Money*, money is a "talisman of the Self."[6]

With these intense feelings about money, it is no wonder that so many of us are confused about its role in our lives. We compulsively strive to amass money, then seem unable to enjoy it when we do—or get rid of it so that we don't have to try. And as a result of such secrecy, people with compulsive and self-defeating money patterns often think they are the only ones struggling with these problems. They carry around a burden of shame and low self-esteem that further exacerbates their compulsive behavior.

Yet, despite the intense emotional charge money carries in our society and the grave consequences of dysfunctional

money patterns, it is surprising how little attention the subject has received. In twelve years of schooling, most students
learn more about isosceles triangles and obscure chemical
elements than they do about the substance they will deal
with every day of their lives—money. People can go through
years of psychotherapy and never talk about money—even
when it's a central theme in their history. Tony, thirty-three,
a video director and the son of Portuguese immigrants, was
haunted by feelings of failure at not earning enough money,
to the point where he became suicidal every time he was
broke. He spent five years in weekly psychotherapy dealing
with his depression—and the subject of money never even
came up.

What is it that we're trying to get from our obsession with
money? What is the payoff that prompts us to make money so
very central in our lives? The answer is not more leisure time,
because the richer we've become, the longer our work week
has grown. It is not the pleasure that affluence can bring, because many rich people *feel* poor, the experience of wealth
having little to do with the numbers. In fact, true wealth has
little to do with *any* of the external symbols of success. Surveys have found that beyond the attainment of a basic standard of living above the poverty level, material riches have
little bearing on one's experience of happiness.[7]

Paul Wachtel, writing in *The Poverty of Affluence,* sheds
some light on what has gone wrong and why our intense
focus on the material hasn't brought us satisfaction:

> Our economic system and our relation with nature
> have gone haywire because we have lost track of what
> we really need. Increasing numbers of middle-class
> Americans are feeling pressed and deprived not be-
> cause of their economic situation *per se*—we remain
> an extraordinarily affluent society—but because we
> have placed an impossible burden on the economic
> dimension of our lives.[8]

We have placed an impossible burden on the economic dimension of our lives—and have not learned to recognize or develop many of our *nonfinancial assets,* such as community, creativity, and self-esteem. We are using money to meet nonfinancial needs for emotional, spiritual, and personal fulfillment. If you look to money for your self-esteem, you'll never be able to get enough, spend enough, or save enough to feel good about yourself. If your sense of power is based on money, you will always crave more. When what you want (money) is different from what you need (self-esteem, a sense of belonging, personal empowerment), you can never get enough.

The heavy emphasis on the financial aspect of our lives has led to growing isolation, an erosion of our social security. I don't mean the government check you receive at the age of sixty-five but a sense of connectedness and security within the larger community. When the goal is to get as much as you can, and the one with the most toys wins, it's hard to be a team player. We want to be rich—but without any collective responsibility. That causes us to become more and more disconnected from the larger community, and that impoverishes us in a very real sense.

It's common today for us to use money as the scapegoat for all our problems. We fantasize that if only we as individuals or we as a nation just had more money, everything would be OK. But money can only solve money problems. It can't solve problems of self-esteem or insecurity, or make our relationships work, or stop us from aging. We simply expect too much of money. Then when it doesn't deliver, we think the problem is that we just don't have *enough* yet, that we still need more.

Conditions in the 1990s have placed some external limits on our money bingeing and present an opportunity for a breakthrough. A stalled economy, paralyzing debt, unemployment, and rising rates of bankruptcy and homelessness are all forcing us to reexamine our relationship to money.

We no longer have the luxury of pretending that money is something we shouldn't talk about, while all along it's running our lives.

But now that we're coming out of denial about our personal and national money dysfunction, we must take care not to fall into another addictive tendency: blaming. Though it's been tempting for the Republicans to blame the Democratic Congress for the deficit and vice versa, blaming is just more addictive behavior. If we are to recover—as individuals and as a nation—we need to be willing to observe our *own* money habits and take action to change what we can change.

I believe there is such a thing as Right Use of Money, much like the Buddhist notion of Right Livelihood. Rightly used, money enriches our lives: it allows us to take care of our material needs, maintain our health, accomplish our life goals, nurture our families and communities, and improve ourselves with education and travel. It is a source of enrichment. Addictively used, money impoverishes us. It drains meaning and purpose from our lives, objectifies our relationships, causes us to neglect our children, steals our leisure, undermines our communities and our environment, and contributes to isolation. It is a source of impoverishment.

To recover from money disorders, we don't necessarily have to make more money, nor do we have to divorce ourselves from it. We simply need to become more *conscious* about money and how we're using it, so that it doesn't unconsciously rule us. We have to acknowledge the role of money in our lives, admit when it's out of control, and learn from that experience, if we hope to diminish the compulsive charge it has for us. Because if we don't confront our increasingly addictive relationship to money, it will continue to fuel our self-defeating patterns unconsciously, undermining our ability to create true wealth—a rich emotional, spiritual, creative, and community life.

CHAPTER 2

MONEY AS A MIRROR

Some people seem to have a gift for managing money. They make good use of whatever funds they have, be they great or small. Other people are forever being pushed around or rendered unhappy by money problems of one sort or another. Is there any basic difference between the two types? I think there is. One regards money as a medium of exchange—nothing more. The other lets money become a symbol of something else.

SMILEY BLANTON
"THE HIDDEN FACES OF MONEY," IN THE
ANTHOLOGY *THE PSYCHOANALYSIS OF MONEY*

Money is as deep and broad as the ocean, the primordially unconscious, and makes us so. It always takes us into great depths, where sharks and suckers, hard-shell crabs, tight clams and tidal emotions abound. Its facts have huge horizons, as huge as sex, and just as protean and polymorphous.

JAMES HILLMAN
"A CONTRIBUTION TO SOUL AND MONEY,"
IN THE ANTHOLOGY *SOUL AND MONEY*

MONEY IS A MEDIUM of exchange, a measure of value that can be traded for goods and services. It's also something more mysterious: a powerful symbol in our psyche, loaded with unconscious meaning, with an immense impact on our personalities. Money is, as Hillman puts it, "a deposit of mythical fantasies. . . . Money is imaginative."[1]

As a symbol, money may be more highly charged than any other substance in our lives. Followers of Carl Jung suggest that the reason money has such weighty mythical meaning to us is because it is a present-day "carrier of soul." How we earn and use money is one of the chief vehicles at our disposal today for expressing and revealing who we are. That may be why the subject of money is so charged with energy; it's our *self*, the projections of our soul, that we're talking about. And according to Adolf Guggenbühl-Craig, whatever the soul is projected onto tends to be guarded by secrecy, driven by fascination (or obsession), and highly charged.[2]

I remember as a child counting the change in my piggy bank and feeling absolutely dizzy with excitement as I walked into Woolworth's to spend my loot. It was, I think, the thrill of possibility, which is, in a sense, a kind of power. What I did with my money was a way of expressing *me*. I also remember the greedy anticipation I felt when someone landed on one of "my" streets in Monopoly, and the powerful feeling of peeling off hundred-dollar bills in order to buy another hotel. Money is intoxicating—and devilishly seductive, which is why I also remember stealing five dollars from my sister's Christmas money, which she had stashed in a kitchen mug. I quickly learned that there were strict rules of conduct governing the acquisition of money.

It is precisely because money is so psychically loaded that people with money disorders have such difficulty acting *rationally* in relation to it. A compulsive spender can look at his ailing checkbook and vow not to spend any more money on luxuries this month. He can voluntarily hand over his credit cards to his spouse for safekeeping, and she will think she's finally gotten through to him with reason, that he's responding rationally. Then—much to her dismay—three days later, her husband brings home an antique rug. When questioned, he admits that he found a way to charge it without having the card with him. His behavior is not rational after all; it is driven by an inner mandate much more powerful than reason.

The word *money* derives from the Latin word *moneta*. *Moneta* is the Latin name for the goddess of memory, who was also mother of the Muses. *Moneta* was also another name for the goddess Juno, who reigned over light, birth, women, and marriage and in whose temple Roman money was minted. The story has it that money was minted at Juno's temple because once upon a time a demoralized, broke Roman army was losing a battle when its leaders consulted Juno, who advised that if the army's cause was just, and they kept fighting, the money would come. The army fought on, money arrived from Rome in time to help them, and they won the battle. In tribute, the mint for money was set up in Juno's temple.[3]

The word *moneta* itself derived from an older Latin word *monere*, which means "to admonish." Money thus has roots in memory, creativity, and warnings. Perhaps we are advised to remember the mystery in money, use it creatively, and heed its warnings.

MONEY AS MAGIC

Money has always been considered somewhat magical. Because it helps make manifest some of our dreams, it is in effect *creative*, which puts it automatically in association with the divine. As others have noted, even our language conveys the special powers that we project onto money. We say that "money talks" and "money opens doors."

Related to our association of money with magic is its connection in our collective psyche with the magic of reproduction, creation, fertility. Many early forms of money, including dentalium shells and red woodpecker scalps, were associated with fertility, reproduction, and the continuity of life. Salt, an early form of exchange with which Roman soldiers and officials were paid, was regarded as a symbol of the procreative powers of sperm, and thus magic. Cowrie shells, whose shape is thought to resemble the female genitals, were widely used as money among Native Americans, and in Europe, Africa, China, India, and the Near East they were often regarded as symbols of fertility, the feminine power of creation, and used as talismans and sacred objects. When a tribal member died, cowrie shells were often buried in the corpse's mouth, as passage money that might be needed on the journey to the next world. Glass beads, used as money in Africa, were additionally thought to possess magical properties in that they represented the sacredness of the earth.

Early coins were often regarded as magic amulets too, capable of warding off illness, poverty, and other dangers, protecting the wearer in battle, and ensuring true love. Ancient Greeks believed the absence of money played a part in causing disease and the presence of money facilitated its cure. In ancient Rome, coins were given out bearing the likeness of Apollo, the god of healing. The Chinese hung a sword made of coins over the sickbed to drive off the fever demon. And in Germany and other European countries, holy coins were distributed by the church during the Middle Ages to protect people from the plague.

Gold and silver were thought to possess magic by virtue of their affinity with the sun and moon, which were themselves considered representatives of the God and Goddess respectively. And kings, in early cultures, were believed to possess magic powers, so coins that they distributed to their subjects were believed to be infused with their magic power.[4]

Even today, though we have lost the association of money with the divine, we still tend to regard money as magic and remain in awe of its powers. Children learn early that all their parents have to do is hand some coins or green paper over to certain people and presto, they get what they want. Even as grown-ups, we still see money as possessing mysterious powers. Some people seem to know how to make it multiply with interest or through the somewhat mysterious stock market. Even the ATM machine bespeaks magic as its "open-sesame" door slides up and crisp new bills are spit out in quarter-note beats.

Credit cards, because they represent the *illusion* of unlimited possibility, have the potential to cast us under their spell too. It's easy to believe that they bestow onto *us* their magic power. Eighteen-year-old Ian describes how he felt when he got his first credit card: "I'm walking around the store thinking, 'I can buy whatever I want! I can buy this whole store! I don't have to think about it right now, I can just *have* it.'"

Advertisers capitalize on our belief in material magic by leading us to believe that this item or that one can transform us magically into someone more attractive, younger, more powerful. A person who feels insecure about his own personal potency, his ability to have an effect on the world, will be all the more concerned with gaining access to the magic of money. It may also be that those people I refer to as addicted to deprivation are instinctively afraid of the magical powers of money and so avoid coming into (or under) its possession.

MONEY AS POWER

I have the power to use 30,000 cash machines.

COPY UNDER PHOTO OF A SMILING YOUNG WOMAN
IN AN AD FOR A BANK'S "POWER CHECKING."

In modern society, money is clout. It is believed to make one more visible, substantial, powerful, a force to be reckoned with. We say that someone's stock is high when he or she has a lot of influence. The flip side is that people without money in our society are rendered invisible, helpless, unable to make themselves heard, unable to influence others, impotent, powerless.

We can look to infancy for our first association of money with power. For the first year of a child's life, if all goes well, his needs are met almost automatically—the breast appears, the diapers are changed, and so on. The mother seems all-powerful and the child is merged with her, so he experiences himself as omnipotent too. Then, as he grows, he begins to experience limits—his own and his parents'—and starts his fall from the early illusion of omnipotence. Psychoanalyst Otto Fenichel suggests that people who use money to gain power are unconsciously trying to regain those infantile feelings of omnipotence. Our drive for riches, he says, is only a disguised drive for power and respect in a society that awards them to those with the most money. "The original instinctual aim is not for riches, but to enjoy power and respect, whether it be among one's fellow men or within oneself. It is a society in which power and respect are based upon the possession of money, that makes of this need for power and respect a need for riches."[5]

In many families, children learn every day that money equals power. I'm reminded of an incident I observed many years ago between a young girl and her father. The sixth grader was about to leave for school when she announced that her teacher was holding a mock presidential election and she intended to vote for George McGovern. The father, a staunch Republican, flared up in anger. "Oh no, you won't," he declared, altogether serious; "not as long as you're living under my roof, you won't." The message to his daughter was that if his money supported her, it also controlled her. Interestingly, this little girl grew up to be a compulsive spender, getting rid of money as fast as she could.

Tony, whom we met in the last chapter, grew up with a father who was a Portuguese immigrant and always stressed the importance of making money as a way to gain power in American society. "He would always tell me, 'If you don't make money in this society, son, you're going to be someone else's slave. I'm not training you to be a sergeant, I'm training you to be a captain. I want you to be a conqueror, not the conquered.'"

The problem is, we've come to believe in money as the *source* of power rather than as a channel through which it flows. And because we mistake money as the source, we think that if we get money *we* will have that power, we will be the power-full. It is this illusion of ourselves as the source of omnipotence that makes us vulnerable to using money compulsively. Jason, a thirty-five-year-old engineer turned full-time stock market player, describes how he came to believe in his own omnipotence:

> I was making $10,000 in a single day. It gave me an incredible sense of power. Here I was, telling my broker, "Send this $100,000 over here," or "Send this $50,000 over there." Then when you double your money in a short time, you come to think *you* made it happen, that it's *your* power, you've got it. It was a kind of perverse thrill, thinking that I could predict the future. It's incredibly exhilarating.[6]

This overemphasis on money as the source of power causes people in its thrall to forgo other pleasures and stifle other faculties that could ultimately be enriching. We fail to develop other aspects of our lives—creative interests, relationships, service, to name a few—then wonder why we feel empty.

Because money is mistaken to be the source of power, people with money attract still other people who want some of that power to rub off on them. Carl, at thirty-two, is a respected businessman in a Chicago suburb. Few of his friends and colleagues know about the ten years he spent as a major drug dealer. Consenting to an interview for this book, Carl spoke about the intoxication available in great sums of money:

> At a very early age I was suddenly making a lot of money. People—girls, other hustlers—were flocking all over me, all ready to do whatever I told them. It's

a phony type of power, of course, but it's power. And you don't realize how addicted you're getting to it. It's very seductive. When I tried to stop dealing, that was a definite part of the withdrawal I had to go through.

And it's not just the greedy who associate money with power. The person I call addicted to deprivation often believes just as wholeheartedly that money is the source of all power—only she avoids it because she fears the shadow side of that power. The person addicted to deprivation thinks she has to forgo money so as not to be seduced and corrupted by it. But that's giving money all the power too, instead of seeing it as a channel through which much *good* can be done as well.

One of the chief benefits that people want from money is control over their own lives, to be free agents. Most people think that if only they could make a certain amount of money (usually double their current salary, whatever that is), they would be free—free from worry, stress, limits, from having to do things they don't want to do, free to spend their time as they like. But more money doesn't always bring greater freedom. One of the young people interviewed for this book, Kara, twenty-four, reflected on why this might be:

> Rich people don't experience much freedom from their money because they're afraid of losing it all the time. If you think that you only have power because of your money, then you have to hang on to that money to hang on to your power, which gives you no freedom at all. But if you can feel your power *without* money, then money isn't power, it's just freedom.

This inner, personal power that Kara refers to is key to what I call Right Use of Money. It's this inner power that frees one from attachment to money as the *source* of power.

MONEY AS SECURITY

Some people seek financial success as a means to emotional security. They are driven to seek and stockpile greater and greater fortunes, perks, and investments, in an effort to ensure that their future will be comfortable. Without money they feel nervous and insecure, and the more money they have, the safer they feel. For this person, money in the bank is something of a security blanket.

According to psychoanalytic theory, if a person fails to get his nurturing needs met during the oral stage of development (roughly the first year), he fails to develop a basic sense of trust and is dogged for life by inner feelings of insecurity and dependency. As an adult, he doesn't trust that anyone else can or will take care of him. Stockpiling money becomes a way of satisfying his hunger for security, for what the British analyst Melanie Klein called the "inexhaustible breast."[7] The irony is that when people pursue security through material success, they often sacrifice their leisure, hobbies and passions, family life, and health—hardly a good tradeoff.

The person who sacrifices everything in order to build financial security is likely to be emotionally devastated if anything happens to his security blanket—a stock market crash or a natural catastrophe, for example. He discovers that money has not given him control, that there is no such thing as a totally reliable, predictable condition of security. Having built his life on an illusion, he is bereft and without his bearings.

Our present exaggerated emphasis on financial security has grown in direct proportion to our decline in social security (not the government check, but a sense of being able to rely on each other). People today have looser community roots and less extended family support and are more likely to divorce than just a generation ago. The more individualistic we become as a society, the more we feel we can't depend on anyone but ourselves. With a growing sense that no one else will (or can) be there for us, we begin to define security in financial terms. "If I ever need help, I'd better be able to pay for it."

A person who suffers the ill effects of financial upheaval or poverty as a child can also come to crave money as security, believing that if she can just get enough stashed away, she can avoid what her parents (or grandparents) went through. Fifty-year-old Syd is a compulsive earner who says he doesn't feel comfortable relying on others. He points out the powerful role his family history played in shaping his relationship to money as a symbol of security:

> I'm Jewish, and Jews often had to buy their freedom during the war. If they had the money, they could get their families out of Hitler's way. If they didn't, they couldn't.
>
> My grandfather got his family out, and I believe my father communicated to me very strongly that money is survival. I think this plays a big part in what gets passed down and communicated about money in Jewish families in general. Money is survival.

According to Herb Goldberg and Robert Lewis in *Money Madness,* people who seek money as security and those who seek money as power have much in common. Both are motivated by unconscious feelings of helplessness and fear of abandonment. The security-driven person is trying to *anticipate* desertion and disaster and prepare himself for it, whereas the power-oriented person is trying to *prevent* desertion and disaster by becoming powerful enough to make others do what he wants.[8]

MONEY AS FOOD

Money is also linked with food in our psyches. In today's society, few people produce their own food. Our ability to feed ourselves depends on having access to money. Where so-called primitive people had to be concerned primarily with hunting and gathering food, we are primarily preoccupied with hunting and gathering money—to get the food. Hence our great fear of not having enough.

An early link between money and meat was forged in ancient Greece and Rome, where divine bulls were sacrificed in religious ceremonies and portions distributed to participants in the ritual. These portions of meat are considered the first known form of money. Later, metal pieces were distributed by various rulers as a substitute for meat; this is how coins came into use. Early coins, as William Desmonde points out, were essentially "sacred relics symbolizing a holy meal among a loyal fellowship."[9] Thus money, God, and community were all linked in a way that they no longer are.

Wealth used to be associated with plumpness. Rich people were often well padded, their wealth evident in the fact that they looked well fed. Now, wealth is associated with

Some of the financial terms we use today derive from times when cattle were still used as a unit of value. The word *pecuniary,* for instance, derives from the Latin *pecus,* meaning "cattle"; the word *fee* is thought to derive from the Gothic *faihi,* which also means "cattle"; and the Indian *rupee* comes from a Sanskrit word for cattle. Even the word *capital* derives from *capitale,* which originally meant "cattle counted by the head." Another food-related derivation is that of the word *fiscal,* which comes originally from the word *fiscus,* which derived from the word for basket. And *salary* may have derived from the Latin word *salarium,* for salt, because in ancient Rome, public officials and soldiers were often paid in salt (hence the expression "not worth his salt").

Other food items that have been used as money at various times and places include wheat, rice, tea, coca, pigs, maize, barley, oxen, butter, and sugar. Our association of money with food finds ample expression in modern English slang too: we refer to money as bread, dough, and bacon.[10]

thinness, and wealth gets reflected not in a plump body but in a plump house, bulging with possessions.

The parallels between self-defeating money patterns and eating disorders are striking. Compulsive eating and compulsive acquiring are both *taking-in* disorders. Like compulsive eaters, most compulsive earners and spenders are trying to fill what feels like a bottomless hole inside, insatiable neediness. But the money and possessions (like the food) can never really fill them up.

Following the death by drowning of the publishing tycoon Robert Maxwell in 1991, the *Wall Street Journal* ran an article about his irrational behavior in buying the *Daily News* at a time when he could ill afford it, aptly using gluttony as the metaphor: "In retrospect, the *Daily News* takeover was a characteristic act of gluttony. In a race to keep up with his archrival, Rupert Murdoch, Mr. Maxwell couldn't resist ingesting another paper—even as debt already was bursting the seams of his empire."[11]

Likewise, the person I call addicted to deprivation is like the anorexic eater: she keeps herself on the brink of starvation so as not to be "fat" like the others. She has a pronounced reluctance to take anything in. Yet her intense focus on avoiding money betrays an immense preoccupation with it, just as the anorexic eater is (paradoxically) preoccupied with food. Though she takes little in, the anorexic's life revolves around *not eating,* just as the person addicted to deprivation revolves around *not having.*

MONEY AS SEXUAL POTENCY

It is no accident that stock exchange floors—in addition to bedroom floors—bring out the noisy blood, the flushed cheek, and the passionate cries of men. Most men are making love when they make "magical" amounts of money.

PHYLLIS CHESLER AND EMILY JANE GOODMAN
WOMEN, MONEY AND POWER

Money has the capacity to turn some people on, excite and stimulate them. That's because in the unconscious, money may also be associated with sexual potency in general and male virility in particular. Some men report feeling more potent when they have money, and inadequate and castrated without it. Syd, the fifty-year-old wealth addict, claims that more money means greater access to sex:

> For me, sex and money are connected. I don't think women have that connection, but for men, sex and money go together. Rich men do have more fun, I think; they get more women. If you have money, you can have multiple relationships without investing a lot of time or emotional involvement. Many women make themselves available for short periods of time if you have money, because of what they can get out of it: nice places to go, fancy meals. They don't mind spending the night if you take them out to a $300 dinner and a show. Money substitutes for emotional involvement.

A study of money and marital infidelity would seem to bear out Syd's theory: Among both men and women the incidence of marital infidelity increases with income. Of married men earning $20,000 a year, 31 percent have had an extramarital affair, whereas among married men earning $60,000 and more, 70 percent have.[12] And though stock market employees are hardly representative of all men, one study of thirty men working in the stock market found that when the market went up, their sex drive went up, and when the market went down, so did their libido.[13]

Anecdotal evidence abounds too. Ken, forty-eight, describes the connection for him: "Whenever I've had money in my pocket, I've found myself feeling much more masculine, virile, freer sexually. It was exciting. I felt exciting. I felt more attractive to women. I bounced in and out of affairs with beautiful women. I had a sports car, money, and women. And there definitely seemed to be a correlation."

Because of this cultural association of money with male potency and access to sex, and of lack of money with impotence, it can be particularly painful for a young man or boy to see his father, his sexual role model, rendered financially impotent. Reggie, at fifty-three, has never successfully met his financial needs. Growing up, he recalls, his father, who owned a shoe store, was forced out of business by a national chain. The day the business was auctioned off Reggie recalls as the most painful day of his life. "I had to leave, just get in my car and drive. It was like watching my father be broken."

Intense competition among men in our society for the largest salary, the biggest house, or the longest limousine may well amount to a struggle for male superiority, or a struggle to avoid being deemed an inadequate (impotent) man. For some men, material resources provide a concrete measure of virility, like the size of the penis. Consider this quote from Donald Trump in his book, *Surviving at the Top:*

> Malcolm [Forbes], for years, had a yacht, called the
> *Highlander,* of which he was very proud . . . Malcolm
> also took many writers, broadcasters, and photogra-
> phers on his cruises around the harbor. As a result,
> he became a darling of the New York press, and his
> 150-foot yacht was legendary—until I came along
> with a much more luxurious, 282-foot yacht and
> stole the spotlight away.[14]

Read on, and you discover that Trump not only had to have the biggest yacht, but also one of the biggest homes and one of the biggest living rooms and at one time intended to build the tallest building in the world.

Financial success as the measure of adequacy is far more pronounced among men than women. That's probably because little boys get the message early on that their adequacy will depend on how well they provide for their families some-day. Little girls, conversely, have often been raised to seek approval rather than resources and may even get the message that earning too much money will taint them as too masculine. And because of the association of financial success with male sexual adequacy, in marriages where the woman earns more than the man, some men feel threatened, symbolically castrated.

This association of money with male potency may be why we refer to financial markets as being soft when they're down, and why, as others have noted, Wall Street traders often refer to the "size" of their gain, as if it were a measurement of sexual prowess.[15] It may also explain our emphasis on financial performance and anxiety about not measuring up. Whether it's making love or making a living, the point is no longer to enjoy the experience but to *perform well,* as duly noted by others.

Because women have been socialized to accept the equation of financial success with male adequacy, it's not hard to find women who are turned on by a man with money. Melinda, a thirty-five-year-old computer programmer, admits she always goes for men with big bucks.

> Being broke is a major turnoff to me in a man. I see it as a sign of weakness, especially for a guy. A woman can be forty-five years old and have nothing to show for it. But for a man, it's inexcusable. I won't even date a man who hasn't made it financially. As far as I'm concerned, he's not a real man. I just don't think I'd feel physically attracted to a man with lots of debts and no money. Money is a turn-on.

Advertisers today gladly capitalize on our association of sex with material success—and may have even helped create it. One glance through any magazine reveals how frequently sexual images are linked with products. According to Philip Slater, that's because sexual pleasure is one thing that challenges the supremacy of money in our culture. Because sex cannot be marketed on any wide scale, advertisers try to make it look as if access to it can be bought with this mouthwash or that liqueur. The result of pairing the primal sex drive with purchasing power, Slater concludes, has been to create "a whole nation of people filled with the kind of obsessive, self-conscious self-dissatisfaction that we usually associate with the onset of puberty and acute cases of acne."[16]

MONEY AS LOVE

In so-called primitive cultures, money was a symbol of the interdependence of members of a community, united in sharing the common meal, dependent on a common god or gods. The sharing of the divine bull was an affirmation of relationship. And though in modern Western society money has been reduced to its practical, quantitative, material purpose alone, perhaps money in our collective psyche is still associated with love, relatedness, community. As has been noted, many English words having to do with finances have a dual meaning in relationship, for instance, *bond, yield, duty, interest, share,* and *security.*[17]

There is another, more contemporary reason for the association of money with love. In the busy modern family, if money is more readily available than love or time, material things may be substituted for attention, so that money becomes associated with love. If a parent appears to value money and business very highly, his child may later emulate him in an attempt to win his approval, attention, and love. In his book *The Art of the Deal,* Donald Trump writes about how his affinity for business helped him get along with his father, evidently a tough, intimidating man:

> Fortunately for me, I was drawn to business very early, and I was never intimidated by my father, the way most people were. I stood up to him, and he respected that. We had a relationship that was almost businesslike. I sometimes wonder if we'd have gotten along so well if I hadn't been as business-oriented as I am.[18]

Money is also used frequently to reward children for good behavior. "If you're good, I'll buy you a toy." Children who are rewarded with money often develop a pattern of rewarding themselves as adults with material things when they feel down or stressed-out. Other people who were rewarded with money as kids react in the opposite way, rejecting money because they associate it with control. The latter kind of person may unconsciously reject money and material possessions as a way of maintaining psychic independence.

A successful rock musician I know used to write his ten-year-old son hundred-dollar checks to leave him alone and be quiet. For the son, this could lead to an ambivalent relationship with money in adulthood: it was his friend, providing many material goods, but it also substituted for love and attention and denied him access to his father.

MONEY AS FILTH

There are many associations in our individual and collective psyches between money and being dirty, unclean, filthy. Many of these also get reflected in language. We say that someone is "filthy rich." Some money, if it's particularly dirty because illegally obtained, has to be "laundered." The taboo against talking about money adds to the sense that the very subject is impolite, a tad dirty. According to Lewis Lapham, Americans are particularly prone to see money this way.

> I cannot think of any other people as obsessive as the Americans about the ritual washing of money. It is as if we know, somewhere in the attic of our Puritan memory, that money is a vile substance—ungodly and depraved. To an Italian, as to a Czech or Brazilian, the fine distinctions between clean money and dirty money belong to the chemistries of the absurd. Money is money, and there's an end on it.[19]

Americans, he adds, prefer to handle money in the "purified" form of a credit card.

It was as power shifted from sacred to secular rulers during medieval times that money made its fall from grace, from something divine to something base, according to Joseph Kulin, writing in *Parabola*.[20] He cites David Carpenter in *The Encyclopedia of Religion:* "Money was increasingly represented as demonic. Feelings of awe before the numinous qualities of gold and silver were transformed into feelings of disgust for gold and silver coins, which were increasingly compared to excrement."[21]

Psychoanalytic theory also sees an association between money and feces. Because feces are the first "possession" a child becomes aware of, premature or excessive demands during toilet training, it is claimed, can leave a person stuck in the anal stage, forever trying to assert his independence and control by holding onto possessions. As an adult, instead of withholding feces, the person with an anal personality might withhold money, attention, emotions, anything of value to another.[22] The codependent spender, I believe, also regards money as excrement, but she tends to spend loosely, especially to please others. And those addicted to deprivation try to wash their hands of money altogether.

MONEY AS SELF-WORTH

Net-worth equals self-worth.

WALL STREET BANKER

Another association people make with money is to see it as the currency of self-worth: "I am what I have. I am *because* I have." With this belief, a person is not worthy just because he exists, he's worthy because he "pulls down six figures." Income becomes a concrete, quantifiable measure. My worth is determined in comparison to your worth. Money becomes a way of keeping score.

According to the cultural mores of recent decades, it doesn't matter so much what you do to get money; what matters is that you get it. If people pay you a lot, you must be worthy, and if they don't, you're worth*less*. What we con-tribute to the common good seems to have little bearing. Money and possessions are the badge of achievement much more than integrity, compassion, or even skill.

Compare the salary of a child care worker with twenty years' experience to that of a twenty-five-year-old stockbro-ker. One can't help noticing that those jobs that have tradi-tionally been considered "women's work," jobs that involve nurturing, teaching, and supporting, are the least valued, and those associated with finance, banking, accounting, law, and brokerage, are the highest.

Long before money was represented in little plastic gold cards, it was associated with status. In those ancient tribal ceremonies where animals were sacrificed, the portions were sometimes distributed to the ritual participants according to social rank. This put money immediately in association with status, and this association is still evident in the collective un-conscious. Eventually, metal coins replaced meat as symbols of status, and gold, silver, and bronze coins embossed with the likeness of the king or with some other symbol of pres-tige would be given to subjects as a symbol of esteem and honor.[23]

We still equate money with status. Those who *look* as though they have money are treated as more worthy than those who don't. Just sit around in any courtroom, welfare office, or bank for evidence. Some people crave this special treatment as a substitute for self-esteem. In the 1980s, many of us compared ourselves to the big moneymakers and spenders all around us and thought we were coming up short. Then, like anorexics who have lost their sense of real-ity, we started starving ourselves spiritually and emotion-ally—working more and more—in order to try and get more of this symbol of status. For many, becoming rich enough to be worthy became an obsession.

The flip side of the equation "net worth equals self-worth" is "negative net worth equals negative self-worth."

People without money who buy into this idea feel shame about their financial situation. "I am what I *don't have*." Tony, a thirty-three-year-old director, suffers acutely from this equation of net worth with self-worth: "When I'm not doing well financially, I feel like a worthless piece of junk. I feel like a bad father, a failure of a husband, no good to anyone— including myself."

According to the writer and poet W. H. Auden, this association of wealth with worth, and poverty with failure, is especially pronounced in America. In Europe, he noted, the poor have not generally been considered personally to blame for being poor, the way they are in the United States,[24] though this may well be changing. And it's not *having* money that Americans have valued (witness our anemic savings accounts) so much as the ability to get it and spend it.

Advertising also exploits our association of money and self-worth, with copy like "You deserve it," "You're worth it," and "You've earned it." A recent American Express commercial features a successful-looking businessman hosting some twenty people for dinner in an upscale restaurant. The voice-over explains what a dreadful failure the host would have been without his American Express card. "Five more people showed up than you were expecting. Not a time when you want to worry about preset limits on your credit card. That would be embarrassing. But with American Express, you know you can handle it. Instead of worrying, you order more wine." The implication is that *limits are embarrassing*, exposing you as less successful and therefore less worthy.

MIRROR, MIRROR, ON THE WALL, WHO'S THE RICHEST OF THEM ALL?

With the varied and powerful associations there are to money, it is no wonder so many intense emotions are played out through this medium. Money represents power, love, potency, magic, self-worth, security, or filth in our psyches. So use your relationship to money as you would a mirror. Hold it up to see what it reflects back to you. It may mirror your lack of self-esteem, your craving for power, your lack of integrity, your feelings of impotency, or your need for nurturing. It may also reveal your yearning for connection, your spiritual hunger, your capacity to love, and your honor.

Remember that the word *money* has roots in "memory," "creativity," and "warnings." Only by refusing to confront the issue of money in our lives do we run a risk, because it's only when we "forget," when we remain unconscious, that money can possess us and take over our lives. And by becoming conscious of our relationship to money, of what we act out through it, we can learn what it has to teach us. All the life-force energy and power that we now expend on our struggles with money can be put to better use in building *true wealth*, but first we have to acknowledge the ways in which we are compulsive with money.

CHAPTER 3

CAN MONEY REALLY BE AN ADDICTION?

> *What is not in doubt is that the pursuit of money, or any enduring association with it, is capable of inducing not alone bizarre but ripely perverse behavior.*
>
> JOHN KENNETH GALBRAITH
> *MONEY: WHENCE IT CAME, WHERE IT WENT*

> *It's a sickness I have in the face of which I am helpless.*
>
> IVAN BOESKY, FORMER WALL STREET
> ARBITRAGEUR

SOME PEOPLE MAY BALK at the suggestion that money can be an addiction. Yet for millions of Americans, it fits the classical criteria common to all addictive behaviors:* (1) *It's an obsession.* Getting it, protecting it, worrying about it, getting rid of it, longing for it has become an almost constant focus, overshadowing other goals. (2) The person *lacks control* over his pattern with money, is driven by impulses seemingly beyond rational control. (3) He *repeats the same pattern over and*

---

*An overview of these criteria as they apply to addictions in general can be found in the book I coauthored with Dr. Arnold Washton, *Willpower's Not Enough* (New York: HarperCollins, 1989).

over, despite negative consequences, and (4) he *denies* that the way he deals with money is problematic.

To call dysfunctional money patterns addictions is not to judge those who suffer from them. If anything, we need to have compassion toward ourselves for being so emotionally and spiritually impoverished that we use money as a mood-changer. Still, the fact that our behavior is having negative consequences for us and is out of control must be acknowledged before we can get better. And what better metaphor do we have for "out of control" than addiction?

Compulsive behavior with money has little to do with the actual amounts involved. A person can be broke and still be driven by money lust, can have lots of money and be a compulsive debtor, and can spend a dollar or a million dollars compulsively. It's *not the amount* of money you earn, spend, or borrow that makes your behavior compulsive, *but the way you use it* and the *effect* it has on your life. Basically, your use of money is compulsive if it's causing problems in your life yet you persist in the pattern anyway.

SIGNS OF ADDICTION AS THEY APPLY TO MONEY DISORDERS

Obsession

Addictive behavior is compelling and consuming. The person with a money disorder spends a good deal of time and energy focusing on money—worrying about it, getting it, protecting it, getting rid of it. Compulsive spenders and debtors worry about where to get money, whether the check will bounce, whether the charge card is still usable. The hoarder is obsessed with how much he has, how much everything costs, how much he is owed. The wealth addict is preoccupied with how much she can make on the next deal. No matter what form the obsession takes, money is a central, absorbing focus, overshadowing other aspects of life.

Even the person addicted to deprivation is obsessed with money. A lot of his energy goes into hating those who have it, trying to survive while rejecting money, dealing with various money crises, and fending off opportunities to make more. In *Wealth Addiction,* Philip Slater tells an old Zen story to illustrate what happens when someone deprives himself out of some dogmatic, ideological conviction:

> Two monks who are traveling together encounter a nude woman trying to cross a stream. One of them carries her across, much to the consternation of the other. They continue in silence for a couple of hours until the second monk can stand it no longer. "How," he asks, "could you expose yourself to such temptation?" The first monk replies, "I put her down two hours ago. You're still carrying her."[1]

The person addicted to deprivation is like the second monk. He thinks he's better than the person driven by greed, but he spends at least as much time focusing on money.

Lack of Control

> *Ambition eclipsed rationality. I was unable to find fulfillment in realistic limits. One frenetic meeting followed another. One deal was piled atop the next. The hours grew longer, the numbers grew bigger, the stakes grew more critical, the fire grew ever hotter.*
>
> *By the time I became a managing director, I was out of control.*
>
> DENNIS LEVINE
> *INSIDE OUT*

The person who is compulsive with money has lost the freedom to choose. He makes repeated vows to change—to spend less, stop charging, stop putting money before the family, stop lending—but seems unable to follow through. He doesn't control money anymore; money controls him.

The compelling urge that an addict is driven by has been described as a "command from within." It's as if you are driven to do your thing despite all rational considerations. Deborah, a forty-two-year-old compulsive spender, recalls that there was no decision involved: "If I wanted something, I felt totally compelled to buy it—regardless of what I could afford. There wasn't even any struggle in my mind about it. I would just block out the reality, go to the bank machine, and get money, even if I had already written checks against that balance that hadn't cleared yet. I was *going* to do it. Period."

Several of the players in the 1980s Wall Street insider trading scandal have said they tried to stop participating at various points but were unable to extricate themselves using willpower. The next time Levine or Boesky or Milken called, they heard themselves going right along with it. The money was just too seductive, and they were no longer in control.

Sometimes, the money addict *can* exert strained control over his pattern for a while, especially if he's trying to prove (to a spouse or therapist) that he doesn't have a problem. The compulsive shopper, for instance, can avoid the stores for several weeks when put to the test. But if he isn't healing the dis-ease within, a return to the old pattern is likely. Or, he may just pick up another addiction—to food, thinness (anorexia), or exercise—to replace shopping.

Repetition Despite Negative Consequences

The primary symptom that sets addiction apart from a harmless habit is this: if the behavior has negative consequences—if it affects a person's physical or mental health, family and other relationships, work and values, or puts him at risk of arrest—and he keeps doing it anyway, the behavior is compulsive. The use of money as a mood-changer can lead to the following consequences:

Physical health. Appetite disturbances, ulcers, high blood pressure, loss of sleep, fatigue, and stress illnesses.

Psychological health. Mood swings and irritability, defensiveness, loss of self-esteem, feelings of guilt and shame, feelings of being a failure, powerlessness, depression and despair. Tony, the young director introduced earlier, grew up in a family that drilled it into his head that financial success was all that mattered. As an adult, whenever he experiences financial strain, his feelings of worthlessness cause him to become severely depressed, even suicidal.

It's not only poor people who suffer negative psychological effects from their money problems. Stories abound of suicide, paranoia, depression, and the like among the rich, the most renowned example being billionaire Howard Hughes, who spent years cooped up in a penthouse apartment, depressed and paranoid.

Relationships. Withdrawal from family and friends, lack of interest in sex, arguments, resentment, communication breakdown, distrust, estrangement, separation and divorce. Carl, the businessman who was once a major drug dealer, says that while in the throes of his wealth addiction, he was altogether incapable of intimacy:

> When you're addicted to money, you can't really have a relationship other than the one you have with money. I remember one night looking at this woman I was sleeping with; she's talking to me, and all I'm thinking about is money: how much I'm making, the meeting I have the next day with another dealer, how I'm gonna handle it so I come out ahead. . . .
>
> Everybody became a deal to me. If you didn't represent a deal, I wasn't interested. I couldn't cultivate any real friendships or relationships. It just wasn't a priority for me. Everything was money . . . making and accruing money.
>
> Besides, I didn't have time for a relationship. I was working at this thing seven days a week, seven in the morning till eleven at night. The whole thing revolved around making money, doing it right, and

getting over. If you weren't helping me do that, then
I didn't have time for you.

Finances. For compulsive spenders and debtors, there are
obvious negative financial consequences—that's part of the
problem. But even acquisition addicts experience negative
financial consequences from their compulsion. In the early
1970s, for instance, the famous Hunt brothers lost their fortunes in a seemingly compulsive drive to get more. Similar
stories on a smaller scale make headlines almost every day.

Values. In the grip of money addiction, people often do
things they wouldn't ordinarily do. The compulsive debtor
kites checks and lies on credit applications; acquisition addicts commit crimes from fraud to murder because what
they have isn't enough; at times even codependent spenders
embezzle money in order to give it to someone else. Individuals abandon cherished beliefs that do not support their
addictive orientation. Cash replaces conscience as the moti-
vating force.

Denial

> *I knew I owed a helluva lot of money, but I preferred not to
> know. On some level, I'd say, "Gee, I must be getting up
> there," but I'd keep going. I didn't want to know, because
> then I'd have to stop.*
>
> LISA, AN INDEBTED SECRETARY

The person with a money disorder doesn't think she has a
problem, or at least she rarely admits it. "Who, me? No, that
jerk at the bank just really screwed me up this month," or "If
it wasn't for XYZ happening, I'd be fine." Or, "Once I get
that record deal, I'll be home free." She denies (1) that her
money pattern is self-defeating, (2) that she's not in control
of it, and (3) that it causes negative consequences for her or
others.

Denial takes many forms. Terence Gorski has described some variations as they apply to alcoholics.[2] I have adapted some of these and added others as they apply to money compulsions:

Absolute denying ("I didn't do that.")

A good defense ("How dare you accuse me!")

Minimizing ("I only charged a few things.")

Blaming others ("You're the one with the problem; you're just too tight.")

Avoidance (just not talking about it)

Rationalizing ("If it weren't for the economy . . .")

Intellectualizing ("See, there's several things you need to understand about money . . .")

Sour grapes ("I pity people who save their money; they live such boring lives.")

When any evidence threatens the addict's denial—confrontation with a spouse, arrest, garnishment of salary—he can become indignant and defensive, because if he doesn't maintain the illusion that everything's OK, he will have to consider changing. To give up one's denial is to turn a corner irrevocably, to ruin the prospect for continuing the compulsive behavior without awareness. It's the beginning of the end; the addict knows it, and avoids it.

That's why it's almost impossible to talk sense into a money addict, as Tracy, the wife of a compulsive spender, is finally realizing. "I kept thinking that if I could just find the *right* way to explain it to him, he would get it. I kept trying to talk to him about long-range goals and budgets. He would seem to be hearing me, then the next thing I knew, he'd be telling me about the speed boat he just put on the Visa card."

Sometimes, a powerful dose of reality will pierce the money addict's denial. For Lisa, a compulsive spender and debtor, this happened at a checkout counter:

I had about $150 worth of goods rung up and handed the clerk my MasterCard. She put it through the machine and said, "I'm sorry, ma'am, it's come back Code 7. You're over your limit." Embarrassed, I groped in my pocketbook and handed her my Visa card, making some little joke. She put that card through, and I saw Code 7 come up again. Meanwhile, the people in line behind me are watching all this. So I made another little joke like "I guess you wouldn't want to take a check from me, huh?" And I ran out of there, literally ran, leaving the cart full of stuff behind me.

I sat in the car, shaking, thinking, "This is it." I knew I couldn't take out a line of credit to pay the cards because I was maxed-out everywhere. It was really a scary feeling.

We see denial at the corporate level too. Recently, a major designer clothing company revealed that it has some $55 million in junk bonds to pay off over the next four years, a considerable sum, given the strained financial condition of the firm. Yet, according to the news report, the company's owner and chief executive exudes confidence. "The debt will take care of itself," he says. In 1984, the same CEO took $12 million in compensation, one year before the company was forced to borrow at high-interest junk-bond rates. And in 1990, with the business tottering, he and his partner took home an amount roughly equal to the company's net loss for the year, despite the financial obligations looming.[3] This is behavior that denies reality, just as surely as that which can be found in any person with a chemical addiction.

OTHER FEATURES OF MONEY ADDICTION
A High

Many money addicts experience a high of sorts. The compulsive debtor feels giddy with relief when he gets approved for a new loan, as though he's just gotten an "injection" of cash. Compulsive spenders describe the high they get from hitting the mall. Even the person addicted to deprivation often describes a thrill achieved from living on the edge. And wealth addicts consistently describe accumulating money as a high. Says stock market junkie Jason,

> There definitely was a high with it, and you get seduced by that. The faster I made money, the more seductive it was. Before long, I was trading stocks very quickly, making three or four trades a day, often holding them for just a few hours. Doing it quickly was a part of the high for me. I was taking a lot more risk, but getting potentially greater gains—and highs.

This short-term investing is rather like smoking crack. Because of the immediate and intense effect, it is all the more powerfully addicting—and subsequently harder to stop.

Fifteen years ago, when Carl was seventeen years old and making $100,000 a month dealing drugs, he says he got a rush from making that much money, a rush that hooked him.

> It was totally intoxicating. It was like speed. I had incredible energy from it. I bet there's a chemical that's released in your body when you're making that much money. I don't know what it is, maybe adrenaline. Whatever it is, it's the highest form of speed and the biggest rush. It keeps your mind constantly working on a certain level. People thought I was on speed, but I wasn't taking a damn thing.

Coming close to getting caught and getting away with it was a rush too. It's like playing a cops-and-robbers game and winning. Every time you get away with something, it's another point for you. Of course, all they need is one point, and the game is over. But as long as you keep winning, it's a rush.

But, as with any drug high, the sense of satiation wears off quickly, and you have to go looking for the next hit. The relief of a new loan wears off after about a week, when the compulsive debtor starts scheming all over again. The thrill of a new deal, a stock market killing, or a great bargain lasts only a little while. As a result, you stay in constant motion with your pattern.

Tolerance (You Need More and More)

In most addictions there exists a phenomenon called tolerance, by which the addict must use increasing amounts of the drug in order to achieve the same high. Money addiction is no exception. The money addict needs to do more and more (spending, borrowing, hoarding, acquiring) to achieve the same effect.

Compulsive spenders say the dollar amounts of their binges increase over time. Hoarders have to put more and more away to feel secure, and the wealth addict has to earn geometrically larger sums to feel satisfied. Donald Trump's sister, Maryanne Trump-Barry, unwittingly painted a picture of money addiction in this description of her brother for *Newsweek* some years ago: "Success brings success, which brings more success. The more he gets, the more he wants."[4]

Carl recalls how his satiation point kept moving farther ahead of him too:

I remember in the beginning, all I wanted was $5,000. Then I said, "OK, I just want $5,000 and a car, $10,000. Then a friend of mine opened up a chain of food stands with $40,000, so then it was forty grand I should have. But the ball was rolling so fast—a hundred grand, and then a quarter million, then a half. . . . Then I lost $200,000 in a deal. Well, I gotta make that up. So like a drug, there was never enough. You get so wrapped up in the world of making money, you don't realize the value of it anymore. It's unreal.

I always kidded myself and said it's a means to an end, and somehow that justified everything. But I was like a shark on a feeding frenzy. I just kept wildly eating, gobbling up money, to the point where I was bloated, overstuffed. But I just kept eating more.

Moodiness

The money addict's moods depend on whether he is able to get his money high or not. The debtor's moods are affected by his ability to get the next loan or get someone to cosign, the wealth addict's moods hinge on whether he's able to cinch the next deal, and the compulsive shopper's moods hinge on whether he can go shopping. If the money addict's usual pattern is blocked by some person or circumstance, he'll get frustrated and irritable. According to Jason, the stock market player, "My moods were completely dependent on how my investments were doing that day. If they were up, I was elated, like I was in a state of grace. If they were down, I was despondent. By the end of the day I was exhausted. Emotionally, it was very draining, because in the course of the day there were so many ups and downs."

Some people describe intense physical and emotional aftereffects when they try to break their compulsive money pattern. Carl describes how he felt when he tried to withdraw from the fast money of drug dealing:

Money was a total stimulant. Then all of a sudden, the stimulant's taken away. I went through severe withdrawal: I was listless; I couldn't get up in the morning; I was sleeping twelve hours a day; I was moody, irritable all the time; I would go off the wall about little things; I couldn't concentrate. It was really hard to get through that period without falling back into dealing, because people were still calling me. I can't tell you how hard it was.

Carl's remarks have implications for our nation's so-called drug war. If we want to help people stop dealing, money addiction will have to be recognized and treated.

Money Becomes an End in Itself

The money addict stops using money as a *means* to an end and relates to it as the *end* in itself. The compulsive shopper doesn't shop to replace an item that's broken, but shops *to shop*. The compulsive debtor doesn't use credit to expand a solid business or acquire assets, but to meet other debts. The hoarder doesn't buy the things he's ostensibly saving for; he saves to save. Dennis Levine was earning $2 million a year *legitimately* while involved in insider trading.[5] Objectively speaking, he didn't *need* the money, certainly not enough to jeopardize his career, family, reputation, and freedom. Yet he risked it all. The only explanation is addiction.

Distorted Thinking: Money Becomes Unreal

Anorexics have what's known as a distorted body image. They can get down to eighty pounds, look at themselves in the mirror, and really see themselves as fat. Likewise, some money addicts have what could be called a distorted money image. Compulsive spenders can be flat broke and still think they have money to spend; compulsive savers can have fat bank accounts and still be haunted by fears of poverty; compulsive earners can be worth a million and still feel poor.

For money-accumulators, huge sums take on an unreal quality, become distorted. One commodities trader reportedly flew into a rage when he got his monthly bonus check, stormed into his boss's office, threw the check on the floor, and spat on it. The check was for $2.1 million, but he thought it wasn't enough.[6] Even J. Paul Getty once admitted, "I've never felt really rich—in the oil business others were all much richer than I was."[7]

Even corporations sometimes behave as if their thinking has become distorted. While the Wall Street firm of Drexel Burnham Lambert was nearing bankruptcy, some executives still received million-dollar bonuses every month. In fact, as the firm's condition worsened, the bonuses grew larger. Less than a month before the firm filed bankruptcy, one executive received a bonus of $16.6 million.[8] The company itself was acting like an addict, denying and defying reality.

Big deal-makers often experience money as unreal, especially in today's electronic marketplace where no real cash changes hands, just computer blips on a screen. Gerrard, a compulsive spender and self-saboteur who made and lost millions in the building trades, talks about how disorienting it can be to deal in such unreal numbers:

> People who are in big deal-making businesses the way I am develop distortions about money. Say I negotiate with this guy, and I just make $50,000 in profit in the deal. So I leave the meeting, and walking by a bookstore, I go in and buy $400 in books, on a whim. What do I care? I just made $50,000. Am I gonna worry now about how much a book costs? After that, how am I gonna deny myself anything? Money takes on an unreal quality.

One September, when I was working as a counselor in a wealthy school district in the early 1980s, a freshman girl named Darlene came to see me, obviously distraught. I gently probed for the problem. Finally, she blurted it out in a torrent of tears: Her parents were poor. They only made $60,000 a year.

Of course, Darlene's parents could not be considered poor by anyone's standards, certainly not mine—I was only making about $18,000. But she was right on two scores: Her parents did make less than most others in this wealthy community, so they were poor perhaps by comparison. But more important, as the school year unfolded, I discovered that Darlene's mother was an alcoholic, and things were quite chaotic and difficult at home. Darlene's family was indeed poor in ways that count. The girl knew she was impoverished; she just mistook the cause as having something to do with money. Darlene's sense of emotional deprivation and impoverishment got projected onto the symbol of money.

Protecting the Supply

The money addict, like any other, goes to great lengths to protect his supply, to make sure nothing interferes with access to his money mood-changer, be it shopping, credit, deprivation, or deals. Compulsive spenders will selectively pay on certain credit cards so as to always keep some in good standing. The hoarder guards his stash behind elaborate security systems. Even the person addicted to deprivation guards her "supply of poverty," sabotaging any success that might threaten it.

Joe, who earned illegal profits through black-market arms dealing, describes the lengths he went to to protect his stash: "I used to bury my money in the backyard, in Platex baby bottles; $10,000 in hundred-dollar bills fits perfectly in each one. And I did it with such care. It was like a shrine, protected. I almost put ribbons on it. A very close friend of mine saw me doing this one day, and he said, 'You gotta love money to do this.' I looked at him and said, 'You're right.' "

Ken, the son of a first-generation millionaire industrialist, describes how his father's behavior with money changed through the years from creating it through work that he enjoyed to being obsessed with protecting it. Because Ken is a former cocaine user, he draws parallels between his father's protective behavior toward money and his own toward cocaine:

> In the beginning, my father seemed to enjoy his money, just as I enjoyed getting high before I got addicted. Then, after the process of addiction set in, his pattern with money became more driven, compulsive, joyless. I saw the way he gathered it around him to conserve and defend it. That's what you do with drugs. You protect your stash, wrap yourself around it. I used to do that with cocaine. Then I saw my father doing it with money. Money certainly is a drug.

Lies and Illegalities

Money addicts will lie if necessary to keep their routine going, just as other addicts will. Debtors lie on credit applications, hoarders lie to family members about how much money they have, and wealth addicts lie on their taxes. One New York City lawyer recently disappeared with $7 million of his clients' funds. He wrote to his clients and told them that he was dying of a brain tumor and had given the money away.[9] This is not unlike the absurd lengths to which chemical drug addicts are driven.

Before their downfall, televangelists Tammy and Jim Bakker lied on the air to get more money from listeners. After making a $149,000 down payment on a house in Palm Desert and spending $100,000 for a Mercedes and a Rolls Royce, Tammy appealed to viewers for money to pay the bills: "Jim and I can't," she pleaded. "We've given everything we have, and literally we have given everything. I have offered to sell everything I have, because things don't really mean that much when it comes to getting the Gospel of Jesus Christ out. But if I sold every single thing I own, Jim, it would probably keep us on the air one more day." "Oh no," said Jim, "it wouldn't be that long."[10]

In addition to lying, the money addict at the advanced stages does other things he never thought he'd do. The compulsive debtor kites checks, manipulates accounts to cover insufficient funds, and reneges on loans. Others shoplift, take kickbacks, embezzle, or participate in fraud. Nothing matters but getting the money, the deal, or the loan. This happens even to people who are considered good upstanding citizens. They simply deny to themselves and others that what they are doing is illegal or unethical.

Blaming

The money addict—like all addicts—tends to blame other people and outside circumstances for whatever problems ensue from her behavior. "Other people didn't cooperate." "The economy is the problem." "If it wasn't for my husband . . ." "How dare the bank bounce my check." It's difficult for the addict to take responsibility for her own actions, because to do so would necessitate giving up denial.

Leona Helmsley, the self-described queen of the Helmsley hotel chain, after being sentenced for tax fraud, cried out to friends in the courtroom, "See what they've done to me."[11] This is a classic addictive response—an inability to accept the consequences of her own actions and an insistence on blaming others. Unfortunately, this blaming behavior keeps the addict stuck in the same self-defeating pattern. As long as she places blame "out there," she is powerless to change herself. And only by changing herself will she be able to alter the behavior that is causing her such distress.

On the national level, we employ blame too in an effort to deny our addictive money behavior. We blame the Japanese for our economic woes, when the growing trade deficit and lost American assets and jobs are really the natural consequence of addictive money patterns at the governmental and corporate levels, as we will see in the next chapter.

A Crisis Point

At some point, most money addicts face a crisis brought about by their self-defeating pattern. It could be an arrest, the threat of divorce, or the shock of discovering that one's bank account has been attached by a creditor. Ironically, after such a crisis, if he doesn't get help, the addict will sometimes actually step up his self-destructive behavior. He'll shop more, or steal or embezzle more, or take out more loans. Grant, a compulsive debtor, describes the humiliation he felt when he got caught kiting checks and how it prompted him to spend all the more recklessly.

> One day the bank manager called me in for kiting checks. Two banks had gotten together and realized what I was doing. He looked at me from across the desk and said, "Grant, what you're doing is a criminal offense." I was so humiliated! But it didn't stop me. In fact, I started spending even more money after that, because I was in so much pain.[12]

According to the *New York Times,* after the congressional check-bouncing scandal came to light in 1992 and the House Speaker called for a crackdown, the number of bad checks passed actually *increased.*[13] Those representatives whose check bouncing was the result not of oversight but of a compulsive pattern may have dealt with their fear, embarrassment, and shame by spending more money, writing even more bad checks.

Geographic Cures

It's common for the money addict to believe that if he just moves to a new area—gets a fresh start—everything will be all right. Leo, after racking up some $200,000 in debt, told his wife he wanted to declare bankruptcy and move to a new state. "I just want to get out of this mess and go somewhere else. I made a mistake." But Leo's compulsive money pattern has been in evidence throughout his life, and his father went bankrupt before him. His fantasy that moving will be a cure-all is just that. He'll surely take his compulsion with him. Recovering alcoholics and drug addicts know well this notion of a geographic cure. They will tell you that nothing is likely to change until Leo faces his compulsive dis-ease.

Secrecy: A Double Life

The person with a money disorder often leads a double life: the one his friends and co-workers know about, and the one only he, his creditors, and *maybe* a spouse know about. The debtor hides the extent of his indebtedness, the shopper hides the extent of her purchases, the hoarder is secretive about what he's got stockpiled, and the codependent spender doesn't tell anyone how much money she gives to her boyfriend.

When New York Mayor David Dinkins's former campaign treasurer, Arnold Biegen, was arrested for stealing campaign funds, many people were shocked, because Biegen was well respected by prominent people, like Governor Mario Cuomo, who'd appointed him to a prestigious panel. According to the *New York Times,* people never detected Biegen's illicit behavior, even though some, like Dinkins, felt they knew him very well.

Because of the secrecy surrounding money disorders, when an incident of white-collar crime comes to light, people are often shocked at such uncharacteristic behavior by this otherwise upstanding person. But in many cases, there was a pattern of previous money dysfunction that was ignored or covered up. For example, it later came out that Biegen had *in the past* defaulted on a $250,000 loan from a

bank on whose board he served, a bank with ties to organized crime, a bank that later failed. This all had come to
light during Dinkins's 1989 campaign but was dismissed by
campaign officials who viewed it as insignificant, a "matter
involving Mr. Biegen's personal business affairs."[14] But a person with a money disorder doesn't turn the behavior on and
off, depending on whether he's working on his personal
business affairs or yours. Like any addiction, money disorders tend to be chronic and progressive. In a culture in
which money disorders are so commonplace as to seem normal, we're just blind to them.

Multiple Addictions: Money and . . .

Many people with money disorders have other addictions as
well. It's common, for instance, for a compulsive spender to
be a compulsive eater who spends a lot on food, for an
anorexic eater to become a compulsive clothes shopper to
further satisfy her body-image fixation, or for a cocaine addict to become a compulsive debtor to get money for coke.
Wealth addicts are often workaholics, and alcoholics typically spend compulsively when they're drinking.

All addictions have more in common with one another
than they have differences—however varied they look on the
face of it. Rather than being wholly unrelated processes, they
are different expressions of the same phenomenon. In other
words, *it's all one disease.* It's not so much the substances
themselves—the food, the money, the sex, the cocaine—that
make us vulnerable to addiction, but our own dis-ease
within, literally, our lack of ease with ourselves. The true
source of addiction lies within us, in our craving for a mood-
changer. That's why, when people give up one mood-
changer, it's common for them to pick up a new one.

One of the biggest dangers of multiple addiction is that
a relapse in one area can trigger relapse in another. "When I
was drinking, I was more likely to be dysfunctional with

money," says Theresa, a thirty-eight-year-old physical therapist who's been in Alcoholics Anonymous for ten years. "And when I'd get crazy with money—not paying my bills, spending wildly, running up debts—that triggered my low self-esteem and all the negative alcoholic thinking, so I was more likely to drink. The two things fed off each other."

Theresa had a six-month slip in both areas several years ago. She remembers how drinking affected her use of money, and vice versa:

> The huge debt I'm in now is a result of six months when I picked up alcohol again and made some really crazy decisions about spending. I put my name on a mutual purchase with this guy I was on a fling with, put about $10,000 of debt in my name. Then the relationship went out the window.
>
> Then again, when I'm drinking, I get into a totally reckless place. "To hell with it, let's do it! Live for today! It'll all work out." A lot of that has to do with the grandiosity that comes out when I'm drinking. It's like I'm not going to let anybody see that I'm hurting, or that I'm having financial problems. Then the fear, anxiety, and shame from the money problems gives me an excuse to drink.

Ross is recovering from addiction to prescription drugs. He's also a compulsive underearner and a shopper with huge credit card debts. The mounting stress of his financial pressures has begun to pose a threat to his sobriety.

> Recently, I started to feel hopeless again, obsessing about the debt. And that triggers my addictive thinking, my negativity. I start to think, "Oh, what the hell, it's hopeless. I'm not worth it anyway. Who am I kidding, I'm not capable." It's the whole negative thinking of the addict. I've been dragging those ideas around for years.

So now I've taken a job at a bakery, just to bring in some regular income for a while and help me pull out of this hole. It's a recovery move. It's not the job of my dreams, but at least I'm taking some positive action. And when I'm doing that, then I'm making a shift in my overall attitude. And that's the best thing I can do to avoid a relapse.

Sometimes when a person becomes abstinent in one area of addiction, say to drugs or alcohol, a compulsive money pattern *emerges*. Polly, a fifty-year-old recovering alcoholic, has noticed the pattern: "When I stopped drinking, I started eating. When I stopped compulsive eating, the spending started. I'm just very addictive. The disease keeps coming out in different ways." That's because when a person abstains from a drug without healing the addict within, the disease is still active. It's bound to emerge in another way. It's like flattening out the bump in a rug: the cravings just pop up somewhere else.

Alison was an alcoholic who went through rehab and then attended Alcoholics Anonymous meetings. During the course of recovery, she started compulsively exercising, bingeing and purging (bulimia), and marathon shopping. People who didn't know better thought she was doing great. After all, she'd gone from being an overweight alcoholic to a sober, slim woman. Says Alison, "There was no telltale smell on my breath anymore, and I wasn't staggering around. My behavior was still off the wall, but no one knew what to attribute it to. From all outside appearances, I was doing great!" What no one realized was that Alison was still an active addict; she merely switched from alcohol to bulimia, compulsive exercise, and shopping. About nine months later, she relapsed to alcohol. Nothing *inside* had changed; she had just switched to more socially acceptable mood-changers.

Incest survivors and adult children of alcoholics both notice that doing work on those charged issues frequently causes their money disorders to be activated. Kirk, a recovering alcoholic, drug addict, and debtor, explains, "Right now I'm dealing with a lot of family issues, which is kicking up intense feelings I never knew were there. So my spending and record keeping are going downhill. It's really a balancing act in certain respects." A person with a chemical addiction is well advised to deal with that first. Without a foundation of sobriety, there can be little hope of recovery from the money disorder, because the alcohol and other chemical mood-changers will interfere with recovery work.

A Dance with Enablers

Money addicts often attract people who support their denial and unwittingly encourage their compulsive behavior. Many compulsive spenders and debtors, for instance, have an enabler who gives them money or bails them out of financial jams. The enabler is nearly always well intentioned. He believes he is helping his friend or relative to get on his feet or get through rough times. Usually, however, this well-meaning person has a blind spot. He doesn't see that the rough times, in the case of someone compulsive with money, are often the result of the person's *own* behavior. The enabler doesn't see that by giving money, he is actually helping perpetuate the problem. As long as any addict doesn't *have* to change, he won't.

Often, the enabler is driven by his own need to feel needed or important or to avoid abandonment. Usually, he's what's known as a codependent. He gives beyond the point where a healthy, self-respecting person would say, "Enough." He is as driven to give as the spender is to spend. On the advice of friends, therapists, or others, the enabler may vow not to do it anymore, but he is typically unable to follow through. The next time the spender/debtor asks for money, instead of "no," he says, "How much?"

During my early adult years, both of my parents unwittingly enabled my self-destructive pattern with money. My mother and I had a finely choreographed dance that we did together around money. We both knew our parts and could be counted on to perform them perfectly. All I had to do was hint that I'd gotten an especially high telephone bill or bounced lots of checks, and I'd get a check in the mail. I would then insist that it be a loan and not a gift, and my mother would reluctantly agree. That would be the last time either one of us would mention it. Somehow, I never seemed to have the extra money to pay her back.

When I was about twenty-five, my name was splashed on the front page of the local tabloids as the city's "Biggest Scofflaw," with hundreds of dollars in back parking tickets (a common distinction of the compulsive debtor). The state threatened to cancel my car registration if I didn't pay up. I employed a variation on my routine: I called my father for money. He met me for dinner, and we joked about how bad both of us were with money, how I was a chip off the old block. Then he gave me the three hundred dollars I needed to get out of the jam—just gave it to me. I believe he meant well, but unfortunately, I didn't learn anything about how to manage my affairs.

By my early thirties, I began to suspect that something was wrong with the way I handled money, but I'd been unable to alter it—until one day. My mother had sent me a hundred-dollar check to pay my phone bill, and I was driving to the telephone company to keep them from shutting my service off. Suddenly, everything became clear. I knew what I had to do. I reached into my purse, pulled out the check— and ripped it up. Then I turned my car around, went home, and called her. I told her what I had done and asked her not to send me any more money.

At first, my mother felt hurt, rejected, and resistant. "I just don't understand," she said. "Other people help their kids." I remember saying, "Yeah, but, Mom, I'm like an alcoholic with money. If you keep giving it to me, I'll never get my life together. Your bailing me out is hurting me, even though you're only trying to help. Look," I said, "even if you can't understand this, please just honor my request, and don't send me any more money, no matter how much I ask or hint."

Reluctantly, she agreed. "Well, since you put it that way. The last thing I would want to do is hurt you." We'd struck a pact, but a pact between an addict and a codependent is not wholly reliable. We've both slipped into our familiar dance from time to time over the years, but steadily we've gotten better.

Then there's enabling at the organizational level. The Wall Street firm of Drexel Burnham Lambert enabled Michael Milken for years. Perhaps because the company was making huge profits from what he was doing, they looked the other way and failed to monitor him. Even after Milken's arrest, top Drexel officials continued to maintain his innocence, and for a while the company paid his legal costs of $3 million a month.[15]

Finally, there's what I call systemic enabling, which is when the larger system enables compulsive money behaviors. Bankruptcy laws, for example, can enable compulsive debtors. Those who know the ropes (and, ironically, can afford the legal advice) know that the system allows them to bail out of their debt and still keep many of their assets.

Further, declaring bankruptcy stalls recovery for the compulsive debtor. It removes the negative consequences from her debting, so she doesn't have to examine the behavior that got her there or take responsibility for changing it. Jerrold Mundis, author of a best-selling book on compulsive debt, estimates that 50 percent of those who declare bankruptcy will eventually wind up in default again.[16] If you don't face the consequences of your spending and debting but employ a quick fix like bankruptcy, you probably won't be motivated to change. An addict only changes when his back is against the wall; bankruptcy, in effect, removes the wall.

In a final example of systemic enabling, in October 1990, some fourteen months before publishing tycoon

Robert Maxwell's apparent suicide, an astute analyst with a London brokerage firm sent a notice to his clients discouraging them from investing in Maxwell's holdings, describing the publishing giant's financial maneuverings as a juggling act. Maxwell threatened to sue the London firm, which then printed a "correction" of the report—and fired the analyst.[17]

Rather than being allowed to experience the natural consequences of his compulsive debt, that is, bad publicity, Robert Maxwell was enabled to keep on the same course. Like any addict, Maxwell fought to maintain his denial but would have been better served had he been forced—by natural consequences—to face up before he stole millions from employee pension funds and got so far out there that he couldn't see any way back.

But such systemic enabling is part of a larger picture of money dysfunction at the level of government and business, a subject that we turn to in the following chapter.

CHAPTER 4

A MONEY-ADDICTED CULTURE

I know of no country, indeed, where the love of money has taken stronger hold on the affections of men.

ALEXIS DE TOCQUEVILLE
DEMOCRACY IN AMERICA

As a nation, we have been partying, with such role models as Donald Trump. In a way, the whole country has been like Trump: Being rich was the fantasy of the 1980s, and Trump, best-selling author and casino entrepreneur, epitomized the dream. But now the party is over, and no one knows precisely how painful the developing hangover will turn out to be.

ALFRED L. MALABRE, JR.
WITHIN OUR MEANS

MONEY DISORDERS ON THE individual level have been all the harder to identify because we have been living in what amounts to a money-addicted culture, in which the use of money as a mood-changer has been pervasive. And dysfunctional approaches to money at the national and corporate level both reflect and help shape our own earning, spending, and debt patterns. The more we hear about compulsive spending and debting at the highest levels, the easier it is to rationalize our own self-defeating habits.

This is not to suggest that all our individual and societal fiscal woes can be attributed to money addiction, for this would be a gross simplification of the complex and varied forces at work. It *is*, however, to venture that the paradigm of addiction is a useful metaphor for understanding something of what motivates people to behave with money in ways that are ultimately self-defeating. Certainly, the way we have been using money as a society is having some serious ramifications for us. And though there are many other interpretations and schools of understanding that could be applied to our current money crisis, I am choosing to look at it here through the lens of addiction.

I am also not implying that we should *blame* society, or the government, or corporations for our individual or collective money habits. Blaming distracts us from taking corrective action in our own lives and denies our collective responsibility for monitoring what our elected leaders do. Perhaps because so many of us have become compulsive spenders, chronic borrowers, and wealth addicts, we have elected—and reelected—leaders who reflect those same addictive orientations. Though blaming is to be avoided, it is important to become *aware* of the addictive patterns exhibited at the level of government and business. The more aware we become, the better able we will be to recognize and reject addictive thinking when we see it and hear it.

There are a number of signs that we *as a culture* have become dysfunctional with money. I will divide the discussion of these signs into three parts: compulsive consumerism, money addiction at the level of government, and money addiction at the level of business.

SHOPPING AS A WAY OF LIFE: COMPULSIVE CONSUMERISM

Since World War II, shopping has become synonymous with the American way of life. U.S. citizens spend more time shopping than the people of any other nation, consume twice as many products as they did forty years ago, and use twice as much energy as either the Europeans or the Japanese. Further, our spending is out of proportion with our earning. During the 1980s, consumer debt tripled and credit card purchases quadrupled, despite the fact that average real wages declined. And though the recession of the 1990s has seen a drop in spending and a slight rise in saving, we're still the number one consumers in the world.[1]

Ironically, however, all this spending hasn't made us more content. According to surveys, the percentage of the U.S. population who reported being "very happy" peaked in 1957.[2] Despite the failure of our consumer culture to satisfy us, there are a number of reasons why we persist in our spending.

For one, there has been a steady shift away from the values of conservation and thrift in favor of consumerism: buying, using up, discarding, and buying more. As we shifted from our identity as citizens to that as consumers, our collective money behavior entered the realm of addiction. If we weren't fulfilled, rather than question the premise that consumerism was the ticket to happiness, we assumed that we simply didn't have *enough* money or possessions yet.

Meanwhile, this myopic focus on the material side of life exacerbated the very feelings of emptiness we were trying to avoid. Like a dog chasing its tail, we could never quite get where we wanted to go. "Enough," as Paul Wachtel observes in *The Poverty of Affluence*, "is always just over the horizon."[3] Our average income is sixty-five times the average income of half the world's population, and well over a million Americans are millionaires. Yet only 0.005 percent of us consider ourselves "rich."[4]

As businesses sought to keep consumers in this expansive, shopping mode, even children became potential consumers. Picture this magazine ad for a kiddie shopping cart: A smiling child stands proudly next to her plastic cart brimming with toys. Above her is the lead copy: "They'll shop 'til they drop." The rest of the ad reads, "The house can become a shopping mall. And every room a store, bursting with fascinating things to buy. All it takes is a preschooler's imagination. And the Shoppin' Basket."[5] We were shaping a new generation of compulsive shoppers. Having grown up on ads like this, no wonder the majority of teenage girls now name shopping as their favorite pastime.[6]

In order to keep people buying in the seventies and eighties while their real incomes were declining, debt was recast as a positive thing. Until then, debt was considered a last resort rather than a way of life, and bankruptcy carried a stigma. But recent mores changed all that. Naomi is a corporate project manager, many thousands of dollars in debt. She describes how she and her husband Edward fell under the influence of the idea of debt as normal:

> In the eighties, all you heard was, "Debt is good"; "You have to spend money to make money"; "The smartest people spend other people's money." And we bought into it all: charge cards up the wazoo, the home equity loan. We had no idea how much we were spending. None. We were charging vacations, dinners out, wardrobes, thinking nothing of it. Then I got laid off, and suddenly we came face-to-face with the reality that we owed a hell of a lot of money.

Our collective behavior during this period seemed driven by an addictlike fantasy of limitlessness, as if we could keep taking on ever more debt—personally and collectively—without ever having to pay it back, as if we could keep using ever more of the earth's resources without depleting them and keep releasing toxic chemicals into the waterways and stratosphere without polluting them. The fantasy of a permanent high with no ramifications is the only way to explain the fact that American middle-class consumers continued to spend more and more throughout the 1980s even though their income was falling, their debt load increasing, and their savings dwindling.

Moneythink, as Philip Slater calls it, was taking hold, whereby everything began to be evaluated almost exclusively

74

by financial criteria.[7] Having money is what mattered; what you did to get money didn't. Whether you enjoyed your work and how it contributed to the greater good—or hurt it— didn't matter as much as how well it paid. And only a sucker or a sappy idealist considered anything like the greater good even to be important. As Laurence Shames quips in *Hunger for More,* "In the eighties, community service seemed to be thought of as something you did in place of jail time if convicted of a white-collar crime."[8]

In the thrall of the addictive thinking of the eighties, some of us were seduced by our own greed, by the fantasy that we were all going to share in the boom, that we were *all* going to be winners now that the killjoys and wimps had been ousted from the White House. Those who didn't buy into the mood of frenzied consumption felt like outsiders, failures, downers, members of the losing team.

But it was an illusion. Like drug addicts lured into chasing an elusive euphoria, we as a nation wanted to believe we would be better off spending than saving, better off consuming than conserving, better off identifying with those driven by greed, acting in their best interests rather than our own.

Like any addict's lifestyle, compulsive consumerism is not sustainable in the long run. As E. F. Schumacher pointed out in 1973, people basing their economic lives on nonrenewable fuels are living on capital instead of income.[9] Now we're not even living on capital anymore, but debt. We've stopped producing much and have been selling off our assets to meet our debts. And we're doing the same thing with the earth—using up and polluting *its* capital—nonrenewable resources—to maintain today's way of life while undermining tomorrow's security and all but ensuring the impoverishment of our children. This is what Gandhi called commerce without morality. "Earth provides enough to satisfy every man's need," said the renowned Indian leader, "but not for every man's greed."[10]

MONEY ADDICTION AT THE LEVEL OF GOVERNMENT

In recent years, many of those in government have managed our finances in ways that suggest money addiction. Compulsive federal spending and debting took the place of sound financial planning and sent our nation plummeting from its position as the world's biggest creditor to that of the world's biggest debtor in just eight years.[11]

According to the economist John Kenneth Galbraith, "the good years of economic management in the United States came to an end with the Vietnam war."[12] From Nixon on, and especially during the Reagan and Bush administrations, national decision makers behaved in ways that I suggest are indicative of money disorders, employing short-term thinking, immediate gratification, blaming, manipulation, and denial. Perhaps because so many of us were also under the spell of these addictive values, we went along with it.

Until the recession of the 1990s pierced the national denial, we pretty much accepted as normal that our country habitually spent more than it brought in, which is exactly what a compulsive debtor does. Enabled by the public's lack of awareness regarding money dysfunction, our government representatives nearly doubled the national debt by 1985.[13]

Still, we kept on the same course. Reagan campaigned in 1984 with the question "Are you better off today?" to which Americans responded with a resounding yes by voting him back into office. People *felt* better off, just as I could feel better off if I went and bought everything I wanted on my credit cards. I wouldn't *be* better, but I could feel better—temporarily. As a nation, we were under the spell of addictive thinking. By the close of the decade, we had tripled the debt, adding more debt in ten years than in the *entire* prior history of the nation.[14]

The key feature of addiction, you will recall from the last chapter, is that the behavior has negative consequences—*yet you keep doing it anyway.* Therefore, it's important to take a quick survey of the profound consequences that money addiction at the governmental level has had for us:

1. The United States is no longer the richest nation in the world; it is the nation with the largest debt. Our combined debt—consumer, corporate, and government—is almost twice our gross national product.[15]

2. Because of this massive debt, constantly compounding interest works against us, as it does against any compulsive debtor. By the close of the eighties, the interest alone on the national debt was *greater than the entire deficit had been in the early eighties.* Two dollars of every five collected in federal income taxes now goes *just to pay the interest* on our debt. That's more than we spend on health, housing, the environment, justice, space, agriculture, and science put together.[16]

3. Also like the individual debtor, we as a nation have little to show for our debt-propelled spending: 37 million Americans have no health insurance,[17] many children attend schools in shameful disrepair, industrial plants have grown obsolete, legions of homeless people bed down in the streets, an infrastructure of roads and bridges is deteriorating, and the environment on which we depend for our survival is in profound crisis.

Most of the federal splurge of the past two decades went to build military might, which gave our country an edge in the balance of power for a short time, but ultimately undermined our security in much more profound, far-reaching ways. Now we are beginning to see that it's not *how much* money a person or a nation accumulates that makes it truly wealthy, but how those riches are used.

The excuse "We can't afford it," when applied to health care, maintaining the planet, and caring for children, simply sidesteps the real issue—that we have made addictive choices. Like the image spender we'll learn more about in chapter 6, we have chosen to put our money into things that enhance external displays of *power* and *image* rather than into things that enhance the long-term health and well-being of the "family." Taking care of basic necessities—bridges, highways, day care, medical care, schools, and the environment—simply has not been our priority. We've behaved like a dysfunctional family in which the parents spend the paycheck on drugs, while the kids go without dental work and decent housing. It's a self-defeating pattern with major negative consequences.

These patterns of compulsive spending and debting have been duplicated at every level of government. States, cities, and small towns alike have gone into hock in order to finance spending, trying to cushion the pain of any deficit with more borrowing. That's exactly what the individual compulsive debtor does. Instead of facing the reality of red ink on a balance sheet, he borrows more.

4. Just as chemical addictions cause a national increase in crime, so does money addiction, because people addicted to wealth are willing to risk the negative consequences of arrest and imprisonment in order to get more of their drug. About 90 percent of all crime in the United States, in fact, is committed for money.[18] Hardly a day goes by that some public official isn't accused of breaking the law in order to get more money: accepting bribes or kickbacks, committing fraud or tax evasion. Yet, like children in denial of their parents' addiction, American voters have often chosen to overlook the dysfunctional money behavior of a politician, naively assuming perhaps that it won't happen again or that it's "normal" to crave money at any cost.

5. As an indirect result of dysfunctional money policies at the level of government, we now have Third World–like gaps in income between the richest and poorest, a condition that historically breeds despair and violence. By 1989, the richest 1 percent of Americans controlled more of the nation's wealth than the bottom 90 percent put together. During the eighties, the bottom 40 percent of the American population saw their incomes decline, so that by 1987, 55

percent of American families had zero or negative net worth. And despite pronouncements in the mid-eighties that there was "no poverty" in America, one in five children born lived in it.[19] Once again, such denial is typical of an addictive psychology.

This widening income gap was exacerbated by what was called tax simplification. In 1986, the tax rate for the highest income bracket was slashed to around 28 percent, placing the multimillionaire and the twenty-year teacher in the same tax bracket. This effectively lowered the tax burden on the rich, so that by 1988, the poorest 10 percent of households paid 20 percent more taxes than they did a decade earlier, whereas the richest 1 percent paid 20 percent less.[20]

The casualties from our dysfunctional monetary policies continue to accrue. As this book goes to press, a record one in ten of us is on food stamps, and hourly wage earners have to put in an average of two hundred hours extra per year (five weeks) just to maintain their 1973 standard of living. In more and more households, people are working overtime, moonlighting, and relying on two wage earners whenever possible.[21] All this means fewer parents looking after the kids. Women, African Americans, Latinos, and younger Americans have taken the brunt of all this hardship, because they are the ones most often affected by layoffs and wage cuts. Between 1973 and 1990, African-American families lost a staggering 48 percent of their real income, compared with young white families, which lost an average of 22 percent.[22]

MONEY ADDICTION AT THE CORPORATE LEVEL

With the tone set at the level of federal government, money dysfunction during the 1970s and 1980s had huge reverberations in the corporate world as well. Ethics and long-term thinking were out of style. Highly leveraged deals (deals financed with borrowed funds) exploded in popularity. Corporations went on an unprecedented spending spree, assuming massive debt, selling assets, and failing to produce new capital, to the point where, collectively, American corporations now have more debt than net worth, and many businesses are foundering.[23]

The federal government *enabled* this corporate spending and debt frenzy in two major ways. The first was through lax enforcement of the country's antitrust laws. The other was by changing the corporate tax codes. The interest paid on debt became tax deductible at a time when other corporate tax deductions were eliminated. That gave companies a short-term incentive to take on massive debt. Company A could buy Company B on borrowed money, and lower its tax bite. In the flurry of hostile takeovers, some companies drained all their cash out and bought their own stock with it, to avoid being taken over. Other companies became the stalkers and went looking for other businesses to gobble up. As a result, for three years running, U.S. companies borrowed as much for mergers, for takeovers, or to avoid takeovers as they did for new plants, equipment, and other assets.[24] Our corporations were becoming compulsive debtors, with grave ramifications for all of us.

One form of debt that corporations widely took on in the 1980s was junk bonds. Junk bonds are high-risk, high-yield securities. Investors buy the bonds from high-risk businesses (usually businesses already in debt), and in return for taking such a risk, they get a high interest rate on their money.

One reason so many people and institutions bought junk bonds during the eighties is that Michael Milken, dubbed the Junk Bond King of investment house Drexel Burnham Lambert, allegedly lured investors by manipulating conditions. He propped up weak, staggering companies with more injections of borrowed cash to keep them from collapsing. This masked serious debt problems and gave Drexel's bonds an unrealistically low default rate. Investors and portfolio managers (also, perhaps, in the throes of addictive thinking) wanted the highest yield in the shortest time. They wanted to believe Milken's projections, so they did. Most of the junk bonds were bought by banks, insurance companies, and mutual funds, which is why many of those companies are foundering today.[25]

Junk-bond financing could also be seen as a form of enabling. It allows corporations that are already staggering under a burden of debt to remain in denial, get another shot of cash, and go on building their shaky empires. Yet when Paul Volcker, as chairman of the Federal Reserve, tried to impose limits on some junk bonds, he was roundly criticized by the Reagan administration.[26] Now, our economy is reeling from the grave consequences of enabling debt-ridden business.

Often the person behind the debt-financed corporate takeover is an image spender, someone with a strong drive for visibility, power, and self-aggrandizement. To cite just one example, in the late eighties, Robert Campeau, a Canadian real estate developer, bought two of America's biggest department store conglomerates, Allied and Federated, which included such prestigious stores as Bloomingdales, Brooks Brothers, Jordan Marsh, and Ann Taylor's. Though Campeau had no experience in retail sales, banks lent him the entire purchase price of $11 billion, *including* most of the down payment. Before long, the conglomerates, which were relatively sound and debt-free when he bought them, collapsed under the burden of debt and filed for bankruptcy. That left 50,000 suppliers and other creditors owed money, 8,000 employees out of work, and a major bank weakened.[27]

Why did so many banks and investment houses, once staunchly conservative institutions, go along with such flimsy schemes? Primarily because the brokerage houses that arranged the deals stood to reap huge fees. One leverage buyout generated almost $1 billion in paper fees alone. And by 1988, mergers and acquisitions produced over 50 percent of Wall Street brokerage house profits.[28] Whether a deal was financially sound for the parties involved didn't matter so much as how the brokerage firms arranging the deal stood to benefit. In a culture where personal, short-term monetary

gain is the accepted criterion in decision making, this could only be expected.

In this atmosphere, business decisions were increasingly based on short-term gain rather than what was best for the long-term growth and stability of the companies. Immediate gratification reigned, just as it does with an individual addict. Get the high now; never mind the consequences later. Soon many corporations had a lot of debt, no cash flow and few assets, setting them up to have to borrow some more. The growing trade deficit and lost American assets and jobs are the natural consequence of our own addictive behavior.

Think of it this way: Healthy businesses generate *true wealth*—jobs, useful products, time-saving technologies. They build factories and modernize equipment. They contribute to the overall well-being of the community and its economic growth. By contrast, business owners operating on addictive thinking just grab money where they can, sucking all the equity out of a business and then moving on.

Another symptom of corporate money dysfunction is the growing gap between executive and employee pay. By the end of the 1980s, according to compensation consultant Graef Crystal, managers made 120 times what the average worker did, compared to a ratio of 35 to 1 in the 1970s. The average salary, bonus, and stock options for chief executives at the thirty largest U.S. companies in 1990 was $3.2 million—nearly three times more than their British counterparts, four times more than French or German executives, and six times more than Japanese executives. In 1987, Chrysler's Lee Iacocca made $17.6 million; Tadashi Kume, head of Honda in Japan, made a mere $450,000.[29]

Such inflated rewards in contrast to the shrinking wages and growing unemployment among the middle class stand as a powerful symbol—like Imelda Marcos's 3,000 pairs of shoes—of the inequality resulting from greed. When a disproportionate amount of a company's income goes into compensation of top executives, it reduces the investment that company can make in new plants, machinery, and other assets—undermining the long-term health and viability of the business and eventually threatening wages and jobs. Consider that in 1990, Steve Ross, then co-CEO of Time-Warner, received $78.2 million in compensation, or 2.5 times the *combined* salaries of *all* the people laid off by the company that year.[30]

Another symptom of corporate money dysfunction has been an epidemic of corporate crime. Fueled by widespread money disorders of compulsive spending, greed, and debt, Wall Street became the scene of the greatest money crimes committed in the history of the United States. Banks lost five times more money to embezzlers than they did to armed bank robbers.[31] By 1987, there were so many wealthy executives in jail that one minimum-security prison was reportedly dubbed Club Fed.[32] It might be funnier if it weren't costing us. But six times more federal dollars are being spent on savings and loan and bank bailouts than are being spent on welfare.[33] And guess who's paying that bill?

As we can see from this brief survey, money addiction at the level of business has had profound negative consequences for us all. Because of steep debt payments, assets have had to be sold and spending for research and development cut back, endangering our nation's future competitiveness. Accelerated corporate crime rates have cost American taxpayers, unemployment is at record highs, and, according to Charles McMillion in a column in the *New York Times,* the United States is no longer one of the top ten most productive nations in output per worker.[34]

RECOVERY?

In some ways, our collective money behavior of the past two decades represents the victory of addictive thinking over rationality, of denial over reality. We seem to want to believe, like the individual addict, that we are collectively invulnerable, that we are always right and always in control. If something does get out of control—like our spending, debting, or greed-driven crime—we simply deny it, and when we can no longer deny it, we ignore it.

Recovery for our money-dysfunctional culture can happen in one of two ways: we can stay the course, and wait until we completely bottom out—perhaps with another Great Depression—and are given an extended opportunity to reflect on our individual and collective money patterns. Or, we can begin now—before such a calamity—to acknowledge the addictive qualities that have pervaded so many of our institutions and start developing healthier approaches to money and to resources in general.

As Thomas Moore writes in *Care of the Soul*, "When a society becomes corrupted by money's shadow, that society falls apart; whereas a society that owns up to its financial shadow can be nurtured."[35] We have to admit that we have a problem before we can begin to nurture ourselves and our society, before we can begin to live by a value system other than greed and compulsive consumerism.

Regaining fiscal sanity and solvency will require that each of us not only take responsibility for our own money recovery but take an active role in monitoring the behavior of those we have entrusted with our national resources. As we do, we can begin to move from compulsive materialism—with all its negative consequences—to the responsible stewardship of resources.

CHAPTER 5

THE FAMILY INHERITANCE
What We Learn About Money Growing Up

In the household where I grew up, the most intense and violent emotions centered around money—the lack of it, the need for it, the desperate difficulty of having enough of it, and the fear of what would become of us without it. Money was power, reality, happiness. Money was a reality stronger than anything else, and the gods of money had no compassion; they were hard, unyielding, hostile. They broke my father's spirit again and again and, through his violent despair and anxiety, they continuously broke my own spirit.

JACOB NEEDLEMAN
MONEY AND THE MEANING OF LIFE

If your parents were inside your head, what would each one be telling you about how you're handling your money?

JUDY BARBER, PSYCHOTHERAPIST,
QUOTED IN *NETWORKER*

JUST AS A VULNERABILITY toward alcoholism can be inherited from alcoholic parents, so too a predisposition toward dysfunctional money patterns is often passed from one generation to the next. Many people who are compulsive with money come from families in which money was used as a means to control others, hoarded as a source of power and security, lavished as a substitute for love and attention, or withheld as a means of punishment.

Most of what we learned about money was absorbed by osmosis, from being around our parents and siblings and picking up on the intense emotional charge often attached to money. Powerful emotions, attitudes, and patterns relating to money are transmitted to us from the time we are crawling around on the floor while our parents are having a "discussion" about money. We also learn from watching them. When what they said ("Save your money") and what they did (spent their money) were at odds, their actions spoke to us louder than their words.

In many households, the most intense emotions—fear, rage, shame, envy, guilt—get expressed through discussions and fights about money. Money can also be a *carrier* for emotions when feelings are conveyed through the medium of money rather than communicated directly. A father withholds money as a way of communicating his disapproval of a daughter's career path. Alienated partners communicate their hurt and rage through brutal financial sparring in a divorce case. And a teenager who's been given money in lieu of attention expresses his resentment by running up Dad's charge cards.

Sometimes the very topic of finances is avoided because it's so loaded with intense emotions. Yet children pick up on the emotions and *feel* the shame, guilt, anxiety, or whatever else is in the air, spoken or not. And living with these free-floating, unacknowledged emotions can be more difficult than living with screaming money fights. If Mom gets fired from her job and is feeling shame and anxiety, and Dad is quietly enraged because he thinks she could have avoided it, and the family needs the income so both are worried, but neither talks about any of this because they want to shield their eight-year-old daughter from it, she will still pick up on all those intense emotions. But because they're not acknowledged, she will have to deny her own perceptions, learning to distrust her own experience. Because she can't talk to her parents about something that supposedly isn't happening, she will have no support in coping with the emotions she absorbs.

Sometimes, our parents had polar opposite money styles: one was an expansive, gregarious spendthrift, and the other the worrier who kept the spender in check. Or one was a taker and the other a codependent giver. Undoubtedly, we received messages from and about each one, and about what we could expect as a member of our gender: "Women are all alike, they just spend your money," "Men promise you everything, but never deliver," and so on.

Often, the associations we formed with money and material things as a result of our family experiences influence us from below our conscious awareness. The man who always makes poor investment decisions and loses money is mystified by the pattern. He doesn't remember receiving the message that he'd never amount to anything or that he'd better not show up a competitive father, but such a buried belief could be what's driving him.

If we come from a money-dysfunctional family, we often become either just like one of our parents—a spendthrift, a debtor, a hoarder, a shopper, a compulsive giver—or their polar opposites, vowing never to be like them. Jill's mother was a driven career woman who seemed to care only about money, so Jill became "not her mother"—a chronically broke underearner. Sometimes, we marry someone with a pattern like the one we grew up around.

When we identify with one particular parent and pattern ourselves after him or her, it makes us feel closer to that parent. We spend on the kind of things our parent spent on, live the way our parent lived. We even elicit similar responses from others. Jesse's father was the stern, hard-working owner of a small grocery store who worried about the future and how he would keep supporting his children. Jesse, the youngest of the family, grew up hearing him criticize Jesse's mother for what he termed her "loose spending." Meanwhile, to Jesse, his mother seemed the warmer, more loving and generous one. Jesse formed the belief that those who spend are nicer, happier people and patterned himself after his mother, becoming a compulsive spender.

Often, our imitative pattern gets reinforced by one or both parents. "You're a chip off the old block," or "You're just like your mother." By identifying with one parent in particular, we also psychically square off against the other. Jesse, for instance, probably acted out some of his anger at his father by becoming what his father disapproved of—a loose spender.

Let's look now at some common family money issues and behaviors. Once again, the point is not to fix blame but to become *aware* of how we acquired our beliefs and attitudes toward money. We then become freer to choose whether to continue them or to establish a healthier approach, truer to our own chosen values.

MONEY FIGHTS

Many of the messages we got about money were absorbed from listening to our parents fight about it, or, if they were repressed types, learning to read the heavy tension in the air. Conflicts about money prompt more divorces than any other single issue, and this is true for *all* income brackets.[1]

Two common money issues fuel most of the fights:

Unmet expectations. One spouse blames the other for not making enough money. The blaming spouse usually feels it reflects badly on them as a couple to be earning less than others, or less than they "should" be at their age. The disappointed spouse feels embarrassed, ashamed, and angry. A study by Philip Blumstein and Pepper Schwartz found that when people are disappointed with the amount of money they have as a couple, it affects their overall satisfaction with the relationship. Interestingly, they found that this is true for heterosexual couples and gay male couples but not for lesbian couples.[2]

Different priorities. It's a common pitfall in relationships to get stuck in rigid, polarized roles. One spouse blames the other for spending too much. One wants to save; the other wants to "live for today." One wants to spend on the home, the other on recreation. One wants to spend on the kids, the other on him- or herself. Oddly enough, if they do break up, such polarized positions often relax. The spender starts to save more, and the saver spends more. Once they've separated, they don't need to balance each other out anymore or prove the other "wrong."

Sometimes, people fight about money to avoid dealing with *other* issues in their relationships. They fight about money rather than face the power and control issues behind their money conflicts. Or, they may fight about money while avoiding their sexual problems. Money becomes the arena where other relationship problems get played out.

FAMILY MONEY IDENTITY

Every family has its money identity: the themes, legends, and unspoken rules that govern how they deal with money as a group. Here are some examples:

"There's not enough." (It's important to save, no matter what.)

"No money problems here!" (It's important to have cash in your pocket at all times, no matter what.)

"We are humble people." (It's important never to look too rich.)

"We are high-class people." (It's important never to look too poor.)

"Rich people are bad/greedy/corrupt/arrogant/wasteful/evil." (It's important not to be one of them.)

"Poor people are bad/lazy/dirty/undisciplined." (It's important not to be one of them.)

"We are middle class." (It's important to look middle class, even if you have to be in hock up to your eyebrows to do it.)

"One side of our family is classy; the other side are bums." (It's important to be part of the good side of the family.)

Whatever the family money script, when one member of the family tries to move outside it, others may react negatively. Cathy was from a family with a "humble" identity. Her parents had disdain for anyone who wasn't what they called "down to earth." People who engaged in intellectual conversation or discussed ideas were considered pretentious, so when Cathy announced that she wanted to spend her junior year in college abroad, her mother exploded in anger. "What the hell do you want to go there for?" she demanded. "You're going to turn into one of those people who think they're better than their family," she warned, revealing the real purpose behind the family injunction. Mother was afraid of being left behind.

MIXED SIGNALS

Trying to read the contradictory signals about money in a family where it's not openly discussed can be a real challenge. Sometimes parents say one thing but do another. Troy's mother was always admonishing him to save half of everything he earned. Meanwhile, she was a compulsive spender who watched Home Shopping Channel far into the night with the telephone close at hand.

In Walter's family, money was never talked about, but indirect and contradictory messages abounded. "I got the impression that money was pretty much a bad thing," recalls Walter, "except that you were supposed to admire the people who had it. It was bad to want a lot of money, but the size of so-and-so's ring was an impressive thing. It was pretty confusing."

Often, children get mixed messages about whether there is "enough" money in the family or not. In Tom's family, where money was never spoken of, he got the impression that there wasn't enough, so he never asked for anything. He felt somewhat confused, though, because his mother had furs and diamonds. And Sharon remembers how her little girlfriends thought she was rich because her father was a doctor. But because her father secretly gambled it away, Sharon always heard her parents fighting about money. She could never understand why the other kids thought she was rich.

Todd's father made a lot of money as vice president of a major corporation but always gave the impression that they were about to run out. "He was always talking about lack of money," Todd recalls, "yet I knew that we had a lot more than my friends' families. So though we had money, I never felt financially secure. I felt that *I* must not be worth a whole lot, that *I* wasn't worth spending money on."

In other families, the opposite occurs: parents give the impression that there's plenty of money when there's not. Jay's step-father always had a couple of hundred dollars in his pocket to show off, but the bills usually weren't paid, and creditors were calling. His step-father was apparently driven to convey the appearance of prosperity, regardless of reality, creating a lot of confusion—and disappointment—for Jay and his siblings. For example, he told Jay he could go to any college he wanted, but after one year at a private university, Jay was forced to drop out because there was no more money for his tuition.

And in Pam's family, whether there was money or not depended on who wanted it. She recalls that there was always plenty of money when her mother wanted to take a cruise or her father wanted to buy an expensive new gadget. But whenever she asked for something, she says, they pleaded poverty. In other families, each parent can be giving different signals. In Lisa's home, her father was always saying, "We don't have enough," while her mother was spending freely. Lisa never knew whether to worry with her father or shop with her mother.

CHILDREN INDULGED, BUT NOT ENRICHED

In some families, children may be indulged materially as a substitute for being given adult time, love, attention, affection, teaching, and other forms of enrichment. A parent who is often away on business may try to assuage his guilt by buying his teenage son or daughter a new car, for instance. Children in such a family end up feeling like "poor little rich kids." They have little true wealth in their lives, and on some level they know it. But because they have access to money, everyone says they're lucky. The result can be pretty confusing. Such children want the cars, toys, and other things but suspect deep down that they are being bought off and deeply resent it. They feel ambivalent about the gifts, may not take good care of them, and—to the chagrin of parents—may act pretty ungrateful.

When I was a high school counselor in a working-class district, a popular, outgoing senior named Tina came into my office one day. The problem? Her father had just bought her a new sports car. Instead of feeling happy about it, Tina was irritable and angry and couldn't help showing it. She already *had* a car, she said, a used car he had bought her the year before, which was perfectly fine. She didn't need this flashy new sports car. Her friends were drooling over it, while she was walking around enraged—and didn't know why.

As we talked, it became clear that Tina was hungering for some real attention from her father. He ran a "bookie" operation from the basement of their home and was always busy. Typically, she said, he was talking on two phones at once, with a phone held up to each ear. As soon as one caller hung up, there would be another call coming in. In order to try and talk to him, she had to compete with this madness. Yet he would reach into his pocket and hand her money quite readily.

What had been hardest for Tina to bear was the seeming discrepancy between what she thought she should feel (grateful and happy) and what she really felt (needy, hurt, and angry). Coming to trust her own feelings and honoring them was a big step forward. She may never get what she wants from her father, but at least she won't be confused about it. Confusion is one of the most debilitating conditions in a dysfunctional family, because it reflects the betrayal of oneself. The signals coming in from others don't match what we feel inside, yet we're afraid to trust ourselves.

Without help, children like Tina, who are given so much materially yet malnourished emotionally, can grow up confusing emotional needs with financial needs. Money, spending, gifts, and material things can come to represent love and emotional support, so that when they're feeling emotionally needy, they indulge themselves materially, which provides only temporary relief. Or, they may pattern themselves after their parents, becoming voracious earners yet never learning how to give to others in any way other than materially.

MANIPULATING FOR MONEY

Most children instinctively adopt a winning manner when asking for something from a parent, knowing the tone and smile most likely to win a yes. But in a dysfunctional family system, such behavior can escalate to conscious manipulation and become the child's chief mode of operation. Sometimes a child is encouraged by one parent to manipulate the other for money and material gifts, as Lydia was:

> My parents were divorced when I was eight. My father came from a well-off family, so my mother wanted me to stay in good with him. Somehow I knew how to play on my father's guilt about not being there for me in other ways. I knew—in whatever way kids know things like this—that he felt inadequate and guilty about his role as a parent and that his way of compensating for it would be with money. I *knew* that. And I knew how to get it.

Manipulating for money is a disempowering approach to gaining prosperity, however. Adults who have learned to get money and things by manipulating someone else often will not have a sense of their own ability to *create* prosperity rather than maneuvering for it.

GIFT GIVING MADNESS

The dictionary definition of *gift* is "anything freely transferred to another person without compensation." But in many families, gift giving is one of the most loaded aspects of family life, laden with hidden messages and emotions, making for a lot of tension and indigestion around gift giving times. Because in addition to expressing simple affection, gift giving can be imbued with various other meanings:

Substituting for other forms of giving. As already mentioned, in some families, gifts are given in lieu of time, attention, or feelings. At holidays, Julian always buys his wife expensive jewelry, even though he can't really afford it. "By giving her sapphires, I feel I earn the right *not* to give in some other ways," he admits. "It's a trade-off. I give her expensive jewelry; she doesn't bother me."

Maintaining power and control. Every year as Christmas approaches, Kate's father sends her and her five sisters a form letter telling them what major appliance he is purchasing for them that year. Kate feels it's her father's way of telling his sons-in-law that they aren't providing well enough for his daughters. *"He* is the mega-provider for the family," Kate says, "and he maintains his position. We get that appliance whether we need it (or want it) or not."

Keeping score. In some families, holiday gift giving has become a competition in which people demonstrate to each other how well they're doing. In such a family, much attention is paid to how much things cost. People with less money often feel obliged to equal the expenditures of others in order to avoid humiliation. In one family I know of, the cost of a present was considered so important that they actually set a *minimum:* no gift should cost less than seventy-five dollars. When one person tried to opt out of this gift giving madness, other family members became quite peeved at her "cheapness" and lack of "spirit."

One very competitive woman actually worried that the gifts she gave to her parents would, after her parents' deaths, be divided among family members. So she announced a policy: the gifts she gave her parents would revert to her when they died. Once the policy was in place, she proceeded to give her parents only things that she herself would someday like to have.

Avoiding abandonment. Rachel has zero self-esteem, resulting at least in part from her victimization in a brutal date rape as a teenager. Now, as the single mother of twenty-year-old Adam, Rachel showers him with gifts. Whatever Adam wants, Adam gets. What makes her behavior compulsive is that Rachel is *driven* to do this. She doesn't feel worthy of her son's love just for herself. She keeps giving to Adam in order to keep him from rejecting and abandoning her. She is, as we shall see, codependent with money.

Preserving rigid roles. In some families, certain people are designated the givers and others the takers. The givers will often complain about the takers but will resist any effort the latter make to give. The designated taker may be told repeatedly, "Don't worry, you don't have any money." It's hard to tell when this is said out of real consideration and when it is meant (however unconsciously) to disempower and keep the designated taker in a dependent role. Paula, who is recovering from addiction to deprivation, knew the difference in how it *felt:*

> I was never allowed to give to other people in my family. "Don't buy anything," my mother would say. "You don't have any money." I was never allowed to treat, or even to bring food to a gathering. The message I got was, "You can't carry your own weight; you have to be taken care of."
>
> One Thanksgiving, after I had been in therapy for a while, I was in touch with how awful it felt to be stuck in this role of the needy, dependent one when I was actually quite capable. I insisted that I be allowed to bring a food dish that year. Even that was breaking the rules and met with a lot of resistance, but I won out through sheer perseverance.
>
> It hasn't been easy breaking out of the role of "Pitiful Paula," but I've done it. First I realized what it was doing to me, then I changed the way I looked at *myself.* Finally, others in my family started to change toward me. But I had to change first.

Not allowing people to give deprives them of the chance to participate in the give-and-take of true community. It takes them out of the flow.

Obligating the recipient. Some gifts—however unconsciously—are intended to bind the recipient in an unspoken agreement. "I give this to you, therefore you will (be my friend, not make waves, be loyal, owe me, etc.)." The giver usually appears generous, but the recipient picks up the sense of obligation that comes with the gift. If she fails to keep her end of the unspoken bargain, the giver may become angry and throw it up to her that "I've given you so much." This is the tyranny of the "un-gift."

Saying "I don't know who you are" or "I want you to be different." Susan is an earthy, counterculture type who grows organic vegetables, wears batik clothing, and writes poetry. Every Christmas, Susan received inappropriate gifts from her family, like polyester leisure suits and fake-suede jackets, which she would exchange for something else. Two years ago, when her mother gave her artificial flowers for her birthday, Susan accepted them graciously. But when she opened her Christmas gifts and found more artificial flowers, she exploded. "Why do you give me artificial flowers," she cried. "Don't you know who I am—*yet?*" Susan may sound like an ingrate, but she was responding to something very real: the incredible pain of feeling unseen or unaccepted by those who purport to love you.

Serving as a medium for fights. Sometimes, conflict between family members is played out through their gift giving patterns. Cathy remembers how "excruciating" birthdays and holidays were in her house growing up:

> My parents always had some kind of scene going, and either rage or crying would be the result. No matter what my father gave my mother, she always made it clear that she didn't like it, or it wasn't enough. That led to accusations that he didn't "make enough." There were always undercurrents that went far beyond the items exchanged. It was excruciating to be around. To this day I hate gift giving occasions.

NO MONEY MANAGEMENT SKILLS TAUGHT

Few people with money disorders were taught much about saving, spending, budgeting, paying, or negotiating when they were growing up. Allowances can be a great vehicle for teaching children about money, but in money-dysfunctional families, allowances can teach the wrong things. For instance, a child whose allowance is automatically replaced when it runs out will learn nothing about limits and will often wind up a compulsive spender (the more he spends, the more he gets). And a child who is repeatedly given an allowance insufficient to meet the needs assigned to it may grow up convinced that there's not enough.

In wealthier families, outside experts—accountants, lawyers, trust officers—often handle the family money. The result is that the children of the rich often have a lot of possessions but very little experience with money. They can feel very inadequate if the time comes when they have to manage their own affairs. Walter, the son of a very successful surgeon, attended an exclusive private boys' school. He had everything he wanted, he says, but didn't have a clue how to earn or manage money:

> Whatever I wanted just seemed to appear, but I rarely dealt with cash. I had a credit card for gas, but I never saw a bill. If I needed an electric guitar or amplifier for my band, somehow I just got it. I never had to work. There always seemed to be plenty, and I never got the impression that I would someday have to *do* something for all this. We just never talked about money. So I walked around with this great air of superiority, but all the time I didn't have a clue what was going on.

HOW ENVY CAN SHAPE LIFE DECISIONS

In a money-dysfunctional family, who has what can be a tremendous source of anxiety, envy, and competition. A grown sibling may enter a high-paying career that he hates solely to make more money than the others. Another child may get the message that it's *dangerous* for her to have anything of value because it evokes such envy and rage from others. She may make an unconscious decision *not* to have anything in life, opting out of the competition and taking on the identity of the "poor relation," hiding her gold, so to speak, in order to feel psychically safe. In some families, the parents may even become envious of the material accomplishments of their children, unconsciously evoking guilt if a child starts to outdo them.

DEPRIVATION AS THE NORM IN DYSFUNCTIONAL FAMILIES

A disproportionate number of those with money disorders come from families in which a parent was addicted or otherwise compulsive. That's probably because deprivation and insecurity is the norm in such families and becomes "encoded" in the child's psyche. As an adult, the person with a haunting inner sense of poverty and insecurity often either reflects it by developing a poverty consciousness, keeping herself broke, or arranges her life to defend against it—through the compensatory materialism of money lust or compulsive spending.

How is deprivation the norm in an addicted family? For one thing, a lot of the available money may go to support the parent's addiction (drugs, alcohol, gambling, shopping, etc.), leaving the family literally deprived. Addicted parents may even borrow and not repay or outright steal money from a child. But of even greater consequence is the emotional and spiritual poverty experienced by the children of an addicted parent.

It did not surprise me to read that Donald Trump's grandfather was a "hard liver and a hard drinker," or that his older brother Freddy was dead by the age of forty-three and suffered from what sounds like alcoholism, though Trump never used the word.[3] Trump's own driven behavior, fierce competitiveness, and tremendous need to be recognized all bespeak the "family hero" or superachiever role, a common response in an alcoholic family. Like other family heroes,

Trump may be driven to defend against feelings of worthlessness, powerlessness, and vulnerability and by an inner mandate to redeem the family.

MONEY AS A MEANS OF CONTROL

In some families, money may be lavished as a reward for acquiescing to the parents' demands or withheld as punishment for resisting them. The promise of an inheritance is sometimes used this way. J. Paul Getty was renowned for making promises to people about what he was going to leave them in his will. Meanwhile, he changed it twenty-one times, always cutting out those who had offended him. In the end, he disappointed a lot of people by leaving most of his fortune to a museum that he had never even visited.[4]

When money is used to control family members, the result can be terribly painful and debilitating. If the child acquiesces in order to win the parent's favor (and money), he experiences a sort of psychic rape, wherein something is done to him against his own will. He experiences in his soul a profound loss of dignity.

POVERTY IDENTITY

In a culture that judges self-worth by net worth, children growing up in poverty often cannot help but incorporate a deep-seated sense of shame, shame that later shapes their own relationship with money. Sandra's parents fought a lot about money, her father having gone bankrupt twice. She remembers people coming to the door to repossess things and hearing that they were going to lose the house, lose the car. For a while, she says, the corner store had a collection box for her family, and at Thanksgiving, they got a box of food from the town. Especially in an affluent society, this kind of experience has a profoundly shaming effect on a child. To feel powerless, impotent, in a society like ours that is based on power is to be shamed. One incident still haunts her:

> I remember one day watching my mother scrounging the bottom of her purse for the last pennies she needed to buy me a stuffed animal for Christmas. That dog became a symbol of shame to me. I could never even play with it. I hated it. It seemed so pathetic to me, the way I felt we were, the way I felt I was.

INHERITED MONEY SHAME

Our family influences regarding money aren't limited to our parents and siblings but can go back much further. We may not have even known our grandparents or great-grandparents, but their money attitudes shaped those of our parents and so had an influence on us. In some families, shame about illegally or unethically obtained money is transmitted for generations. In others, fear of not having enough is what gets passed on.

Some families have money skeletons in their closets: a grandparent who went bankrupt, a great-uncle arrested for theft, a suicide following financial loss, a falling-out over an inheritance or other major money rift. These incidents may not be talked about, but the emotions attached to them— the shame, fear, anger, envy—remain highly charged and continue to shape current family patterns and relationships.

Deborah is forty-two and addicted to deprivation. Her family had a skeleton in the closet that, though never talked about, undoubtedly affected her and her siblings. When her mother was seventeen, her father (Deborah's grandfather), who was treasurer of the local steelworkers' union, absconded with union funds. Just before the front page story broke, he skipped town, never to return. From that point on, he lived under an alias in another city. Subsequently, his wife, from whom he remained estranged, lost the family home to foreclosure because she was unable to keep up the payments on her own.

Undoubtedly, the shame Deborah's mother suffered as a result of this episode had an effect on her and subsequently on what she learned about money, about her family, about who she was. Shame gets transmitted from generation to generation, especially if it's not acknowledged and worked through. It's possible that Deborah picked up the unspoken but intense feelings of shame and lived them out through her own commitment to struggle and deprivation.

IMMIGRANT ISSUES

The children of immigrants often absorb powerful messages about money. Usually, the first generation had a great struggle to make it in America and communicate to their children a great deal of fear about not having enough, shame about being an outsider, and tremendous emphasis on making it.

The second generation either tries to live out the parents' dream or rejects it and lives in reaction to it, as Tony did. You'll recall that Tony, whom we met earlier, is the child of Portuguese immigrants who relentlessly harped on the importance of making money and being accepted. Because so much seemed to be riding on it, Tony absorbed not the message itself but the shame that fueled it.

> My father instilled in me the idea that I had to work my fingers to the bone and never question anything. The most important thing to him was to become assimilated, to be accepted as an American. He would beat me and my brother if we didn't live up to his expectations. My reaction was to reject his values and reject money. I said to myself, "If I can't be part of this family for who I am, who needs it?"
>
> My brother did the opposite. Even as a kid, he made up incredible stories to his friends about who

and what we were. He plucked his eyebrows because he didn't want to have heavy, Portuguese-looking eyebrows. He wanted to be accepted more than anything. As an adult, he wholly bought into the American dream. He made a million dollars by the time he was thirty, but then he lost it.

Me, I've always struggled with money, always scrambled to pay last month's rent. I'd like to come to terms with this and find some balance. My father and brother made money a god, and I reacted by making money evil. I'd like to find the middle ground.

GENERATIONAL ISSUES

Every generation has its own money history too, which helps shape patterns. Among the generation who grew up during the Great Depression of the 1930s, a residual fear of running out of money caused them to place a high value on frugality, caution, thrift, and security. Partially as a result of this frugality, the next generation, the baby boomers, enjoyed a childhood of relative affluence. Then the pendulum swung. After watching their parents live what seemed like overcautious, restricted lives, many boomers came to place a high value on expansiveness, risk taking, freedom, and spontaneity. As adults, they tended to spend more, save less, and incur debt cavalierly.

WEALTH PROBLEMS

Contrary to all the rags-to-riches fantasies about America, 80 percent of household wealth is inherited.[5] But that's not to say that coming into money is *easy*. Many people from wealthy families inherit their fair share of money dysfunction.

The charge of history. For one thing, children of the rich often have to "carry the shadow of their parents' wealth," as

Joel Covitz points out in "Myth and Money," an essay in the anthology *Soul and Money*.[6] Any guilt, discomfort, or ambivalence the parents and ancestors had relative to the money is inherited too. Often these shadow feelings are never talked about, because of the discomfort surrounding them. The resulting silence leaves children to grapple alone with the weight of these charged emotions that come attached to the money. It is possible, Covitz maintains, that the high incidence of self-destructive behavior (drug addiction, alcoholism, suicide, money self-sabotage, etc.) among the offspring of the rich reflects the tremendous difficulty of dealing with this shadow energy without support.

A tough act to follow. Then too, the person who inherits a fortune often has doubts about his ability to measure up to the original fortune maker. Though the question of measuring up may never arise overtly, undercurrents of competition and fear of inadequacy can get played out. As John Sedgwick writes in *Rich Kids,* "They can never get out from under the shadow of their elders; they will always, in some sense, live in their fathers' houses."[7]

This sense of being in the shadow of the successful one especially affects children of the same sex as the achiever. Because in our culture men have had much greater access to money, it's usually men who have made the fortunes and their sons who have suffered from fears of not measuring up. Again, one can't help but think of the association of money with male potency in our culture and the consequent competitiveness for the role of "dominant male."

An embarrassment of riches. Many children of the rich inherit a strong sense of entitlement, which in turn contributes to their continued prosperity. But others are embarrassed about having "too much too easy." They fear other people's resentment and yearn to blend in with those who have struggled to get where they are. The latter tend to keep their trust funds a secret, afraid that others will think less of them if they haven't earned all their money.

Inheritance manipulation. Another challenge for the children of the rich has already been touched on: maintaining some sense of personal autonomy when the prospect of an inheritance is used as a means of control. The seduction of an inheritance can be very hard to resist, yet altering one's behavior in order to stay in the benefactor's favor can only leave a person feeling "screwed." Ken, the son of a wealthy industrialist, whom we met earlier, explains:

> They constantly made demands on me. I should go to law school, marry this one from that family, attend this, invite that one, and so on ad nauseam. They never said, "Do this or you won't get the money," but somehow that's how I read it.
>
> So I did all those things, or most of them. In effect, I postponed living my own life, always thinking I'd be a wealthy man someday. Then my father died, and everything was left to my mother. So now I'm forty-eight years old, in the unenviable position of waiting for my mother to die. I just can't do it anymore, yet life has passed me by. Instead of having money, money has had me.

"Wealth-fare" mentality. We hear a lot about how receiving welfare and food stamps can have a debilitating effect on poor people, but it's just beginning to be clear how the children of the rich can also be negatively affected by a sense of entitlement, loss of incentive, and dependency on the checks they receive. Again, Ken talks about how ill prepared he was for life because of his wealth-fare mentality:

> Growing up, I had the equivalent of about $200 a week allowance. I had charge accounts in all the stores, a new sports car at sixteen. Basically, I could have anything I wanted. I thought beds got made by themselves, and if you left your clothes on the floor,

they'd disappear and come back clean. Grades didn't concern me, because my father was rich, so my future was assured—or so I thought. I assumed it was a free ride, and that was a big mistake. I became passive, just waiting to come into money "someday," and that was disabling. It disabled me to a large degree, and for a long time.

Children who expect to inherit a fortune, like Ken, often develop this sense of entitlement. They expect to have money no matter what they do, so they lose the incentive to create and achieve things and then miss out on feelings of accomplishment.

No limits. Though it's hard for anyone without money to imagine a lack of financial limits being a problem, many who grew up wealthy say that knowing there is no limit to what they can do adds a lot of pressure. There are no external limits, so they have, in effect, infinite choices—and no excuse for failure.

Money and abuse. The children of the rich who probably have the most ambivalence toward money are those whose wealthy benefactors also abused them—emotionally, physically, or sexually. Louis inherited millions from his father's industrial fortune when he was just twenty-five. You would never suspect he has any money, though, as he dresses shabbily, drives an old car, and works at a low-paid menial job. He appears dark and brooding much of the time, never talks about money, and if anyone brings it up, becomes moody and irritable.

Louis's father, it turns out, was a violent alcoholic who beat Louis's two brothers quite severely whenever he was drunk. Louis managed to avoid most of his attacks by being extremely controlled, keeping a very low profile, and never crossing him. When his father died, he left the bulk of his fortune to Louis, which created a lot of hard feelings in the family. Now he lives with the guilt of having avoided the worst beatings and inherited a fortune from a "bad man." That's a lot of baggage.

With money functioning as the carrier of such intense emotions in our families growing up, it is no wonder that so many of us developed dysfunctional money patterns. If we witnessed people fighting about money instead of dealing with their feelings, if we got mixed signals about money, if we experienced it as a weapon of control or a substitute for love, if we had models who hoarded or borrowed or spent compulsively, we are bound to have incorporated some of these patterns into our own lives.

This is not to suggest that we blame our families of origin for the money habits we have assumed, but rather that we invite compassion and understanding toward ourselves. There are probably good reasons we developed our money madness. What we can do now is not to blame our families or beat ourselves up but turn our attention to *change*. For unless we identify and transform these dysfunctional beliefs and patterns in our own lives, we are liable to pass them on to yet another generation.

PART II

The Money Disorders

There are two ways to really know people. One is to live with them; the other is to handle their money.

JOHN D. SPOONER
SEX AND MONEY

OUR MONEY STYLES—whether we hold on tight to every dime or spend the mortgage money on kitchenware—are, as we have seen, metaphors for who we are and how we relate to the world. They often have less to do with money and more to do with aspects of our personality that get played out through the *vehicle* of money. The compulsive debtor doesn't get into the red simply because he doesn't have enough money, although he often thinks of it that way. If money alone were the solution to his problem, there wouldn't be so many wealthy people in serious debt. The compulsive debtor borrows because of what *being in debt* does for him, as we'll explore in chapter 7, "Beyond Their Means."

Often, one's money style is evident at a surprisingly early age. I was about seven years old when I began slipping away from the church hall where my Brownie meetings were held each week, escaping to the local five-and-ten store with my girlfriend Bonnie. There we would spend our Brownie dues on candy, hang around the store, and get back to the hall just in time to be picked up by our mothers. Eventually, I was dropped from the roll for nonpayment of dues—my first debtor experience. I told my mother I just didn't want to go anymore.

It is important to understand that having a money disorder doesn't make us bad people or failures; it simply makes us people who use money in some self-defeating way. To explore this aspect of our behavior is to learn about our approach to *resources* in general. Recovering from a money disorder ushers in a healthier way of using not only money but *all* resources—relationships, talents, and other sources of nurturing and gratification.

It is also important not to overstate the problem. Saving, spending, giving, and earning are each in themselves normal and necessary activities. They only become problematic when we operate *solely* in one mode at the exclusion of others, when we have lost balance.

Those of us with money disorders rarely fit neatly into just one category. Usually, we have symptoms of two or more patterns at once. Compulsive spenders often borrow heavily, money codependents spend compulsively on others, and so on. Still, for the purpose of furthering understanding, in the chapters that follow we will discuss each self-defeating behavior separately.

A word about recovery from money disorders: alcoholics recover by not taking a drink, a day at a time. As incredibly challenging as this is, it is at least clear what must be done. But those of us with money disorders can't stop spending money altogether. We can't keep money out of our homes or avoid places where money is being spent. Indeed, we have to continue to live in a society that revolves around money. Still, in each case, there are some actions that can be taken that support change.

At the close of each chapter in Part II, specific recovery actions related to that pattern will be listed. Then, in the last chapter, we will explore the broader attitudinal changes that can help all of us regain fiscal sanity—and solvency.

CHAPTER 6

MONEY TO BURN
Compulsive Spending

A native of the United States clings to this world's goods as if he were certain never to die. . . . He clutches everything, he holds nothing fast, but soon loosens his grasp to pursue fresh gratifications.

ALEXIS DE TOCQUEVILLE
DEMOCRACY IN AMERICA

The consumer of commodities is invited to a meal without passion, a consumption that leads to neither satiation nor fire . . . and he is hungry at the end of the meal, depressed and weary as we all feel when lust has dragged us from the house and led us to nothing.

LEWIS HYDE
THE GIFT

NORMALLY, WE SPEND MONEY to acquire the goods and services we need or desire, and that we can afford. But when we are *driven*, "have to" buy it, do it, spend it—regardless of our resources—our spending is compulsive. According to a 1989 study, 6 percent of Americans are compulsive spenders, people who say they are "continually unable to control the urge to buy despite the overwhelming burden of debt."[1]

A compulsive spender generally spends whatever he has, whether it's $10 or $10,000. There's not a point at which his urge to spend is satisfied and he relaxes into enjoying what he has. He spends on things he doesn't really need, and he spends regardless of whether he has the money to pay for them. Splurging on nightly dinners out and deluxe vacations, the spender can seem self-indulgent. But he often neglects his more basic needs—like paying the rent or saving the down payment for a house.

Some compulsive spenders are rich and have the money to support their habit. Others spend far beyond their means and run up big debts. Some spend little bits of money compulsively; others spend on a grand scale. Many break no laws in the course of their spending; others are lured into illegal activities to get more money for lavish spending.

It is often thought that most compulsive spenders are women (and men just pay the bills), but this is not true. Though compulsive clothes shoppers tend more often to be women (and even here men are gaining), men spend compulsively on big-ticket items, from electronic toys to sporting goods and vehicles. And a very high proportion of money-related crime is committed by men trying to get more money to spend. Spending is an equal opportunity mood-changer.

Paul doesn't have the money to pay his rent this month, but he just bought a hundred-dollar pair of sunglasses. He knew at the time he was doing it that it was crazy but felt that he had to do it. Last week he bought three pairs of shoes, even though he doesn't need them, and last month he purchased an electronic keyboard, though he doesn't know how to play it. When he went on a ski trip recently, some of his friends brought lunches. "Not me," he says with mock pride. "I always spend more than anybody else—in the snack bar, on a vacation, or out to dinner . . . I don't know what it is."

He has been married for eighteen months, and his wife, Wanda, is starting to catch on to the fact that he's got a problem. "At first, I thought he was just fun-loving," she says. "And because I tend to be a little tight with money, I thought it was good for me to be around him. Now, though, it's getting scary. I've had to come up with more of the expenses the last couple of months." Last month, Paul promised he wouldn't charge anything else and put his credit cards in the couple's safe deposit box. But three days later, he came home all excited because he'd just bought a telescope. He'd used the account number without the card. "If I try to talk to him about his spending," says Wanda, "he gets defensive and tells me I'm just cheap or that I don't know how to live. I bought into that for a while, but now I'm starting to wonder, Who has the problem here?"

Deborah has always had trouble holding onto money. Even as a kid, she spent her allowance within a day or two of getting it. By the time she was twenty-seven years old, Deborah was tens of thousands of dollars in debt—mostly from department store and airline credit cards. In one year alone, she took eight airline flights, mostly long-weekend getaways. Besides travel, she's spent a lot of money on self-improvement courses and dinners out. Often, Deborah picks up the tab for a friend just to have company.

Now she's forty-two and is starting to feel as though she's missing out on some things that matter to her. Other than a closet full of clothes she's barely worn, Deborah has little to show for her spending. Though she wants a home of her own, she has no savings and still rents. But every time she makes up her mind to save, it doesn't work. On her way home from work, she'll swing into the shopping plaza to pick something up for dinner, and before long, she's cruising in and out of stores. Last night, even though she doesn't sew, she bought forty dollars' worth of material, and today she went to the warehouse store and bought patio chairs—her second set. She only has ten dollars in her savings account, because every time she makes a deposit, she draws it out within a week to buy something.

INDICATIONS OF COMPULSIVE SPENDING

A Penny Earned Is a Penny Spent

The compulsive spender typically spends whatever is available—whether that's $5, $500, or $5,000. As his income goes up, so does the amount he spends. It's as if he's trying not to have any money left over by the end of the month. Says Steve, a dancer, musician, and compulsive spender:

> Whatever I get is gone; $800 can go in twenty-four hours. It's like I'm hemorrhaging money. If I've got money in my hand, I never think about saving it for next month's bills. I think, "What can I buy?" The notion of spending less than you earn is a total revelation to me. I always assumed that whatever you had was what you spent.

The Need to Buy *Something*

If there's an opportunity to buy, the compulsive spender has to take it. She can't walk through a souvenir shop, a mall, or even a grocery store without buying *some*thing. Naomi, a project manager and compulsive spender: "I *cannot* go into a store and not buy something. I feel I'm missing out. At my worst, I buy twelve somethings. And I become totally nonselective. If I can't decide among three suits, I buy them all."

Inability to Tolerate Frustration and Accept Limits

The compulsive spender has trouble accepting limits. If he sees something he wants in a catalog or a store, he feels as if he *has* to have it—immediately—even though he's gotten along without it until now. Things that other people (even people with more money) might consider luxuries, the compulsive spender experiences as necessities. He has to have that imported coffee or exotic vinegar, has to take the latest self-improvement course or buy the new lens for his camera.

Tracy was astounded when her compulsive spender husband came home with a new toaster recently. Only days earlier, he had agreed not to charge anything else. When Tracy asked, "What about our agreement?" he replied with all sincerity, "But this is an emergency!" "A toaster—an emergency?" Tracy repeated, incredulous. To him it was. He couldn't stand to want something and not have it. *That* was the emergency.

One reason the spender has trouble with limits is that he tends not to be able to tolerate feeling uncomfortable or frustrated and wants to do something about it right away. Albert Ellis and Patricia Hunter, in *Why Am I Always Broke?* call it "discomfort anxiety," a horror of feeling uncomfortable. If the compulsive spender sees something he wants and can't have, write Ellis and Hunter, the resulting feeling of frustration is to him a "horror," to be avoided at all costs.[2]

Once a craving to spend is triggered, a compulsive spender has great difficulty not gratifying it. Even if she manages to walk away, she often comes back and buys it soon after or buys something else. Amy describes what happened to her recently when the urge to splurge was triggered:

> The other day while waiting for a friend, I was looking in the window of this antique shop. I wanted to buy my son and daughter-in-law a silver frame for the picture of their first baby, and I saw one in the window, a beautiful silver frame. But it had a price tag on it of $350. I said, "Oh, I just can't do this anymore. I can't do it!" So I walked away, didn't even go into the store. But I was still waiting for my friend, so I walked across the street into an antique jewelry shop. And within three minutes I bought myself a pair of earrings—for $350.

The spender also dislikes limits, because she never wants to grow up, and limits are a clear sign of adulthood. She prefers to stay in a fantasy world where there are no limits on her behavior and she doesn't have to take any real responsibility. Amy puts it this way: "I really believe, deep down, that there should be no limits on me. It's like the princess thing: I should be able to drink seventy milkshakes and not gain weight or write fifty checks and never run out of money."

Paradoxically, it is our rejection of limits that confines us to a lifetime of relentless gratification seeking. We can't relax and just accept ourselves, because we continue to think we should *have* more, *get* more, *be* more. In a world without limits, we can never get enough.

Vagueness

The compulsive spender avoids clear thinking that might interfere with her spending. She doesn't keep her checkbook tallied and is usually unclear about how much she is spending. Says Polly, "I blank out, go into vagueness. If I'm clear, I'm afraid I won't get what I want." Recently, Polly ordered lots of clothes from a catalog and put it on a credit card. She didn't total it up, because she knew it would come to more than she should spend. "That's generally how I've lived my whole life," she says, "never knowing how much money I have or how much I need. If I know, I might have to put limits on myself. If I stay in denial, I won't have to take responsibility. Something powerful in me resists knowing."

Compulsive Energy

Some spenders describe a vague, uncomfortable awareness of being out of control when they're spending. They know what they're doing is crazy, but they can't control it. Rosalyn describes it as "compulsive energy," a feeling of being "driven":

> It's something inside that starts to drive me. It's a sense that if I just do this or get that, I'll find relief, I'll be happy. I've been like this since I was a kid. I can feel this thing on a cellular level, like it's imprinted in my cells. It's a feeling that I *have to* buy

this stuff, or fly to the Virgin Islands, or whatever. I have to, have to.

I think this compulsive energy clicks in whenever I'm uncomfortable with things as they are, when I'm feeling not in control, especially of my feelings. Keeping down the feelings must be what I experience as compulsive energy.

This compulsive energy can be exhausting, she adds. "There is like a speediness to it, an aggression. It gets really tiring. I mean, you blow yourself out after a while."

Spends Most When She Has Least

Compulsive shoppers tend to spend more when they are feeling hopeless and powerless. So ironically, when their finances are in the worst shape, they tend to spend *more,* as Deborah describes: "Inevitably, I fritter away the most money when I'm in the biggest hole, tottering on the edge of financial disaster. When I have money, I guess I feel some sense of control over my life, more hopeful, and so I spend less."

Satisfaction Short-Lived

Satisfaction from a purchase never lasts long. Shortly after buying the cross-country skis, the compulsive spender's interest shifts to motorcycles, or photography. Perhaps that's because much of his spending feeds fantasies he has about himself. He harbors some vague hope that the next purchase is going to change his life, make him more interesting, fulfilled, but it never does. As soon as the high wears off, another craving sets in.

Often Spends More Than Planned

The compulsive spender pays very little attention to spending plans. In fact, planning at all is anathema to him. Michael went out to buy a rug for his living room, for example, roughly figuring he'd spend one or two hundred dollars. Instead, he came home with a thousand-dollar rug. "I don't know what it is," he said afterward. "I would never dream of saying, 'I can't have that one because it costs more than I *planned* to spend.' If I see it and I want it, I have to have it." That would be all right if Michael had the money to pay for it, but he doesn't.

Pays Down Debts in Order to Spend Again

Just as the alcoholic tries to control his drinking so that he never has to give up alcohol, the compulsive spender often pays selectively on some accounts so that he always has one or two credit cards still under their limits, maintaining his access to spending.

Saves Only to Spend

The notion of saving money is foreign to the compulsive spender, even if she earns a lot. If she saves at all, it's usually to buy a big-ticket item. When the compulsive spender does have money in savings, it eats away at her. Usually, she'll only be able to keep it there for a short period of time, then she'll use the money for something. Deborah: "Every year when I get my income tax return, I open a savings account. And each time, it's gone within a month. I use up all my withdrawal slips and still have all the deposit slips."

Spends Not Just Earnings, But Windfalls and Capital

The compulsive spender tends to regard all resources—income *and* capital—as spending money. If he comes into a windfall—an inheritance, royalty check, lottery winnings—he spends it rather than reserving it for investment or a cushion. Reuben is a successful writer. After his first best-selling book, he invested a small portion of the royalties, but drew the money out before the term was up, losing the interest.

The rest he spent—on nothing much in particular. He lived off the money for four years, rather than generating more. Recently, he fell on hard times and was evicted from his apartment. While that was happening, he saw himself as the victim of an unfair landlord. He was unaware of the part he played in it.

Compulsively Spends Time and Energy

Compulsive spenders tend to spend freely not only money but time, energy, and even sex. On the positive side, their expansiveness has a creative aspect to it and can make them very appealing and interesting people. According to Ernest Borneman in *The Psychoanalysis of Money,* spenders actually get some creative enjoyment from "expelling" (spending), which is probably why they tend to also expel (spend) time, energy, and sexuality more freely than other people do. Conserving is just not their thing. According to Borneman, such people tend to experience spending as a creative *achievement* rather than a loss.[3]

This tendency to constantly expel has its drawbacks too, in that compulsive spenders tend to deplete themselves in many ways. To keep any available resources in reserve is unthinkable. Reuben is a good example. He's as generous with his time as he is with his money, rarely taking into account the overall picture of what he has to get done. Then, by running out of time, he often has to *spend more money*—for overnight delivery because he didn't get something mailed on time, for dinner out because there's no time to cook, and so on. Recently, because he overspent his time he missed a flight (with a nonrefundable ticket) and had to spend an additional $1,000 to get on another one.

Angry If Confronted About Spending

The compulsive spender erects a wall of denial around himself and tends to get irritated if anyone tries to dismantle it.

Doris's husband, Leo, is building a house for them that is turning out to be three times the size of the original plan. They're now $200,000 in debt, with little income to offset it. Whenever Doris tries to question what he is doing, Leo verbally attacks her: "He gets angry if I question the spending, even though we're approaching bankruptcy at this point. As soon as I say something, he snaps, 'You're just like your mother. You're just tight, money-grubbing.' Then I think, 'Maybe he's right. I should stop worrying.'"

Cross-Addictions

Many compulsive spenders have other addictions as well. Thirty-two-year-old Bill is a compulsive eater who amasses enough food at home to stock a small grocery store. Twenty-five-year-old Nicole spends compulsively on cocaine and alcohol, dropping half her paycheck each week at the nightclub she goes to. She rationalizes that as a single person, she has to have some fun, but actually she is supporting drug and alcohol addictions.

Anyone who spends to support a primary addiction to another drug or process—alcohol, cocaine, prostitutes, gambling—must address that compulsion first. Otherwise, any effort to arrest compulsive spending will only lead to repeated failure.

There are several subgroups of compulsive spenders, including image spenders, compulsive bargainers, bulimic spenders (who spend to stay broke), and compulsive shoppers. Mostly they differ in what the person seeks—consciously or unconsciously—from his spending. Some spend to fulfill fantasies of themselves as successful; others spend to get rid of their money because they feel more comfortable being broke. Still others are in it for the hunt, seeking victory in the exchange itself, or shop to distract themselves from unwanted feelings.

IMAGE SPENDING

Image spenders are *trying to be seen.* They put their money into designer clothes, fancy cars, vacation homes, luxury items, jewelry—anything that is a visible symbol of success. Driven by an insatiable need to be noticed and approved of, to be seen as significant, successful, important, valuable, they spend on things that turn heads and impress people. Donald Trump is a classic image spender. In his heyday, he bought and built only high-profile assets—flashy hotels, luxury high-rises, gambling casinos, airplanes, yachts—all emblazoned with his name: Trump Tower, Trump Shuttle, Trump Castle.

But not all image spenders are rich. Lisa, the secretary who ran up tens of thousands in debt by the age of twenty-five, is also an image spender. Whenever she vacationed (which was often), she would stay on the concierge level of the finest hotels, even though she was going into massive debt to do it. Here, in her own words, is what mattered to her: "We had our own key to the elevator, an open bar—all top shelf—people to carry our bags, a fully stocked refrigerator, full cable service. And it was a suite, not just a room. I felt on top of the world. I was the elite. It cost $140 more than a regular room, but I didn't care. I had to have the $300 suite in order to convince myself I was worth something. But it was only temporary relief. I still hated myself."

Because it is important to the image spender to be "among the elite," she craves preferential treatment, whether it's getting the best table in the restaurant, flying first class, or staying in luxury suites. And she is particularly vulnerable to any marketing pitch that plays on this. She loves getting credit card applications that start "Congratulations, you have been preapproved . . ." Gold cards carry special appeal. She likes to be able to flash them in front of other people.

The image spender also likes to shock people by being outrageous. Ivan Boesky, when out to dinner with friends once, couldn't decide what he wanted to eat, so he ordered one of every entrée on the menu. When the trays of dishes arrived, he tasted them all, decided what he wanted, and sent the rest back.[4] That's something an image spender would love to do.

Because of his focus on success, the image spender is impressed with big shots and often uninterested in or even contemptuous of people who don't have any claim to fame. Deep down, of course, the image spender fears that he himself may be rather ordinary, and his spending is in the service of putting him in the league with "important people." For this reason, image spenders often gravitate toward glamour careers such as those in film, recording, publishing, Wall Street—whatever their version of the happening place is. Even if they remain at the lower levels, they enjoy being associated with a glamorous career and often fancy themselves more successful than they are or imagine great success as right around the corner, about six months away.

The image spender defines himself by his lifestyle. In a sense, he believes "You are what you spend." He figures if he *looks* successful—has the right house, car, and clothes—then he *is* successful. Because his self-worth hinges on this fantasy, he is driven to keep up appearances, no matter what. The image spender will often overextend himself with his prestige purchases, taking on huge debt to buy impressive homes, fancy cars, gleaming jewelry—anything that people will admire. In opening a new business, he may prematurely sink money into such things as luxurious offices at an impressive address, three-color brochures, company cars, and expense accounts. Then he's surprised when the books show he's not able to sustain such expenses. He makes excuses: it's the times, or that business. It's never his fault.

Jesse is an image spender. The youngest of four sons in a high-achieving family, Jesse has always been trying to prove to his siblings that he's as successful as they are. An aspiring screenwriter, he fancies himself a Hollywood success story for whom a big sale is always just around the corner. The trouble is, he spends as though he's already sold a dozen smash hits, even though he's years behind in his taxes and months behind in his rent. Jesse came close, he always says, to selling a script once, but blew it when he slept with his agent's girlfriend. Still, he has no awareness of his money dysfunction and loves to revel in the Hollywood life of his dreams:

> For a while there, I got into the good life. I'd go to nightclubs in limos, put on a tux, and have champagne in the back of the car. I went to Europe seven or eight times: Hamburg, Rome, Paris. Going back and forth, international phone calls. I once sent a limousine to the airport to pick up a girlfriend. It ended up costing me a fortune, because the plane was late coming in. But I was just living that life, and I didn't care what happened. I didn't care. I just did whatever I had to do to live the life.

Spending isn't the only thing Jesse was excessive about. He got into compulsive drinking, drugs, and compulsive sex too. Jesse recalls that cocaine played a big role in his Hollywood flings. "I always made sure I had enough to go around. I used drugs for power. I'd buy in bulk for parties, using it to get in with producers, directors, actors, anyone I wanted to impress. I used cocaine as currency, as money, basically."

For the image spender, it is very important to be seen as generous. To be considered cheap would be humiliating. Consequently, he tends to pick up the tab in restaurants whether he can afford it or not, give lavish gifts, and lend money to virtual strangers, even if he himself owes others money. And he will keep lending money even when there's evidence that it won't be paid back. For Michael, a business owner, all these have been central aspects of his spending pattern, which he now wants to change:

For fifteen years I grabbed every check with every friend and acquaintance. That was my identity, the "successful guy." And I'm very competitive, so it was my way of showing others that only *I* could afford to do this.

I've also been excessive with gifts. Last Christmas, I gave every member of my family a thousand dollars, gift-wrapped with ribbons. It's definitely my role in the family to be the strong, competent male. I'd lend anyone money on the spot. The worst thing to me would be to be considered cheap.

The image spender is very competitive. He has to pick up the tab or give the most expensive gift because he has to compare well to others—or else he's worthless in his own estimation. He has to win, or he feels like a loser. Lisa was admittedly in competition with her mother: "When I was out there splurging, I always thought, 'Well, if my mother can have it, why shouldn't I? I can be just as good as she is, or as she *thinks* she is. I can keep up, and even do better, I can show *her.*'" Even as she declared bankruptcy, Lisa saw herself as winning by virtue of the fact that she shocked her parents with the size of her debt: "When they found out the dollar amount I owed, it about landed them on the floor," she says. "That was my coup d'état. I thought, 'They couldn't have done this if they tried.'"

Sometimes, two image spenders get together and collude with each other to stay in denial, as Naomi and Ed did throughout the Roaring Eighties:

With Ed and me it was all show. Whenever we were out, Ed treated everybody, bought drinks for the whole bar. If I went shopping with my girlfriends, I bought the most. We rented limos to take us all to shows. It wasn't "what can we afford?" Honest to

God, the question never occurred to us. To be cheap was *the* worst thing.

This one couple we were friends with, Arlene and Bob, really did have lots of money. We'd make fun of them and call them tight because they didn't spend the way we did. Arlene shopped at Marshalls, while I shopped at Saks Fifth Avenue. They probably had forty times as much money as we did, but they must have thought we had money to burn. That was almost like a high to us, to act as though we had money to burn. It was an acceptance thing.

Meanwhile, we were taking out home equity loans and running up more and more credit cards to do it. When I lost my job, the whole show collapsed.

Because the need to maintain an image of success can override their better judgment and integrity, image spenders are vastly overrepresented among those arrested for white-collar money crimes like embezzlement, insider trading, and tax fraud. Alvin Ashley, a former New York divorce lawyer, stole millions from friends, relatives, colleagues, and clients in an investment scam. For ten years, he solicited large sums to invest in various business deals, promising 50 percent returns in just two years. Most of the investments turned out to be nonexistent. He paid off previous investors with the money raised from new scam victims, then encouraged everyone to roll over their "profits" into new deals.

Meanwhile, Ashley lived a life of conspicuous consumption, frequenting pricey restaurants, dropping names, ordering Dom Perignon by the case, touring the French Riviera, shopping, gambling. When the scam was finally exposed, one shocked and betrayed colleague asked how he could have stolen money from even his closest friends. Ashley answered, "Because it was so [expletive] easy."[5] This too is typical of some image spenders: if he *can* get money, he may be compelled to do it—whether it's legal or ethical, or not.

COMPULSIVE BARGAINING

Other compulsive spenders are in it for *the hunt,* gaining an inordinate sense of victory from finding bargains. This is not the person who shops wisely for the best prices but the person who spends lots of time (and money) buying things he neither needs nor uses—*just because* he can get them cheaply. Often, the bargainer can well afford to pay full price but gets specific satisfaction from talking the seller down. Nola, an admitted bargainer, explains the appeal bargains had for her:

> For me, it was my victory. I'd say, "I got this shirt for ten cents. It was a steal." Getting over, finding something *dirt cheap,* making a killing, that was my rush, my drug. It was me in the jungle, beating the odds and surviving. It gave me this sense of prowess, like I really was the victorious hunter.

Note the multiple references Nola makes to aggression, power, and control. To the bargain hunter, it's not the article itself that matters so much as the *act* of getting it "at a steal," of getting the best of the seller. Victory is the prize.

The ultimate bargain hunter may be the one who gets the "five-finger discount," the shoplifter. She often has the money to pay for the items, but it's not the item itself that she seeks so much as victory over the system. Rosalyn explains:

> When I was in my teens and twenties, I used to shoplift a lot. I did it just for the sake of doing it. Sometimes I wouldn't even need the item or want it, but I would steal it if I could. There was something triumphant about it. I felt, "I deserve this." It was as

though the world owed it to me. I took pride in being good at it.

The psychoanalyst Edmund Bergler, in *Money and Emotional Conflicts,* maintains that underneath, the bargain hunter is actually harboring a masochistic wish to be refused but covers it up by appearing to be the tough bargainer who gets (or steals) what he wants. It's "defensive pseudo-aggression," says Bergler. "To circumvent the inner conflict, created by masochism, the problem is shifted to the act of wrestling something from a hostile mother" (or, presumably, a hostile father).[6]

According to Bergler's analysis, the seller represents the withholding parent of childhood, and the bargainer sets out to finally *get something* by outsmarting him with aggressive bargaining. First the bargainer devalues the article by pointing out its defects. Then, if the seller won't give it to him for the price he wants, he rejects it; he walks away. *He* is in control, because he doesn't really care if he gets the object or not. His main goal is to defeat the seller.

Philip Slater, in *Wealth Addiction,* suggests another interpretation. He says the bargain hunter has fallen prey to an entrenched way of thinking in America he calls "moneythink." The rule of moneythink is never lose a chance to make a buck, regardless of how you *feel* about what you're buying or selling.[7] As a result, says Slater, people fail to make decisions based on their true desires. They end up with a lot of stuff they don't really want or need just because they applied the principal of "moneythink," buying things because they can, or because the things are cheap.

Regardless of which interpretation we accept—the intrapsychic, the sociopolitical, or some combination—the fact remains that the compulsive bargainer's behavior is self-defeating. First of all, he spends a lot of time and energy tracking down these bargains. And because the real purpose is to outsmart or beat the seller or system, he often doesn't even care much about the item. Shortly after getting it home, he may lose interest in it. So though the compulsive bargain hunter thinks he's saving money or getting the best of someone, the only one he is actually fooling is himself. As Bergler puts it, he has only "purchased a defense mechanism." And he's spent a good deal of money, time, and energy doing it.

BULIMIC SPENDING

Some people spend compulsively for the main (unconscious) purpose of *getting rid of their money*. Whether they have $5 or $5,000 in their checking account, they spend it as quickly as possible in order to get back to broke. I call this bulimic spending because, like the bulimic eater, the bulimic spender may allow herself to take in a lot of money, so she may be a good earner. But she "vomits" it right back up—by spending it—so in the end is always broke.

Brian won several hundred thousand dollars in a lottery at the age of twenty-nine. Three years later, he had nothing to show for it. He threw a few outrageous parties, bought a couple of fancy cars, and gave some away to friends and family. But he didn't save or invest a penny. "I just wanted to get rid of it as soon as possible and get back to normal," he says.

Normal? What does Brian mean? He's not sure himself, but it's probably got something to do with feeling comfortable, familiar. For the bulimic spender, having money creates an inner tension that isn't relieved until the balance reads zero again. It probably has something to do with avoiding the feeling of being out of control, the compulsive energy Rosalyn described earlier, as if money is toxic. Getting back to being broke gives Brian a sense of limits again.

It's a terrible feeling, really, to spend money in the extreme. It's like I have no controls inside, which is a scary thing. It's excess all the way, then horrible feelings of guilt and shame afterward that I've done this again.

I think that's why I got rid of the money as fast as I did, so I could feel back in control again. At least if I'm broke, I can't spend like crazy and put myself through that. There's some built-in control in being broke.

Someone who grew up in a cold, loveless environment but later comes into an inheritance may get rid of it as quickly and as foolishly as possible so as to send a message to the dead parent: "I don't want your stinking money." Forty-five-year-old Amy relates to this:

> My father's been dead now for four and a half years, and I've managed to spend a lot of my inheritance in those years. It's been like an ongoing drive to get rid of the money. It's like I'm still paying my father back in a way, because nothing would be more disturbing to him than my pissing away his money. *That's* how to get back at him.

Once she is "spent," the bulimic spender often feels profound guilt and shame that she didn't handle the money better. During the boom in real estate in the early eighties, Pamela sold a co-op in New York City for ten times the purchase price. Suddenly, she had $400,000. Over the course of the next three years she frittered it all away—without generating any new income. At the time, she couldn't seem to control it, but when it was over, she was left with tremendous shame and remorse. "I felt so ashamed that I didn't do something better with that money. Like here I had all this money and couldn't make use of it properly. That's how I've been all my life. I always end up feeling like a bad little girl." Perhaps feeling bad is what the bulimic spender is driven to seek.

COMPULSIVE SHOPPING

Compulsive shoppers are yet another type of spender. One of their main (unconscious) purposes seems to be to use the stimulation and distraction of shopping to *avoid unwanted feelings.* "When the going gets tough," as the saying goes, "the tough go shopping." Without thinking it through, any unwanted feelings of depression, anger, fear, loneliness, or boredom get translated into the itch to shop. Once at the mall or department store, or tuned into the Home Shopping Channel, they lose themselves in the appealing merchandise, the visual distractions, the fantasies of what this coat or those shoes will do for them. Shopping provides enough ritual and distraction that they don't have to feel, while simultaneously providing enough stimulation to feel alive. Using shopping as a distraction from uncomfortable feelings is often learned at home as a child.

While in the act, the compulsive shopper often feels a sense of well-being, excitement, and control. But after the spree, as she drives home or puts away the goods, she begins to feel anxious and guilty about how much she's spent, confused about her loss of control, vaguely let down that the new items aren't magically transforming her moods or life, and shame that she can't seem to get her spending in control. In short, she emerges from the experience "spent." Then her cravings to shop are only fanned by this complex of uncomfortable feelings, and so the cycle perpetuates itself.

After decades of being laughed about and dismissed as the naughty behavior of incorrigible wives, compulsive shopping is finally being recognized as a serious and painful problem. And it's not only women who can become compulsive shoppers. On any given day, a full third of the people wending their way in and out of stores at the mall are men.[8] Kirk, when he felt rejected by the woman he was dating, went shopping and bought five compact discs—even though he didn't have a CD player! "I knew something was going on with me when I did that," he admits. "Whenever I have some shame or lack of self-worth kicking up, I spend money like crazy, much more than when I feel OK about myself."

One of the most common rationales for a shopping binge is the feeling that "I deserve it." That's because compulsive shopping often comes on the heels of stress buildup and feelings of deprivation. The compulsive shopper can see shopping as his reward for putting up with an otherwise stressful, dull, or ungratifying life. He may not have what he wants in life (or even know what that is), so he tries to compensate for this nagging lack of fulfillment by shopping. Shopping becomes a sort of pseudopleasure.

It can also be a way of acting out anger. Ian's mother died when he was fourteen years old, and at sixteen he was sent to live on his own while his well-to-do father went off to Europe with a new wife. Ian was given rent money and his father's American Express card. He looks back on that first year on his own and how tremendous resentment got expressed through his spending:

> I had no regard for money whatsoever. If I saw the sign that said, "We take American Express," I'd rush into that store and buy something. I figured, "Hey, my dad's out there having a good time. I'm here busting my butt just to get by, so I'm going to stick it to him with the credit card bills. I'm going to have what I want."

Ian felt understandably deprived of the nurturing he needed from his father. Such a sense of deprivation is usually a core issue for compulsive shoppers. Because he harbors such feelings of deprivation, he may feel he deserves his indulgences.

Even though the compulsive shopper tends to be intelligent and creative, she often harbors deep suspicions that she is unlovable as she is. It's not that she doesn't have enough, but she fears she doesn't have *what other people have*—and that's what matters. She tries to wear the most stylish clothes and furnish her house just right in order to be acceptable, accomplished at something. Hillary, a one-time actress, felt like a failure because she never really made it on the stage. After a second career in design failed to bring her the recognition she sought, she felt like a failure on that score too. Then she turned to aerobics and running for feelings of mastery and achievement. By compulsively starving herself and running ten miles a day, Hillary shrank from a size four-teen to a size three. Then she started shopping. She ran three Visa cards and five department store charge cards up to their limits and had closets full of clothes, half of which she never wore more than once.

> I felt I couldn't do anything right in my life, had nothing in my life, but at least I could *look* good. I got a sense of accomplishment from this. Everyone made a fuss about the clothes and my new figure. I have a need for approval—it's like a hunger—so this was extremely important to me. I wanted to present a perfect picture outside, because things inside me felt so imperfect. If I couldn't control anything else in my life, I could control the way I looked.

Pamela, an incest survivor, suffers from extremely low self-esteem. She shops most when she fears being judged and rejected. When she gets into a new love affair, or is going to visit family or friends, she is compelled to splurge on all the right clothes and accessories—whether she can afford them or not. She poignantly describes how she always tried to get her self-worth from clothes:

> Before I left the house I would literally total up how much the clothes and jewelry I was wearing were worth and sort of "put that on" as my value for the

day. I knew it was crazy, but I couldn't help doing it in my head. Because I had no sense of intrinsic value, I looked to clothes for my sense of worth, because price is a measurable thing.

Now that Pamela has been attending Debtors Anonymous for over a year, she is starting to be able to recognize this syndrome of fear and anxiety *before* it turns into the urge to splurge. She picks up the phone and talks to someone about it, so she's not so likely to act out the compulsive energy.

Amy has been in money recovery for about six years too, and in therapy for four. She's just starting to uncover what she believes fuels much of her shopping: the need to avoid feelings of loss. Amy says she can't stand to yearn for anything, because to do so puts her in touch with intense feelings of loss suffered as a child.

When I was four years old, my nanny was suddenly fired. Just one day, she was gone. I think she may have been having an affair with my father, I don't know. Anyway, I was incredibly attached to this person, loved her deeply, then suddenly she never came back. It was like losing my mother, really, only no one acknowledged that it was any big deal. So I was never allowed to mourn.

Recently I got in touch with what a profound loss this was to me and the fact that there's still a lot of pain around it. I think ever since that unmourned loss, whenever I've *wanted* for anything, *longed* for anything, it's tapped into that excruciating reservoir of grief. As soon as that longing comes up, I buy— quick—so as not to feel it.

Because the compulsive shopper is more invested in the *act* of shopping than in the details of what she buys, clothes may hang in the closet with their tags on, and recreational equipment can sit in the garage after one or two uses. She didn't really need the items; she just needed to go shopping.

Some compulsive shoppers describe a shopping blackout, a kind of altered state during which they don't remember what they've bought, as Lisa describes:

> One night, I went to the mall and bought a new pair of Reeboks. When I got home I found the identical pair of Reeboks in a bag in my bedroom; I'd apparently bought them the night before. I didn't have the faintest memory of buying them, but there they were, with my signature on the charge slip. This happened a few times. It was pretty scary.

For other people, it's more of a fog-out, as Polly, another compulsive shopper, describes it. Polly is a recovering alcoholic and sees similarities in how she fogged-out and rationalized during both drinking and shopping binges.

> When I'm about to go on a shopping spree, I kind of glaze over. It's like slipping into a trance in which any thoughts that would interfere with my shopping are blocked out and I'm just moving through a fog; nothing matters but mixing and matching.
>
> I remember one day walking by a store that was having a 50-percent-off sale. I went into this glazed-over state and started amassing merchandise. In the end, I walked out with $1,000 worth of clothes. By fogging out, I think I lower my inhibitions, like drinking a little used to do. Somehow I think I won't be responsible for my actions that way. Because of the sale, I rationalized that I could let myself go because, "How bad could it get?" It's the way I used to rationalize that it was OK to drink beer, because I wouldn't get "that drunk."
>
> But I suffer afterwards, just as I did from a drunk. The more unconscious, fogged-out, my spending has

been, the more guilt I feel at the end, even if I could afford it. Because it's a cop-out from taking responsibility for my actions.

RECOVERING FROM COMPULSIVE SPENDING

In addition to joining a Twelve-Step money recovery program that can provide ongoing support, invaluable shared experience, and a spiritual foundation for recovery, the following are some supplemental steps that can aid the healing work.

Admit That Your Spending Has Negative Consequences

We joke a lot about compulsive spending in our society, so it's hard to take the problem seriously. But now that the 1980s are over, perhaps we can take stock of the damage we've done on this bender, how it's cost us some relationships, marriages, children, health, hobbies, peace of mind, leisure, and credit ratings. That doesn't mean we should judge ourselves harshly but just admit that our lives have become unmanageable as the result of our spending.

Write It Down

Start keeping a journal of your spending. Buy a small, inexpensive pocket notebook, and carry it in your purse or pocket. Each day, write down everything you spend. This sounds like a harder task than it is. It just takes a moment when you leave the grocery store, mall, or gas station to quickly jot down the figure. Do this nonjudgmentally. It is not meant to be an opportunity to berate yourself but a tool to learn about your spending habits.

At the end of a week, take fifteen minutes to total your spending in various categories: groceries, clothes, gas, office supplies, haircuts, and so on. At the end of a month, take another fifteen minutes to total up your weekly sums. For a maximum investment of two hours per month, you will gain valuable awareness of your spending.

Is the picture that emerges one of someone who spends in ways that enrich her life? Or is it someone who spends money in nonsatisfying ways that ultimately perpetuate feelings of deprivation and lack of fulfillment? Is it someone who spends lavishly on gifts but hasn't had the dental work she needs? Is it someone who deprives herself of money for cultural enrichment like films, theater, museums but splurges on makeup and clothes to make herself more acceptable to others? Is it someone who spends sparsely on groceries but is hemorrhaging money for the phone bill? What are the patterns?

Keeping track of your spending can be very grounding, because it helps keep you conscious of what you are doing. If you can do it without berating yourself, it will become a valuable tool by which to *evaluate* and *choose* how you want to spend your money in the future.

Enrich Yourself for Real

Having identified the problem as too much spending, one might assume that the solution is an austerity budget. But in truth, this kind of solution is actually just an extension of the same addictive thinking. What's required to recover from compulsive spending is not simply more self-control and discipline but greater *enrichment*.

Enrichment goes far beyond consumer spending. Enrichment means not just placating yourself with more things but giving yourself what you really want—a less stressful, more gratifying life. True wealth consists not only of financial assets but of nonfinancial ones as well—relationships, creative outlets, a sense of belonging, self-esteem, hobbies, interests. These are the best antidotes to the feelings of deprivation that drive compulsive spending. And many of these kinds of riches can't be cultivated easily while we're overfocused on consuming *things*. Recovery for the compulsive spender, then, means learning to spend only on those things that will truly enrich life.

When we spend money on those things that reflect important values to us—beauty, workmanship, personal growth, whatever it is—those purchases enrich us, enhance our sense of well-being. Conversely, when we spend money on things that reflect not our own true values but a need for others' approval, those purchases are liable to be less satisfying to us. For instance, the person who spends $3,000 to travel to the Galapagos Islands because of a lifelong interest in tortoises will undoubtedly obtain more gratification from it than will the person who spends $3,000 to travel to the Galapagos because it's the "in thing" to do. The latter person isn't wrong; he's just not honoring his own values. Therefore, he will receive less satisfaction and spend a lot of money doing it.

Beverly places a high value on aesthetics, quality, and beauty, so she only buys things that meet those criteria and never buys things just because they're cheap. That, to her, would be throwing money away. "I never buy anything temporarily. I'd rather wait, save the money, and buy something really beautiful, something of quality that will last and hold its value. And because I don't waste money on cheap, worthless things that break, in the long run I probably don't spend as much as other people." There's an old adage that Bergler cites and that Beverly seems to follow: "Unless you are rich, you cannot afford to buy cheap, therefore poor, merchandise."[9]

Living rich means shifting your orientation from having everything you want—right now—to delaying some impulsive purchases in order to have more of your heart's desires over the long run. When we indulge ourselves with un-needed or unworthy items, we pay a cost beyond the price tag. For that extra money, we have to work more hours, which means giving up some freedom, and we also have to give up time (and more money) to maintain, protect, and store those items. In the long run, compulsive spending can deny us some of the things we want most.

Ride Out Cravings to Spend

It's important to recognize that even with the best resolve to stop compulsive spending, the urge to splurge will continue to strike from time to time. That's the nature of compulsion: it doesn't go away just because you decide it should. Cravings to spend will be triggered by people, places, things, feelings, and situations previously associated with your spending. When you drive past the mall on the way home from work, you may still be seized with the sense that if you don't buy that new Turkish rug for your living room or that antique ring, things somehow won't be right. And when you feel angry at your spouse for never being home, your first impulse will still be to go out and buy yourself those $300 boots. The goal is not to become strong enough never to experience such cravings, because willpower is a poor defense. It's much more effective to *expect* cravings—and *be prepared* to deal with them constructively when they occur. Here are some key points to remember:

1. When the urge to splurge comes on, it does not have to lead to spending. You can respond to it in a new way, such as talking it over with a trusted friend or going for a walk on the beach or in your favorite park.

2. Cravings to spend or shop will tend to reach peak intensity within an hour of onset, and they *will pass* if you ride them out without indulging them.

3. When you get the impulse to spend, think it through to its likely conclusion. What will it feel like *afterward?* Think

past the fantasy of how you'll look in those gorgeous new outfits to how it will feel to have spent all your money again, to be further than ever from your long-term goals, and to have frittered away another three hours of your life.

4. Because willpower is a poor defense against cravings, it's best to remove yourself from the circumstances triggering the urge to spend. Get in touch with someone supportive and talk it through.

5. The compulsive urge to splurge will diminish in frequency and intensity over time as you work a recovery program and begin to heal your addictive dis-ease.

Avoid HALT

Many recovering alcoholics and addicts have learned through the wisdom of Alcoholics Anonymous and other self-help groups to avoid staying in a state of "hungry, angry, lonely, or tired" because these conditions seem to make addicts more vulnerable to relapse. The same is true for compulsive spenders, who tend to spend more in these depleted and vulnerable states than they do when feeling rested, satisfied, and cared about. Therefore, in recovery from compulsive spending, if you find yourself feeling hungry, angry, lonely, or tired—HALT, and do something about it.

People, Places, and Things

Compulsive spenders in recovery also do well to avoid anything that triggers the urge to spend: malls, souvenir shops, checkbooks, credit cards. If you spend through the Home Shoppers Channel, you may want to cancel cable service for a while. If catalogs are triggers for you, toss them in the recycling bin before they even get into the house. Avoid going on a shopping excursion with a friend you used to shop with. Take a different route so you don't have to drive by the mall on your way home from work.

Even if you don't have a problem with debt, limit the number of cards you carry to one or two at most. If you are a compulsive debtor, cancel them all (more on that in the next chapter). Using credit cards exacerbates compulsive spending because it fuels the fantasy of unlimited spending potential. Using cash makes you more conscious of what you're spending, so you're more likely to stay within your means. Kirk, a recovering compulsive spender and debtor, insisted on keeping one of his charge cards in his wallet, "just in case." The first two times he felt like spending, he was able to resist, though he always thought about it. The third time, he gave in and charged several hundred dollars' worth of items he didn't need.

Ask Yourself, What Will Happen If I Don't Buy It?

According to Albert Ellis and Patricia Hunter in *Why Am I Always Broke?* the compulsive spender often "catastrophizes" in his mind about what will happen if he doesn't get what he wants. He can even be driven by an unconscious, irrational belief that "if I don't get what I want, I will die." An important step in recovery is to learn to recognize such irrational beliefs in action and counter them. Ellis and Hunter recommend countering the compulsive belief with positive self-talk, which I have summarized and adapted here:

1. If I don't get it, I won't die.
2. I can get other things that I want.
3. If I *never* get what I really want, I can still be happy, though maybe not *as* happy.
4. What I want is important to me—but not *all*-important or sacred.
5. Other people often don't get what they want and still lead good lives, so I can too.[10]

Finally, Ellis and Hunter remind us that recovery from compulsive spending doesn't mean we can't buy the things we want. We simply switch from *compulsively demanding* them to *preferring* them. We can prefer to go out to dinner twice a week even if we only go twice a month. We can prefer to buy expensive holiday gifts even if we buy moderately priced items this year. Perhaps at another time, we will have what we prefer, but in the meantime, we won't demand it.

Request a Purchase Order

Several years ago, I started playing with the notion of psychic purchase orders. Because businesses issue POs for purchases approved by management, I thought maybe I could issue psychic POs for the purchases approved by my higher self. Here's how it works:

Let's say I'm in a store and something catches my eye and tickles my urge to spend—a new kitchen gadget, maybe. Instead of rushing off to the cash register with it, I think, "Do I have a PO for this?" In other words, have I given prior consideration to this purchase and decided that (a) it would benefit me sufficiently and (b) there are funds available to pay for it? If the answer is yes, and I have a psychic PO for it, then I need only ascertain (like a good purchasing agent) that this is a good model for a good price—and buy it.

But if I don't yet have a psychic PO for the item, I must pass it up for the moment. At a later time, I can go to my inner management and propose purchasing it. If management finds it meets the criteria of (a) benefiting me substantially and (b) being affordable, then I can issue a psychic PO and go back and get it. If management decides it's not a wise purchase at this time, however, I can let it go, knowing that to have bought the item would have been unsound, so I've spared myself a net loss. As George Clason writes in *The Richest Man in Babylon,*

> Therefore, engrave upon the clay each thing for which thou desireth to spend. Select those that are necessary and others that are possible through the expenditure of nine-tenths of thy income. Cross out

the rest and consider them but a part of that great multitude of desires that must go unsatisfied and regret them not.[11]

Regret them not. Purchasing unnecessary or unfeasible items only hurts us in the long run! If any item will benefit us, we *can* have it; we need only *plan* for it, like any sound business. Today is not the only chance!

Get Ready to Know Yourself

Not consuming so many goods and services can give you a chance to find out who you are—apart from the person with a great wardrobe, an expensive living room set, or a newly renovated bathroom. That can be scary. Lots of compulsive spenders don't really *want* to know who they are, because they suspect that they are not worthy. They haven't learned to cherish and value themselves apart from their image. Moreover, not consuming so much means having the *feelings* that lie beneath the urge to splurge, being willing to tolerate discomfort instead of seeking immediate relief. Amy, in her recovery, is committed to doing what it takes to heal:

> Now I'm letting myself feel the longing that's been so hard for me to tolerate in the past. I'm allowing myself to sit with feelings of longing and loss, to reexperience *not having something I want.* As a result, I'm finding my cravings to spend are diminishing. I'm freer and freer to spend in ways that are good for me.

Consider Saving

Compulsive spenders are used to getting what they want when they want it. The compulsive spender's inclination is to *get,* to *use up all* of his resources. To put aside, to keep reserves, rather than just to get equates (in his psyche) with missing out, with deprivation. Saving is anathema to him.

But living prosperously doesn't necessarily mean we indulge ourselves with everything we want. Another important shift in consciousness is coming to see *not buying* as a legitimate way of being good to yourself, and saving not as deprivation but as *real* indulgence. "If you would be wealthy," wrote Ben Franklin, "think of saving as well as of getting."[12]

Saving is also a chance to reduce your dependence on work. If you refrain from spending a hundred dollars and save it instead, that's a hundred dollars less you'll have to work for in the future. If you're good at holding onto money, you can *choose* to earn a lot, but you won't *have to* earn a fortune just to support your spending habit. As Jean Jacques Rousseau wrote, "As long as the money in my purse lasts, it assures my independence . . . the money which a man possesses is the instrument of freedom; that which we eagerly pursue is the instrument of slavery."[13]

For a compulsive spender, it's a good idea to get at least six months' income put aside in what I call "freedom funds." That's what Rosalyn, a recovering compulsive spender, has done, and she says it feels better than any spending binge: "I'm not even tempted to draw it out," she says, "because there's nothing I want more than the freedom of having a savings account. That's the shift that's happened inside me." Rather than the freedom to buy whatever she wants on the spot, Rosalyn is opting for the freedom to choose what she really wants.

CHAPTER 7

BEYOND THEIR MEANS
Compulsive Debting

He was not lazy and he was thoroughly respectable. He was a good father and a good husband. He neither gambled nor drank to excess. . . . But he simply could not live within his income.

EDGAR JOHNSON, DESCRIBING JOHN DICKENS,
FATHER OF CHARLES DICKENS

No man is rich whose expenditure exceeds his means; and no one is poor whose incomings exceed his outgoings.

THOMAS CHANDLER HALIBURTON

- Consumer debt nearly tripled during the 1980s.[1]
- Credit card purchases increased fourfold during the same period.[2]
- By 1987, 44 percent of American families were concerned about the extent of their indebtedness but many kept incurring new debts anyway.[3]
- The amount of debt in default quadrupled in ten years. By the close of the 1980s, mortgage defaults were at an all-time high.[4]

- A record 900,000 Americans declared bankruptcy in 1991.[5]
- Debt collection is a growth industry, with 6,000 companies nationwide.[6]

WHAT EXACTLY IS compulsive debting? When is borrowing just a necessary feature of sound financial planning, a way to make ends meet in tough times, and when is it a self-defeating, compulsive pattern? Jerrold Mundis, author of *How to Get Out of Debt, Stay Out of Debt and Live Prosperously,* defines compulsive debting this way: "You repeatedly incur new debt despite the negative emotional and financial consequences that follow. Each time, you find a way to justify the new loan or late payment or use of credit, or turn to them in order to obtain relief from pressure you perceive as intolerable."[7]

The compulsive debtor is not the person caught *unexpectedly* in a cash-flow crisis by a downturn in the economy, a job layoff, or an illness or the person who charges the children's school clothes out of necessity and pays them off over several months. The compulsive debtor is someone who digs himself into a hole by *excessive* borrowing and the *misuse* of credit, who seeks relief from the mounting stress with yet another loan. He borrows even when he could avoid it just because he doesn't want to face the reality of limitations.

The compulsive debtor finds the truth regarding his finances *intolerable.* Rather than say, "I can't afford it," he puts it on his credit card. Rather than face a creditor, he borrows from one line of credit to pay another. Rather than generating more income, he relies on credit, borrowing to take another vacation or buy another expensive toy.

Compulsive debtors rationalize that they have no choice, but the fact is, *you cannot get out of debt by continuing to incur new debt.* The quick-fix solution of more credit only makes the debt greater, along with the pressure and stress. Rather than go through the discomfort necessary to get off the merry-go-round, compulsive debtors opt for short-term relief—over and over again.

People with high incomes are as likely to borrow compulsively as others. Amy, with a six-figure savings account, still bounces checks regularly—not because she doesn't have the money to cover them, but because she is a compulsive debtor, driven to repeat this pattern regardless of her financial resources. It's not economic necessity that drives the compulsive debtor, but the *process* of spending and owing.

The aggressive marketing of credit in America over the past twenty years has fed this compulsion. Credit cards are very lucrative for financial institutions, producing some 26 percent of profits.[8] So while many developers and investors default on high-risk loans, we are keeping the banks afloat by paying our 19 percent interest charges every month. The average American credit card holder pays *$465 a year in finance charges* for the privilege of using plastic![9]

Debt is psychologically easier to acquire when the lender is not a relative or neighbor but a faceless corporation miles away. If we're late with payments, we don't feel we're really hurting anyone, just getting the best of some rich corporation. But who's fooling whom? Studies show that we spend 23 percent more when using plastic than when using cash.[10]

What are the negative consequences that compulsive debtors typically incur? Stress illnesses, strained relationships, insomnia, loss of freedom as the growing monthly debt payment obligates them to work at jobs they dislike or work longer hours, shame and isolation, victimization by con artists pushing quick-fix schemes for bad credit and easy loans, depression, anxiety—even suicide. Some debtors physically endanger themselves by borrowing from unscrupulous loan sharks. Perhaps the worst consequence suffered by the compulsive debtor is the loss of a light heart. Harangued by creditors, ashamed to run into friends and relatives whom he owes, hopeless about finding any solutions, the compulsive debtor finds it increasingly difficult to enjoy the simple pleasures of life.

Joyce, a divorced mother of two sons, is an administrator in a large civic organization. She is also $30,000 in debt—from credit cards, loans, and store credit. Joyce operates under the policy that as long as she can still get money out of the magic money machine (ATM), she's not broke. She pays only the minimum due, but now her balances are so high that she can't even do that.

In a classic compulsive debtor move, rather than face her overextension and halt the borrowing, Joyce recently started taking cash advances to meet her monthly payments, incurring more debt. She rationalized that she had to do this to protect her credit rating. All the while, of course, she's sinking further into debt, and that can't be good for her credit rating in the long run. But she's opting to avoid today's cash squeeze with the quick fix of another credit hit.

At this point, Joyce has exhausted all credit lines and is receiving insistent calls from her twenty-odd creditors. At work, she pretends to be someone else when she answers the phone and offers to take messages for "Joyce." At home, she screens incoming calls with her phone machine. Recently, her telephone was shut off (incurring new fees to restore service), and her electricity has been turned off twice.

Last week, Joyce went to cash a check at the bank and discovered her account had been attached by the state for an income tax assessment she had long been ignoring. As is often the case, this kind of public exposure and loss of control came as a very painful shock that pierced her denial:

> I thought I was going to faint right there in the bank;
> I really did. I felt nauseated and dizzy. It was so hu-
> miliating to have this person say this to me so matter-
> of-factly. The other people in line were all looking at

me. It was the worst feeling I ever had. I knew I owed the money, but I preferred not to think about it. This hit me like a really scary reality. I'm thinking, "What am I going to do? This means my credit rating is shot." For the first time in my life, suicide actually occurred to me.

Despite the severity of Joyce's debt problems, few of her friends were even aware of it, and none of her business colleagues suspected a thing. She dresses Manhattan-chic and drives a sporty car. The few friends who know about her debt tend to make jokes about it. One friend bought her a key chain last year engraved with the words "I'm using my Visa to pay MasterCard."

Joyce says she's made the decision to file for bankruptcy protection. She's remarrying soon and rationalizes that she can file for bankruptcy under her own name, then later take her husband's. What she doesn't realize is that unless she gets help, she's likely to repeat the same chronic debt pattern.

Grant got his first credit card at the age of nineteen. He loved clothes and electronics, and within five years he'd run up $28,000 in credit card debt—an amount equal to his annual income. So he took out a consolidation loan to pay off those debts, swearing never to let his debt get out of control again. His monthly payment for the consolidation loan was less than all his other payments had been, so he felt some immediate relief. He went a month without incurring any new debt, but then one evening he wanted to take his girlfriend out to dinner, so he put it on his newly paid-off Visa account. Within a year, he had large balances on all his credit cards again—*and* he was still paying off the consolidation loan.

The woman Grant was dating, Nancy, knew little about the extent of his debt. One Christmas, he took a loan from a high-interest finance company in order to buy her an expensive necklace she wanted. Grant liked to take her to the theater and out for dinner, and he juggled debts to pull it off. She knew he was under some financial pressure but didn't know the extent of it.

When they got married, it was agreed that Nancy would take over paying the bills, bringing her money management skills to bear. The long-range plan was to get the couple into the black and save money to buy a home. This worked for a while, but being a compulsive spender, Grant had trouble staying within the budget. He once bought a CD player, then lied and told Nancy that a friend gave it to him when he got a better model. Grant started slipping back into his old spending patterns, which required more money than their budget allowed. At one point, he borrowed money from his mother and didn't mention it to Nancy.

On one occasion, Nancy gave Grant the bill payments to mail, but he didn't mail them. Instead, he wrote checks against that money, paying off some people at work that he owed, and the rest just seemed to go. Failing to mail the bills and spending that money was an irrational act, guaranteed to be discovered. The next month, he started coming home every day at lunch to intercept any new bills from the mailbox so that Nancy wouldn't find them and discover that he hadn't made the last payments. As his days began revolving around the mailman's schedule, his work productivity diminished. At night, he tossed and turned, worrying about how he was going to get out of this mess. Eventually, Nancy got the inevitable call from a creditor, wanting to know when they would pay the bill. She, of course, insisted that it *had* been paid, but several days later, Grant told her the truth. Shocked and confused, Nancy insisted they go together to a psychotherapist, who in turn suggested Debtor's Anonymous meetings. That turned out to be a good move.

Now, five years later, Grant and Nancy are still together, and a good deal of the debt has been paid off. Following DA's suggestions, the only debt they have now is collateralized, such as the mortgage on their house. And Grant's business is thriving. "The serenity that comes with solvency," says Grant, "helps you get a good night's sleep."

Troy is a young high school teacher. Six years ago, when he was a sophomore in college and out of spending money, he was approached by a credit card company representative outside the student union who suggested he take a minute to sign up for a Visa card. It didn't matter, the salesman said, that Troy had no credit history or source of income. Those requirements would be waived. Troy thought for a second.

> I knew I needed books and spending money for weekends, and my car needed a few repairs. So I figured, "Great, where do I sign?" It was easier than I thought. A couple weeks later I had my card, which I rapidly maxed out buying a new stereo and whatever.
>
> At first, making the monthly payments was no big deal. I paid the minimum, like twenty-five dollars. I thought, "No problem. When I graduate, I'll pay off the balance." I didn't even consider the possibility of a recession.
>
> Then I started getting invitations for credit cards from everyone: "You have been preapproved . . . ," "A card in your name is waiting . . . ," "You're one of a select few . . . ," and all that. So I'm like, "Cool," and I sent some more in and ended up with three major bank cards, two airline, and four department store cards.
>
> I thought this was the greatest thing—my name embossed on all these credit cards. "I'm someone now, you know, I'm really an adult." You don't think about the fact that they expect *payment* on all these things, and if you don't pay, they come after you. You just think, "Wow, I can buy whatever I want. I don't have to have money."

By the end of his junior year, Troy was starting to do what a lot of students do: using his credit cards to cover basic living expenses like rent, groceries, and gasoline, not to mention parties, a new wardrobe, and some compact discs. His payments became sporadic, and soon he had a drawer full of final notices. Troy graduated with over $10,000 in credit card debt and a bad credit report. Now, he's moving back home with his parents until he can get on his feet financially.

At the time of this interview, Troy was counting on willpower to turn things around. He put himself on a stringent budget that called for paying off the entire debt within one year. It allowed for no entertainment, no new clothing, no gifts—nothing beyond the bare essentials. He sounded determined, but he admitted this was the third time he had tried a budget.

INDICATIONS OF COMPULSIVE DEBTING

Gets a Special "Charge" out of Using Credit

Compulsive debtors use credit whenever possible. Early in the progression of their dis-ease, they usually have multiple cards, far more than necessary to handle emergencies, and charge more than they can easily pay off, given their incomes. Form letters announcing preapproved or special customer status are irresistible. Lisa, the secretary who accrued $35,000 in debts by the age of twenty-five, once had a contest going with a friend to see who could qualify for the most credit cards: "I had thirty-two of them, and he only had thirty. I'd call him whenever a new card came in, saying, 'Guess what they sent me,' as though I'd won a prize. When a new card came, it meant I could go out for dinner, go shopping, or plan some exotic vacation. I thought of it as free money, not like I'd ever have to pay it back."

Uses Credit as Income

Like Lisa, many chronic debtors think of a new credit card, a line of credit, or overdraft privileges as found money rather than as debt that will have to be repaid with interest. When Jesse, the screenwriter heavily in debt from his spending, was two months behind on his rent, he got one of those form letters informing him that he was preapproved for $2,500 on a Visa card. He remembers thinking, "Oh great, this is going to save me from going out to get a regular job." Now that Visa account is maxed-out, along with several others.

Most tellingly, compulsive debtors use credit to pay for normal living expenses like rent. Rather than *create* income, they use credit as income. If a compulsive debtor has overdraft privileges, rather than save it for emergencies or to cover any math errors, she'll intentionally write checks against it. Within a month, the balance usually hovers at the maximum overdraft permitted, and she has lost all the benefit of a cushion. Now she just tries to keep up with her interest payments each month.

Jay, a dancer and massage therapist, is trying to get a friend to cosign a loan for him. "It would be nice to have a buffer," he says, "to take care of a couple months' rent, and have some money." He thinks of taking a loan as having money. He doesn't see that next month the rent will be due again, and then he'll have to pay not only *that* rent but the loan payment too.

Pays Only the Minimum

It never occurs to the compulsive debtor to pay more than the minimum due on her bills. To her, that's staying current. I still remember being dumbfounded when a friend told me she paid her MasterCard account off in full each month. I thought, "Why do you do that if you don't *have* to?" Of course, the bank doesn't mind if you just pay the minimum, because they make tremendous profits on the interest. According to a bulletin called *The Banker's Secret*, if a person with $2,000 on her credit card pays only the minimum due, she will eventually pay a whopping $9,125.[11]

Maintains No Margin of Safety

The compulsive debtor tends to spend 125 percent of his income, so there never seems to be a surplus or "cushion." That keeps him operating perilously close to the edge. Any unexpected car repair or medical expense, or even the quarterly insurance bill, precipitates a crisis, which usually results in either unpaid bills or yet another loan.

Always Maxes Out

A compulsive debtor also tends to use the maximum credit available. She may exercise restraint for a while, especially if trying to prove to a spouse or someone else that she's in control, but eventually the credit gets used. If she pays down a balance, she usually runs it right back up again.

Enters a Self-perpetuating Cycle

Because the compulsive debtor is overextended, making his debt payments often leaves him without enough money for everyday living expenses, like groceries, gas, utilities, or rent. So he borrows more money to get through the month, which only adds to the debt burden, or he writes bad checks, hoping to cover them in time.

Writes Rubber Checks

Many of those who are chronic check bouncers are compulsive debtors. This, again, is not the person who bounces a check on rare occasions and only when she's made a mistake in her math. Compulsive debtors bounce checks knowingly, and chronically. If the bank extends overdraft privileges to them, they simply run *that* up to the maximum and then bounce checks from *there*. Rosalyn, the travel agent in recovery for compulsive spending and debting, describes her pattern:

I used to write checks even when I knew they would probably bounce. There was the same kind of feeling as shoplifting—very rough on your nervous system. I'd try not to look at the person I was writing it to. It was like fear and guilt, which is strong energy to oppose. That's how I bought most of my clothes. I would put it on layaway and then bounce a check to get it out.

Along with bouncing checks, many compulsive debtors play near-constant games with the bank. "Let's see, by the time this check gets to my bank, I'll cash a check at the grocery store and deposit that cash to cover it. I'll get paid on Wednesday, so that deposit should clear before the grocery store check gets there . . ." And so on. Sometimes it works, sometimes it doesn't. It always hangs in the back of the mind as a source of low-level anxiety. As a result, some people get what they call *bank sweats*. Just walking into a bank makes them feel uneasy and anxious, and they can literally break into a sweat.

If the compulsive debtor gets bank notices about insufficient funds, she often just ignores them, because they don't fit with what she wants to have happening. She sees the familiar envelopes arrive in the mail, but she doesn't let them register in her mind.

Develops Tunnel Vision

The compulsive debtor only considers those bills that are due *now*. He rarely plans ahead to meet periodic bills for taxes, insurance, or car repairs that will come due *next* month or next quarter. Each month's income is treated almost like a grant that must be spent in full by the end of the period or be lost. The notion of saving or planning ahead is foreign, so when periodic or emergency expenses do come up, they inevitably cause a crisis, which usually leads to more borrowing.

The compulsive debtor operates on the principle that he should spend what he wants and needs to and then pay his bills with what's left. You may recall a TV commercial some years ago featuring a pubescent Brooke Shields in Calvin Klein jeans, lying on the floor in a provocative pose. "I'm saving my money for more Calvins," she cooed intimately to the camera. "And if I have anything left over, I'll pay the rent." That's exactly how the compulsive spender and debtor thinks, that he shouldn't let details like paying the rent interfere with having the things he wants. Kirk, a compulsive spender and debtor, remembers that commercial well:

> That's exactly how I used to live, only my version of "designer jeans" was eating out in fancy restaurants seven nights a week. I put that before paying the rent or going to the dentist. It didn't matter if the money was there or not, there was just a voice in me that said, "Do it." The question, What can you afford? never occurred to me. I just did it.[12]

Charges and Then Pockets the Cash

The compulsive debtor operates under the delusion that using a credit card is like not paying, like getting something for nothing. She charges purchases and dinners rather than parting with the cash. If dining out with friends, she may collect cash from everyone then put the bill on her credit card. She likes having the cash in her pocket—and spends it without regard for the bill she will get in a month. In contrast, the person who is not a compulsive debtor can collect cash and put the bill on her credit card, but she pays the bill when it comes in, so she's no worse off.

Spends Based on *Expected* Income

Compulsive debtors may be the world's most relentless optimists. They always believe that relief from their financial strain is just around the corner, days or weeks away. Charles Dickens, himself the son of a debtor, captured this optimism—which in the compulsive debtor's case is really a form of denial—in *David Copperfield,* in the character of Mr. Micawber, whom he described thus: "I have known him come home to supper with a flood of tears, and a declaration that nothing was now left but a jail; and go to bed making a calculation of the expense of putting bow-windows to the house, 'in case anything turned up,' which was his favorite expression."[13]

Accordingly, the compulsive debtor often spends money based on income he *expects* to get rather than on income in hand. Then, if the money he expects is delayed or turns out to be less than expected, he is thrown into crisis—and more debt. Sometimes his expectations for future income are unrealistic to begin with; at other times he may expect an advance, royalty payment, dividend, or insurance settlement that just doesn't come through or is substantially less than expected.

When Grant was in college, before he got married, his father sent him money to pay his spring tuition, but Grant spent it on a ski trip between semesters. He figured he'd be getting a stock dividend soon—he got it every year at this time—and would pay his tuition with that. But as luck would have it, the stock decreased in value that year, so the statement arrived without a check this time, throwing Grant into his first major debt crisis.

Pam did something similar. She was expecting to receive a chunk of money from an insurance settlement, so she ran up substantial debts that she planned to pay for with that windfall. But it never materialized, leaving Pam $20,000 in the hole.

Stays Vague About Finances

The compulsive debtor suffers from what one debtor calls "terminal vagueness" when it comes to finances. He's usually not entirely sure how much money he has, how much he has spent, how much he owes, or how much he will need next month—and he prefers not to know. He generally doesn't reconcile his checkbook or keep a tally of his balance. He rarely knows the rate of interest he pays on his credit accounts. That, to him, is a pretty irrelevant detail; what matters is that he *got* the credit.

He uses this vagueness to delude himself about how much money he has available. Troy, for instance, doesn't keep the tally in his checkbook. When he needs cash, he requests his "balance available" from the ATM and draws on that. He blocks out the fact that he may have written checks against that balance that haven't cleared yet.

Jerrold Mundis coined the term the *Ostrich Syndrome* for the debtor's habit of not opening his mail for fear of finding more bills and past-due notices.[14] The debtor sticks his head in the sand rather than face reality. I remember tossing a half-dozen bounced check notices in a drawer once and leaving them there for weeks before finally getting around to figuring out what was happening. Not opening the mail, of course, exacerbates the debtor's problems, as he misses important deadlines and fails to take appropriate action. Reuben, an active debtor, recalls:

> As a general policy, I don't pay my bills for three months or so, even when I have the money. Part of it is that I'm lonely since my girlfriend broke up with me. I believe I shouldn't have to live alone and pay my own bills—so I just don't.
>
> Last year, I got put in jail because my license and registration had been revoked due to a traffic infraction that I failed to respond to. I got pulled over and wham—off to jail, strip-searched, the whole deal. All because I hadn't opened my mail. That was pretty extreme.

People observing the debtor's ostrich behavior may mistake it for a devil-may-care attitude. But those bills and notices actually weigh heavily on his mind. Though he hasn't opened them or dealt with them, he's often well aware of them at a deeper level. One debtor described the bags of unopened bills he had stuffed in a closet as "pulsating" there in his imagination, growing more insistent, like a throbbing abscessed tooth.

Misuses Consolidation Loans

Theresa got a consolidation loan to pay off her credit card balances. It seemed like a good idea at the time, because she was falling behind in her payments and getting a lot of pressure from her creditors. When she got the loan, her intention was just to cut up her credit cards and pay the loan off, but that's not what she did. Instead, she ran all five of her cards back up to the max, so that now, a year later, she has the loan plus all that new debt to pay back.

This behavior with consolidation loans is pretty common among compulsive debtors. The loan intended to lighten the load of overwhelming debt becomes instead a way to free up accounts to be used again. The person really believes at the time that she's not going to incur new debt. But if she is a compulsive debtor, she inevitably does, because she is—by definition—compulsive, not in control. She ends up more in debt than ever, defeating the original rationale for taking the loan.

Gets on the Budget Merry-Go-Round

Mark Twain once wryly observed, "It's easy to stop smoking. . . . I've done it hundreds of times!" He was referring to his own nicotine habit, but his point applies to all compulsive behaviors. Typically, two-thirds of those who try to break a bad habit are back to it within three months.[15]

Likewise, the compulsive debtor finds it easy to start a budget . . . he's done it hundreds of times. Troy, the young teacher many thousands in debt from his college days, explains that as of this week, he's drawn up an "incredibly detailed budget," the goal of which is to pay off all debt within a year. But just like Twain with his smoking, Troy has made similar vows before. *Deciding* to go on a budget is the easy part. It's the follow-through that gets tricky.

One major mistake compulsive debtors like Troy make is committing themselves to an unrealistically stringent plan. Such a plan backfires when it fosters feelings of deprivation that in turn spark the urge to splurge. They tend to see paying off debt fast as the number one goal and lose sight of the fact that the best way to be responsible to creditors is to devise a *realistic* plan that they can actually adhere to. Some misguided debtors even keep incurring *new debt,* thinking (or rationalizing) that the goal is just to pay off *old debt.*

The most successful tool for recovery from compulsive debt is not a punishing budget but a realistic spending plan that puts *not incurring new debt* as the number one goal, along with having a real life and allotting money for items and activities (including saving) that contribute to overall well-being and gratification. The difference is that now one must pay for those items and activities in cash rather than add to overall indebtedness. Only after new debt has been stopped and the need for a gratifying life recognized can one expect to make lasting headway in reducing overall indebtedness. More on spending plans can be found in the recovery section of this chapter.

Resorts to Desperate Measures

If the compulsive debtor gets in deep enough, he may be tempted to engage in unethical and illegal activities in order to keep himself afloat. I'm reminded again of Robert Maxwell, the publishing magnate accused of stealing from his company's pension funds to try and keep his flagging companies afloat, or the New York school chancellor who lost his prestigious position for chronically borrowing from staff, or the compulsive debtor who withdrew all the money from his and his wife's joint savings account without telling her, figuring he'd pay it back later.

Wayne, a small-business owner, ruined his credit with unpaid bills, then finagled new cards by creating fictitious names and businesses. He kept track of the information he put on different applications, gave out phony social security numbers, used various post office boxes, made up names of companies and supervisors, and had friends on call for verification. He got eight new cards that way. Then he took a cash advance on one of them to make a down payment on a new car and got a car loan.

Examples like these of illegal and unethical activities by compulsive debtors are growing in number and will continue to do so until the problem of compulsive debt is recognized in our society and more people find help.

Blames Others

The compulsive debtor often blames his creditors for being "on his case" about a debt. "What is he making such a big deal out of this for?" Or "How dare the bank bounce my check!" He turns it around in his mind so that *he* is the one being wronged. He claims the anxious creditor is just overreacting.

Roger, a West Coast carpenter, took an advance from a couple to build a garage onto their home but never did the work. At the time, he was desperate for money to pay some debts, so he agreed to build a garage for them even though he didn't actually have the experience or tools for such a big project. So he just kept blocking it from his mind, trying not to think about it, and dodging the couple's calls. Finally, the pair complained to the police, and Roger was arrested. Instead of owning up to his dishonesty, he became outraged that the couple "opened up a can of worms by being excessively vehement."

In another example, Julia ran up phone bills last year while living temporarily at a friend's house. Now she can't understand why her friend is getting so pushed out of shape about it. "She's really been getting on my case," says Julia. "I don't understand why people get so uptight about money. I feel so shafted."

Both Roger and Julia managed to turn things around and feel victimized by their creditors. They feel like victims and rationalize that other people just put too much emphasis on money. And though there can be some truth in this accusation, the compulsive debtor uses it as a way to justify his own self-defeating pattern with debt, one that has negative consequences for himself—and others.

Maintains Secrecy and Pretense

The compulsive debtor fools a lot of people. Outside of his banker, his creditors, and possibly a spouse, most people who know him don't suspect that his finances are in such chaos. He especially tries to keep any evidence of his debtor pattern from anyone he wants to impress. Jesse, for instance, would bounce checks to his creditors or the utility company, but *never* to his father or brothers, because he wanted to appear successful to them. "One way or another," he says, "I would always cover that one."

Some compulsive debtors even keep their debt secret from a spouse. Bob knew when he married his wife, Gloria, that she expected to be supported in style. His manhood, it seemed to him, hinged on how well he filled his role as provider. So he kept her in luxurious homes, taxis, and decorators—while secretly accruing massive debt.

Such secrecy causes the debtor to feel isolated and ashamed. And because other debtors are likewise secretive, few people are aware of how widespread the problem is. Each debtor thinks he's one of the few around who has trouble managing money.

Expects a Bailout

Most compulsive debtors harbor the belief that someone is going to save them, that they ultimately will not have to be responsible for themselves. They have an "out" in mind—a relative, a friend, an insurance settlement, an inheritance—something or someone that will come to the rescue.

Lydia always knew her father would bail her out, and she felt he owed her that much: "There were times when I literally went out and ran up debts, knowing that I could get the money from him. Money was all my father ever gave me, so I guess I had some investment in keeping this routine going."

When and if the debtor starts recovering and taking responsibility for her own debts, the rescuer(s) in her life may unconsciously try to resurrect the old dance by somehow (and unwittingly) encouraging the old behavior. When Deborah joined Debtors Anonymous, her mother, who had paid Deborah's bills off for years, must have sensed that Deborah was on the verge of changing, though the daughter made no mention of the meetings she was attending. But several weeks into the program, Deborah got a letter from her mother offering to pay off all of her debts. This was surely a tempting proposition for a compulsive debtor, but by this time, Deborah knew that she had to take responsibility for herself if she was ever to become financially sound and sane. The compulsive debtor only recovers when she stops taking bailouts and takes back her own financial power.

Uses Debt as Distraction

Some people—curious as it may sound—use debt as a *distraction* from feelings and other problems they don't want to face. The constant crisis and pressure of being in debt become so absorbing that they don't have to think or feel anything else. When Kirk was devastated by a breakup with his girlfriend two years ago, he concentrated on his debts to keep from feeling:

The debt and its problems became such a strong focus in my life that I hardly thought about anything else. I wasn't using drugs anymore, so debt became like a drug. It was a major distraction, and it worked very well. Someone with higher self-esteem might have chosen to find distraction some other way, like working or making money. But having low self-esteem, I found being in debt fit me perfectly.

In my family growing up, people were always fighting about money as a smokescreen for other issues. I guess I learned from them to focus on money rather than on whatever else is wrong in my life.

Uses Debt as Revenge

Theresa's parents send her $500 each month to keep her creditors at bay. Theresa, who is now in recovery, is starting to become aware of how and why this pattern persists. She grew up feeling that her mother resented her and withheld affection and money. "I think I keep myself in debt so they'll keep sending me this money, which I'm sure my mother resents sending. My father is the one who insists that they can't let me sink. It's like my way of getting revenge on her, like I'm saying 'I'll drain you, Mom, I'll *get it* from you—one way or the other.'"

There is often a "screw you" attitude implied in the debtor's behavior toward creditors. Creditors can be stand-ins for parents, spouses, or whomever the compulsive debtor seeks to punish. She feels she's been "screwed" in life, got a bad deal, and now she's getting hers.

Uses Debt to Reenact Shame and Fear

In early Christian thinking, the word *debt* was used synonymously with sin, as in "Forgive us our debts, as we forgive our debtors." Even today, one of the definitions of *debt* in *Webster's Dictionary* is "neglected moral duty, sin, trespass." So despite our much more cavalier attitude toward debt in the 1970s and 1980s, it still carries a lot of heavy baggage. Deep within, we associate debt with failure, shame, guilt, and fear.

So why would anyone set themselves up for such stigma and feelings of failure? Because those feelings may be familiar, according to Dean, a coin dealer who compulsively writes bad checks and piles up debts. Dean was sexually molested as a boy and still struggles with a toxic level of shame. He draws a connection:

> There's a lot of shame in bouncing checks and being a deadbeat. It's public exposure as a person who is actually worth less than he said he was. The truth comes out. It's a reenactment, I think, of being shamed as a kid. It's my way of saying, "Yes, I really am worthless." The fear and anxiety of living in constant debt feels familiar too. The more fear and shame I have, the more I spend and debt, which creates more shame and fear—which feels right.

Debts More When Feeling Hopeless

When a person doesn't feel much hope for the future, financially or otherwise, she may develop a "screw-it" attitude that drives her into debt even more. When Theresa wasn't able to make even her minimum payments, she sank further into hopelessness—and more debt.

> After my boyfriend broke up with me, I didn't do anything but run up debts for three and a half months. I went out to get cash advances and buy groceries, and the rest of the time I slept. I was very depressed. And the fact that my debt was climbing and I knew my credit rating was being shot just compounded it. I felt like, "Why bother trying?"
>
> Then, as I started coming out of the depression and seeing some light, some hope that I could live a

good life after all, my attitude toward debt started to shift. Now I'm not debting anymore, a day at a time. Today I do have hope.

RECOVERING FROM CHRONIC DEBT

Some compulsive debtors assume that all they need to do to get out of debt is generate more income. But the fact is, when compulsive debtors do get more money, they tend to deal with it *exactly* as they did less money: they spend more than they have coming in and get into further debt, as Jerrold Mundis aptly explains.

> Jim makes $25,000 a year, but consistently spends $30,000, borrowing and going ever deeper into debt. . . . His debts are a constant source of pressure, pain, and unhappiness. If his salary jumps to $50,000 next year, he will almost inevitably begin to spend $60,000, borrowing and going ever deeper into debt. The behavior patterns that resulted from his distorted attitudes about money and self, which led him into debt in the first place, are still wholly intact. He will continue to incur debt, and the pressure, pain, and unhappiness this brought him will still be there. All that will change are the numbers.[16]

Other debtors think that to get out of debt they must adopt a stringent budget, get a debt consolidation loan, or switch to credit cards with lower interest rates. They assume they will be able to *control* their debting if they just learn how to do it smarter. Consolidation loans and budgets might work for the person who got in debt solely as a result of a job layoff or an unexpected injury, but *compulsive* debtors are by definition out of control. Suggesting that the compulsive debtor "debt smarter" is like suggesting an alcoholic "drink smarter." He may control it for a little while, but if he isn't on a recovery track, relapse is all but inevitable.

Increased income by itself, consolidation loans, or strict budgets are not the way out of compulsive debt. The way out is to stop incurring new debt and start developing new attitudes toward money, debt, and ourselves. Let's turn now to some specific suggestions that people in recovery have found useful.

No New Debt—Just for Today

Far more important than how quickly you pay off existing debt is not incurring any *new* debt. This is the single most important step for the compulsive debtor in recovery. Stopping the accumulation of debt is like applying a tourniquet to a wound: the goal is to stop the bleeding. You can't expect to begin healing until you've done that. It may seem a self-evident step, but it's profound for the compulsive debtor.

Before I went to a self-help group for my money problems, it honestly never occurred to me to simply stop incurring any new debt. I thought I had to find a magical way to keep the creditors at bay, hit the Lotto and pay them all off, or become a better money manager. At my first self-help meeting, I heard the speaker say that after she stopped incurring new debt, her total indebtedness only grew *smaller* as she paid on it, never larger. This was a revelation.

If you don't have enough money to cover your monthly expenses, you may think you have no choice but to borrow more money. But if you are committed to not incurring any more debt, you can either cut expenses or generate more income. Both are more possible than you think. The important thing is to close the door on the quick fix of borrowing money or bouncing checks. As Mundis writes, "You can not get out of debt by borrowing more money. No more than an alcoholic can become sober by having another drink."[17]

If there's no money for debt repayment now, remember this: building a sound financial future by not incurring *new* debt is the most responsible thing you can do for your creditors, because it best ensures that you *will*—as you become financially stable—be able to repay them in full.

There is one exception to the "no debt" rule for recovering compulsive debtors, and that is secured loans, a loan for which collateral is pledged. Collateral is property, like a house or a car, that you sign over to the lender until a debt is paid. If you fail to pay the money back according to the agreement, the property becomes the lender's. An example of a secured loan is a mortgage, or a car loan for which the car is pledged. It's not so dangerous a debt for the recovering compulsive debtor, because it is balanced off with an asset. If you don't pay back the loan, the asset is taken from you by the lender, and the debt is resolved.

But even secured loans should not be taken lightly. Whether it's secure or not, a debt can still become a terrific burden if you don't have the money to keep up the payments. Why put yourself through that? The wise money manager takes even a secured loan only when it contributes to her overall well-being. Last year, I was able to buy a house for the first time, so I now have a mortgage, a collateralized debt. Having my own home contributed substantially to my overall well-being, providing me with a sense of roots, a yard for gardening, and a greater sense of self-determination. It was a wise purchase, in line with my long-term goals and life purpose—a far cry from the finance company loans I used to take for the sole purpose of paying other debts and enjoying a few dinners out.

Not incurring any new unsecured debt—a day at a time—turns out to be a tremendous gift if it moves you closer to having your heart's desires. So rather than thinking of forgoing credit as something that deprives and restricts you, begin to look upon it as something that nurtures and liberates you. Keep one eye on the greater pleasures and gratification you are moving toward by abstaining from new debt. Dare to make some long-range plans based on not debting for *today*. Start expecting true wealth as a result of solvency.

Spend Less Than You Bring In

And he told me, I remember, to take warning by the Marshalsea, and to observe that if a man had twenty pounds a year and spent nineteen pounds, nineteen shillings and sixpence, he would be happy: but that a shilling spent the other way would make him wretched.

CHARLES DICKENS, RECALLING WHAT HIS FATHER,
JOHN DICKENS, TOLD HIM FROM MARSHALSEA, A
DEBTORS' PRISON

Unless you can instantly raise income, spending less than you bring in means cutting back on spending. As harsh as this sounds, there's usually a lot more leeway in the debtor's expenditures than he thinks. It's just a matter of getting creative.

In his book on recovering from debt, Jerrold Mundis tells how, soon after starting his recovery from compulsive debting, he needed $5,000 in dental work and didn't know how to get it without running a tab with his dentist (thus incurring a new debt). But because he was *committed* to not incurring any new debt, he found a way. He got the most urgent work done at a dental college for greatly reduced rates, then had his own dentist complete the work gradually over the course of a year, as Mundis had the money. He paid for each visit on the spot, for a total of $3,500. That was $3,500 in new debt he did not incur.[18]

Pay First Things First

Compulsive debtors are used to reacting to insistent creditors by sending them money that was earmarked for rent, mortgage, food, or the kids' school clothes. But this only perpetuates the pattern, because it inevitably results in *more* borrowing in order to meet those basic needs. In recovery we learn to get off this merry-go-round and pay *first things first*. That means taking care of your basic living expenses like food, shelter, clothing, and medical care before you even *think* about debt repayment. Otherwise, the gnawing anxiety, fear, and sense of deprivation will fuel more spending and debting, keeping you trapped in the cycle.

Perform Plastic Surgery

Cut up your charge cards and *close the accounts*. Paying cash ensures that you don't incur new debt and makes you more conscious of what you're spending. Note that for the compulsive debtor it is crucial not just to get rid of the cards but to close the accounts; otherwise you can just get the account number out of the file and charge anyway. I know; I've done it.

Open Your Eyes

Clarity is another friend of debt recovery. Without clarity, you remain powerless to change anything. As hard as it is, as much as you don't want to see, it's crucial to open your eyes and take inventory of your income, expenses, and debts. Get out your statements, bills, and check registers; give yourself plenty of time to pore over them; and keep breathing. Tell someone when you're going to do this so you feel connected to a support system, even if you're doing it by yourself.

Rather than think of this process as an exercise in self-torture, think of it as a wise, loving, nurturing thing to do for yourself. Staying foggy, vague, and in denial is the only thing that can hurt you at this point. With your eyes open, you can find the way out. By *seeking the truth* you make contact with your own higher self.

Learn About Spending Plans

For the debtor, a budget is based on tightening the belt, deprivation, and sheer willpower. He relies on short-term fortitude rather than on a transformed relationship with money. Most compulsive debtors who go on budgets end up putting the debt back on (just as dieters often put weight back on), as feelings of deprivation give way to bingeing.

In contrast, a spending plan is based on *prosperity*—financial and emotional. It invites you to make choices about how you will spend your money—choices that support your long-term well-being. Where a budget usually calls for cutting out all "extras" and "frills," your spending plan may *include* things like fresh flowers, a movie, dinner out and a play, a new book, a college course—whatever it is that truly feeds and nourishes you. (Of course, you will now pay cash and not put these expenditures on a credit card!) It is in your best interest—*and your creditors'*—that you enjoy a good quality of life. Otherwise, you'll have no incentive to continue the spending plan and eventually make full repayment. That's the paradox of debt recovery: the way out is through true prosperity rather than deprivation. A spending plan enables you to indulge your heart's desires rather than your impulses.

I remember how as a fledgling writer struggling with debt, I never seemed to have the money for books, office supplies, postage, and other business expenses. I used to buy those items only if there was money left over, or I would incur new debt for them. After developing my first spending plan with the help of friends in recovery, writing expenses became a priority, even above debt repayment, as they would ultimately contribute to both my life satisfaction and my income. That one change in how I spent money presaged a shift in my overall financial priorities, signifying my growing respect for my own skills and career, which in turn made me feel more prosperous and cared for—by me! It's amazing, but once you've identified what's really important to you—whether it's getting an education, buying a house, studying music, adopting a child, launching a career—the money will be there for it. But *you* have to make it a priority first, take it more seriously than constant consumption of perishable goods.

Providing there is enough income to undertake it, a part of the spending plan may include debt repayment. Most debtors are used to paying the creditors who shout the loudest. But a spending plan is just that—a *plan,* based not on who shouts the loudest, but on what's truly available for repayment!

Resist Bankruptcy and Become Committed to Debt Repayment

For a compulsive debtor, thinking of bankruptcy as a solution is pure fantasy. It's like throwing out an alcoholic's liquor supply and supposing the problem is over. Eventually, of course, the alcoholic will just get more booze. Likewise with debt. Estimates are that some 50 percent of those who declare bankruptcy do so again, usually as soon as possible under the law.[19] That's because bankruptcy is just another quick fix. So resist the temptation to file for bankruptcy protection. It gets you off the hook but impedes long-term recovery. Instead, become committed to repayment of your existing debts and to not incurring any more. This commitment will restore your sense of pride, self-esteem, and responsibility, and *that* will do more to ensure future cash flow than any bailout!

The word *credit* comes from the Latin verb *credere,* which means "to trust, to believe." It's a good feeling to know that your word is trustworthy, that people can believe in it. And when you become committed to repayment, you'll be surprised at the way your clear intention opens up new possibilities. You may not know yet *how* you will repay those debts, but as Goethe is often quoted, "Whatever you can do or dream you can, begin it. Boldness has magic, power and genius in it." When you move forward boldly, courageously, to keep your word, somehow it becomes possible.

Just out of college, Dan and his friend Ralph started a small house-painting business in Florida. After a couple of successful years, they took a substantial bank loan and bought two hardware stores. Such expansion was probably premature, and they were inexperienced at retail business. Within two years, both stores failed. The two young men were stuck with these bank loans and other debts, for which they were each 50 percent responsible. Dan and Ralph handled their portions of the debt differently, with startlingly different results.

Dan went to the bank officers and to his other creditors and told them he was committed to repayment. "However long it takes," Dan said, "I'm going to do it." He returned to painting houses, made a realistic debt repayment plan (one that still allowed him a life), and kept to it. In the area where Dan lived, word spread among homeowners and contractors of his integrity and trustworthiness. More and more work came his way, as one referral led to another. Within four years, his debts were completely repaid and his reputation enhanced. One of the homeowners for whom he did work turned out to be on the board of a national fast food chain, and Dan wound up with a contract to paint all the chain's restaurants. Today, Dan and his wife are multimillionaires.

Dan's partner, Ralph, assumed the same amount of debt when the hardware business failed, only he declared bankruptcy. At the time, it probably seemed like the smart thing to do, to take advantage of the laws that allowed him to wipe the slate clean. But perhaps because he never had to deal with the negative consequences of his debt, Ralph didn't learn much from that early experience. He has continued to struggle with money and debt ever since, and recently declared bankruptcy again.

As I think has been made abundantly clear, the way to recover from compulsive debt is not to avoid your creditors or to declare bankruptcy and have the slate wiped clean, it is to accept complete responsibility for your debts and become totally committed to repayment. That does *not* mean to judge yourself harshly for having these debts. Neither does it mean that you pay these debts sooner than is financially sound for you.

The best way to be responsible to your creditors is to begin today to handle your financial affairs *soundly*. That may mean that, for the time being, no debt repayment is possible, while you work on stabilizing your income, taking care of basic expenses properly, and getting a real, gratifying life. That doesn't mean more indulgence; it means *enrichment*. For only when you stop going in debt to *yourself* will you become consistently able to act responsibly toward your creditors.

Take Back Responsibility—and Your Power

When the compulsive debtor refrains from incurring new debt and devises a sane plan for repayment of existing debts, he takes real responsibility for his life—perhaps for the first time. Along with responsibility comes power, real power, the kind that comes from within and inspires others by example, not domination or "power over." No longer are you a servant of the banks, the advertisers, or your creditors; you have the power that a responsible, self-determining person enjoys, as Deborah, a recovering compulsive debtor, explains:

> I used to relate to my bills as though they represented some big, bad authority that was out to get me. Naturally, with that attitude, I resented paying them.
>
> Recently, I've begun to turn that around. I finally see that debt repayment is not something I have to do for them, but something I have to do for *myself*, to maintain my own power. It's like I'm not the underdog or the victim any longer. I'm in charge of my money. And one day at a time, I spend it "soberly."

Understand That You Are Not Your Debts

We have developed yet another prejudice in our nation, which I call financialism. We judge people—including ourselves—on the basis of financial worth. It's important to remember that *you are not your debts* or your credit rating, any more than you "are" the color of your skin or eyes. If you became a millionaire tomorrow, you would not be any more deserving of respect than you are today. People might show you more attention and superficial respect, but that's because our society generally associates self-worth with net worth. To recover from money disorders, you can no longer afford this kind of thinking. You are neither your debts *nor* your fortunes. You are something much greater than either of these symbols. Refuse to judge yourself on such hollow criteria.

If you're still saddled with debt, instead of seeing it as a disaster and a horrific burden, start to look at it as a vehicle through which you can transform your relationship with yourself and others, as Rosalyn did:

> I used to walk around feeling like such a piece of shit for being in debt, like I had a scarlet letter on my chest, only it was a big "D" for Debtor.
>
> Now I realize that a lot of my debting behavior was learned, generations of attitudes toward money that got expressed through me. And it doesn't seem like such a humiliating thing anymore. I can have a good life, feel happy, feel confident, enjoy myself—and still have debts. The goal is not to incur any *new* debts. And I don't feel I have to pay creditors more than I can sanely pay anymore, or else be a bad person. I am not my debts.

Consider Saving a Necessity, Not a Luxury

To avoid being caught without money for car repairs, root canals, home emergencies, and other surprises, the recovering compulsive debtor does well to consider saving a *necessity* rather than a luxury. Saving is a greater priority for recovery, in fact, than paying off past debts quickly, because without a contingency fund you will be setting yourself up to borrow again, undermining long-term recovery. Saving 10 percent of all incoming money is a good goal, but you may want to start with 5 percent and work up. You'll be surprised at how great it feels to be taking care of yourself this way.

Act, Don't React

> *Now I take the actions I have to take, even though I don't always want to. I call my creditor even though I don't want to; I apply for the job even when I don't feel like it—because hiding from problems was part of my disease, and taking action is part of my recovery. As long as I stay out of hiding, I'm going to be getting better. I don't have to be perfect; I just have to be out in the open. Recovery is mostly about doing things, rather than just hiding out.*
>
> ROSS, RECOVERING COMPULSIVE DEBTOR

Compulsive debtors are used to *reacting*. We react when we get an angry phone call from a creditor by putting a check in the mail—even if it's going to bounce, or even if it means we don't pay something else, like the rent. We react to our spouse's complaints by going out and charging something else, just to "prove" our independence.

In recovery, it's important for us to take back control by acting in our own best interests, instead of reacting. That might mean calling creditors rather than waiting for them to call us, or pursuing the job we really want, or balancing our checkbooks *before* we start getting bank charges for insufficient funds, or totaling up our debts to see where we stand, or closing a charge account.

We tend to put off taking action because we're afraid the result won't be to our liking: maybe we won't get the job we apply for; maybe the bank statement won't balance; maybe our creditors won't agree to the repayment plan we propose.

But these are all outcomes that we cannot control. The only thing we can control is whether we take the action in the first place. The result is not ours to worry about. We need to take the action and let go of the results.

I remember when I got my first free-lance assignment to write an educational videotape script. I had no training as a professional writer and wasn't sure if the script I had written was at all acceptable. As I dropped my script in the mail to the client, I remember repeating to myself over and over, like a mantra, "Take the action, let go of the result." I found it comforting to remember what the parameters of my responsibility were. I'm not powerful enough to know what everyone wants and to provide it—perfectly—every time. My responsibility is to do the best I can. How it is received is not up to me. If we don't accept the limits of our power, we can be paralyzed—and not do anything.

Come to Terms with Taxes

Like many compulsive debtors, I ran a tab with the Internal Revenue Service for a number of years. My money recovery, however, forced me to examine my attitude toward taxes. I discovered that *in principle,* I don't disagree with the concept. It is my responsibility to contribute to the functioning and well-being of the larger community—my state and nation. Because community is an important value to me, I realize that evading taxes is actually at odds with my own values. As former Supreme Court Justice Wendell Holmes once said, "With my taxes, I buy civilization."[20]

Where things have gone wrong is that many people no longer trust that the money they contribute to the national coffers *is,* in fact, buying civilization. In the past twenty years, as compulsive spenders and wealth addicts gained political power, the bulk of our tax money went to buy power and control for a few, rather than to enrich the whole nation. But instead of getting angry and evading taxes, perhaps we're better off affirming the principle of community and holding those in power *accountable* for how they collect and spend our money. If current tax laws allow the ultrarich to amass private capital at the expense of our collective well-being, let's lobby to *change the tax laws* and elect people who will do it. Rather than further undermine the stability of the nation, let's do the right thing—and then see that the right thing gets done by staying informed and politically active.

Become a Credit Skeptic

Sharpen your awareness of and skepticism about credit advertisements. Remember, when you use a credit card or a credit line or overdraft privileges, you are *borrowing* money. Do you really want to borrow money—and pay interest on it—just to go out for dinner? Remember, if you only pay the minimum due, you could end up paying *twice* the original cost of that meal (or more!) before you've paid it off.

Going into debt for consumer goods that don't add to your lasting assets is unwise. You'll be paying for that item long after the item or service has been consumed and will have acquired no assets to offset the debt. If you're a recovering compulsive debtor, the only good reason to borrow money is to contribute to your long-term well-being or that of your family, and even then the debt should be collateralized, so that your assets always outweigh your debts.

Join the Club

In recovering from compulsive debt, it's crucial to get emotional support. Many of those who have succeeded at breaking a compulsive debt cycle have done it by attending Debtors Anonymous. DA, as it's known, is a Twelve-Step recovery program modeled after Alcoholics Anonymous, but it is for people who want to stop incurring debt. It is free and anonymous, has chapters in many cities, and is growing fast.

178

See your local telephone directory to determine if there is a chapter near you.

There are also other self-help groups for people with debt and other money issues. Just be sure that if you have a history of compulsive borrowing, you don't join any group that endorses what I call controlled debting or bailouts. If the advice is to get a consolidation loan or declare bankruptcy, you're in the wrong place.

Obtain Further Information on Debt Recovery

There is much more to know about the specific steps to take in debt recovery than can be covered here. I suggest reading *How to Get Out of Debt, Stay Out of Debt and Live Prosperously.* This clear, concise guide to recovery from compulsive debt, written by Jerrold Mundis with wisdom, compassion, and humor, contains all the details about debt recovery, from dealing with creditors, collection agencies, and the IRS to designing a spending plan. It is a must-read for anyone committed to debt recovery or closely involved with a debtor.

Cultivate True Wealth

I love the term *true wealth.* I first came across it in a book of that name written by Paul Hwoschinsky. According to him, "Money is just one part of the total system that produces a feeling of well-being. The challenge is earning money to live life rather than living to earn money." Wealth, according to this philosophy, is something we *experience* rather than possess. "'Having' is not at all bad," writes Hwoschinsky, "it simply is not 'it.'"[21]

He also writes about "nonfinancial assets," which are different things for different people but might include education, talents, creativity, friends, family, community, self-esteem, health—those nonmaterial aspects of our lives that contribute to our overall well-being, even to our ability to earn money!

In contemplating this broader definition of wealth, I realized that in the course of my life, I have built up many assets indeed; they just haven't been financial ones. Now I'm restoring health to the monetary aspect of my life too, and I'm glad to be doing it. But without the self-esteem, communication skills, creativity, and community I've cultivated for twenty years, this healing work on my finances may not have been so fruitful or rewarding.

You don't have to wait until the debts are paid to begin building true wealth, either. *Being in debt has nothing to do with prosperity* and needn't interfere with it. Prosperity, or true wealth, is something much broader and more profound than the bottom line on a balance sheet. Cultivate the *experience* of prosperity even while you're broke or in debt. As the saying goes, "I've been broke, but I've never been poor. Being broke is a temporary situation; being poor is a state of mind." True wealth is a state of mind too, one that Rosalyn, the travel agent and recovering spender and debtor, is cultivating:

> I've taken the "charge" off of having debts. I figure I have the rest of my life to pay them off, and my goal is not to incur new ones and not to agree to send any creditors more than I can reasonably pay. In the meantime, I can still feel happy, even ecstatic, now and then! I don't have to wait for my debts to be paid off to live.

CHAPTER **8**

LOVE AT ANY COST
Codependent with Money

> *Love buyers love to play Santa Claus. Money and gifts are to them the means of making others happy and thus winning their friendship and affection. . . .*
>
> *In the final analysis, love buyers get what they pay for—a substitute.*
>
> HERB GOLDBERG AND ROBERT T. LEWIS
> *MONEY MADNESS*

> *Many of you love to give to others, yet it is harder to allow yourself to receive from them. You empower others by letting them give to you, for they then have the opportunity to demonstrate their abundance.*
>
> SANAYA ROMAN AND DUANE PACKER
> *CREATING MONEY*

PEOPLE WHO ARE codependent with money use money to try and win others' approval, companionship, loyalty, or love. They are often compulsive givers, spending lavishly on others and granting loans that never get repaid, while neglecting their own financial needs. The codependent spender *looks* generous, but his giving may actually be a way of trying to control the relationship. He feels more comfortable in the role of "rescuer" or "provider" than in the give-and-take of real intimacy. By making himself needed, he carves out a niche for himself that he hopes (unconsciously) will buy him approval and stave off rejection or abandonment. He doesn't believe he is worth someone's love and loyalty just for his own sake.

But isn't there a place, you might ask, for selfless giving? Must it be seen as compulsive or enabling? Can't a person put others' needs before her own simply out of compassion or altruism? The answer is yes, indeed. But there is an important distinction here. If a person freely *chooses* to give, and gives out of a sense of her own wholeness and fullness, she is *enriched* by it. But a money codependent gives not from her fullness but from her neediness. It is a way to control the relationship rather than a simple expression of love or service. Healthy giving energizes the giver, resulting in feelings of vitality, fullness, gratification. Codependent giving depletes the giver, leading to feelings of resentment and exhaustion.

Healthy giving also enriches and empowers the recipient, making him feel loved and cared for, whereas codependent giving is an "investment" that seeks a certain return—approval, gratitude, cooperation, or control. Chronic codependent giving cripples the recipient, eliciting feelings of confusion, depression, ambivalence, and resentment.

Mother Teresa, to cite a well-known—albeit extreme—example, strikes me as a good example of apparently altruistic giving. In serving the needy all over the world, she appears to be doing what she chooses, fulfilling her life's purpose and serving a higher set of values. Despite whatever material poverty she endures, Mother Teresa is a wealthy woman in the sense of true wealth; you can see that in her countenance. But another person living such a materially impoverished, selfless life, focused only on taking care of others, might be doing it out of compulsive "shoulds," not the free choice of a higher self. Again, the difference can be seen in the result: the altruistic giver is enriched and empowered; the codependent giver is depleted and impoverished. The recipients of the free giver are enriched and empowered as well, and experience gratitude; the recipients of the codependent giver are disempowered and impoverished and experience resentment.

Of course, in order to make the distinction, I have cited extreme examples. Most of us will be neither a Mother Teresa nor a 100 percent codependent giver. But if our *tendency* is to feel compelled to use money in ways that win us approval, or if we are chronic recipients of codependent money, we stand to benefit from exploring the material in this chapter.

Both men and women can be codependent with money, though women are perhaps more vulnerable, because they are often trained to take care of others at their own expense. But the provider role that men have grown up with can also be a setup for money codependency. Such men may feel that to be adequate providers they must never say no, even though they resent giving and give with strings attached.

Here again, examples of money codependency can be found in the news. In the summer of 1992, the well-known socialite Edward Downe, Jr. (husband of the automobile heiress Charlotte Ford), was accused of reaping millions in illegal stock market gains by trading on inside information. But there was more to the story. According to an article in the *New York Times,* Downe, "apparently out of a need to be liked," helped dozens of other people—from close relatives to mere acquaintances, from celebrities to the hired help—to cash in on the scheme. Ultimately, it was this lack of discretion that led to a leak to the authorities and his subsequent arrest. Downe was also known for giving loans and gifts "almost willy-nilly." Even when he was reportedly having financial problems in the mid- to late 1980s, his apparently compulsive giving continued unabated.[1]

As Downe's story illustrates, a person can be codependent with money whether he has a little or a lot. A wealthy person can give compulsively at less obvious cost to himself, although I maintain that the effect on his and the recipient's life is still impoverishing. And a person who is broke but money codependent will simply go into debt to do it. Let's look at a few other examples.

Eric, a twenty-eight-year-old insurance salesman, has noticed a pattern in himself. He repeatedly winds up with partners who don't give as much to the relationship as he does: "I am the giver. I give more emotionally; I give my time to helping her do things, fix things; I give expensive gifts; and it's not coming back. I don't want to say, 'You owe me,' but I am aware that I give much more than she does. And this is not the first time. All my relationships have ended up like this."

Eric recalls how, growing up in an alcoholic family, he was never allowed to have any boundaries, in particular with money.

> My father always said that he was going to send us to college, so anything we had was his. If we got some money from working or something, he'd say, "Who do you think you're kidding? That's not your money!" Anything we had, he considered his, and if we wanted anything for ourselves, he said we were selfish. There were no boundaries.

Eric spends the most, he says, when he's afraid that someone is mad at him or is going to reject him. He especially tries to avoid conflict. Rather than dealing with such uncomfortable feelings, he says, "I just go out and buy her something. I figure if she's getting enough out of it, maybe she won't leave me." He bought the girl he's dating an expensive audio system for her car last month, even though they'd just begun seeing each other. "I know that blew her away," he says, unable to conceal his pride. "But still, I wish I'd meet someone who would return the favors a little too."

Thirty-three-year-old Judy is the child of a compulsive gambler. Even in elementary school, her codependence with money was evident: she gave her lunch money to other kids so they could buy treats—and be her friend. As an adult, Judy developed a pattern of bailing men out financially, even at her own expense. At twenty-five, she moved in with Frank, a thirty-two-year-old man who told her he "used to have a gambling problem." Though it quickly became evident that his gambling was ongoing, Judy continued living with him for eight years, paying all the bills for both of them and going without basics like new clothes and dental and medical care.

Meanwhile, she was making a pretty low wage herself as a temporary worker because (like many money codependents) she's also a compulsive underearner. At the urging of friends, Judy tried moving out several times, but she always felt guilty, as if she was "letting Frank down." And even though she was supporting them both, Judy also had an irrational fear that she couldn't make it on her own, without a man. Recently, she did make the break, though she's fighting a strong urge to return. She says the very thought that Frank might need her is still "unbearable."

Judy struggles with her inner demons: "I feel like I don't deserve any good stuff, like prosperity or abundance," she says. She traces her feeling of not deserving to a time when she was six years old and her father punished her severely for looking in his suitcase for a present when he returned from a business trip. "I learned that if you love someone, you never expect or ask for anything."

Judy is a classic codependent, acting out her self-rejection, dependency, desire to be needed—and to control—through this financial entanglement with her boyfriend. She's now attending CoDA meetings (Codependents Anonymous, another self-help group based on the Twelve Steps) and is starting to see some possibility for recovery ahead.

INDICATIONS OF MONEY CODEPENDENCY

Fails to Set Limits

The person who is codependent with money finds it extremely difficult to set limits with anyone who makes financial demands or even requests of her. She is unable or unwilling to tolerate the anger or disapproval that might result from saying no. She thinks that to turn someone down for money is cold and mean, and she doesn't want to see herself that way. She is a people pleaser.

Colleen and Julie were living together for a long time. Colleen would repeatedly lend Julie money even though she resented it, because she felt she shouldn't say no to a friend or lover.

> At one point, I was paying the phone bill, and she was making long-distance calls and running up a huge debt. But I didn't think I could say anything about it, because I was the one with the job, so of course I had to pay the bill. I had no boundaries. All I had was "shoulds" in my head. I thought I would be a mean, bad person if I didn't do it.

Sometimes a person behaves codependently with money because he feels guilty about something else and thinks he has to make up for it financially. Larry, a recovering alcoholic, says that he spent lavishly on his kids, rarely saying no to them, because he felt guilty about his drinking. "I failed them in so many ways. I felt I had to make it up to them somehow, so I gave them whatever they wanted." Other money codependents are terrified of conflict and spend to keep peace at any cost.

Because of her inability to set financial boundaries, the money codependent is liable to keep herself broke most of the time. That's the only way she feels she can legitimately say no. To have boundaries means you have to disappoint others sometimes, and the codependent isn't willing to pay that price. She'd rather stay broke and deprive herself if necessary, just to avoid the whole dilemma. If she doesn't have anything, she can't be expected to give it. Therefore, she doesn't have to suffer the discomfort of trying to set boundaries or the pain of failing to.

Compulsively Seeks Acceptance

The person who is codependent with money is driven to spend whatever is necessary to create the perfect meal, perfect holiday, or perfect vacation for others—regardless of whether he can afford it or not. He doesn't feel as though he has a choice. He *has* to do it. If he is having people over for dinner, he will spend whatever is necessary to be approved of, rather than whatever is available in his budget. The overriding motive for the money codependent is to gain acceptance, belonging, and approval—and avoid rejection.

Holidays are a particularly dangerous time. He doesn't feel he can decide what to buy on the basis of his resources but is driven to please the other person, no matter what it takes. Michael, for instance, is deep in debt and has been paying his rent with cash advances from his credit card. Yet he feels compelled to get his girlfriend an expensive gift because she wants and expects it: "I *have* to buy Carol this turquoise necklace," he explains. "She'll be really upset and hurt if I don't. I'll just put it on the ol' credit card again, and top that one off."

John, another man who is codependent with money, became involved with Stuart, an alcoholic director who was something of a celebrity in film circles. Though his films were critical successes, they tended to be commercial failures, and he drank and gambled away whatever proceeds there were. John, meanwhile, kept them afloat with his job as an assistant editor at a publishing company. He remembers spending his whole paycheck one day on a lunch for Stuart's friends at a four-star restaurant.

One day we went to the Four Seasons with an agent, his girlfriend, and a very famous actor who'd appeared in one of Stuart's films. When the bill came, Stuart didn't have any money with him, so I rushed to the rescue and pulled out money I'd just gotten from the bank. It was my entire week's pay. Talk about codependency! But I felt I had to do it; I couldn't let Stuart suffer that embarrassment.

Neglects Personal Needs

While the money codependent spends lavishly to please others, she often goes without basic necessities herself, like medical and dental care or the security of having her rent paid. Kara, a young musician, and Elaine, an office worker, lived together as partners. Elaine was the only one bringing in a steady income, and she took on the role of provider. Elaine gave and gave, until she didn't have anything left. She kept their house stocked with gourmet groceries, paid for tickets to plays and concerts, and took Kara out for dinner in fine restaurants. She encouraged Kara to develop her career, while she covered the bills. It's not that Kara demanded it, but Elaine felt compelled to take care of her. And Kara, being an aspiring musician, couldn't resist the opportunity to pursue her career while someone willingly covered the bills.

The problem is, though Elaine felt compelled to be the all-giving provider, she was quietly building up resentment. And she wasn't really covering the bills. Her own meager income didn't allow her to pay for the kind of lifestyle they enjoyed *and* pay the rent and utilities, so she fell into arrears but didn't tell Kara. Eventually, the pair got an eviction notice, and their phone was shut off. By this time, Elaine felt very resentful and abused, and Kara was confused. She'd never asked for such sacrifices in the first place and had been led to believe that what Elaine was doing wasn't a strain.

I guess it was her way of showing her love to me. Except that she was putting us both in the position to be homeless. She just gave and gave, as if there were no consequences. I would rather have had the rent paid, even if she had told me, point-blank, "I can't carry us. Get a job." She ended up resenting me for taking, even though she *told* me to take. In the end, the whole relationship crashed and burned, so she didn't do me any favors.

Often, the person who is money codependent makes major life decisions based on how they will benefit someone else. Sally decided to apply to medical school when her boyfriend, Dennis, a struggling artist, was having financial problems. In trying to sell him on the plan, she told Dennis the reason she wanted to go to medical school: "Then I can buy you the things you want, because I'll be making a lot of money." But her readiness to make such a major life decision based on how it would benefit him made Dennis understandably uneasy. He started backing away from the relationship.

Underearns

Ironically, though the money codependent spends compulsively to please others, she often doesn't earn much herself. That's because she is a compulsive giver at work too, tending to work long hours for low pay. This is just another expression of her codependency, her need to please, her low self-esteem and lack of a sense of entitlement. She'd rather feel exploited by her employer than risk having "too much," more than she feels she deserves. She's much more comfortable as a victim than as a victimizer, and she thinks it's either-or.

Spends Time Codependently Too

The person who is codependent with money is often codependent with time too, spending more of it than she really wants to in order to please others. It comes from the same lack of boundaries. She doesn't feel she can set her own limits, say no to a request on her time and run the risk of "letting the other person down" and incurring disapproval. As a result, she often ends up depleted of energy as well as money.

Has Difficulty Asking for Anything

People who are money codependent don't like to ask for anything. They try to get their own needs met indirectly, by hinting around or otherwise manipulating. This can be extremely irritating to other people who must try to read between the lines and figure out what they really want. The codependent does this to protect herself. If she asks for what she wants and doesn't get it, she's afraid she'll feel shamed and devastated. And if she asks for what she wants and *gets* it, she's afraid of being out of control, in unfamiliar territory. So it's most comfortable to get her needs met indirectly. She takes care of others so they'll take care of her.

Buys High, Sells Low

The money codependent is often not a smart consumer. If a salesperson pressures her, she tends to buy rather than say no and risk the salesperson's disapproval. This is especially true if the salesperson has been nice to her or given her a lot of time. As a result, she often pays more than she should have for things of questionable value. Similarly, if the codependent tries to sell something, she settles for whatever price is offered rather than insist on the price she wants. She'd rather please the other person, even if it costs her.

Forms Relationships with the Financially Needy or Demanding

People who are codependent with money almost always get involved with partners who can't give much and/or who need to be taken care of financially. The pattern may not be obvious at first. A new partner may seem to "have it together" financially. But somewhere along the line, owing, no doubt, to a dance that both people participate in, an imbalance develops wherein the money codependent ends up taking a much larger share of the financial responsibility. Theresa explains:

> I always end up with people who are impoverished. I become the fixer and the caretaker. I've never been supported by anyone else, and I've never gotten into a relationship with a guy who has money. I filter those guys right out. I tend to be the one holding everything up.
>
> Several years ago, I moved to California with this guy, even though I knew already that he was out of work, in debt, and all that. Anyway, we get out there and start setting up a home. He tells me that his ex-wife ruined his credit, so he doesn't have any. There I was with all these credit cards. So I furnished the whole house: living room, dining room, bedroom sets, TV, VCR, the whole thing.
>
> Then comes Christmas. I let him charge stuff for his kids, because I say, "You have to give them presents." The short of it is, I ran up thousands of dollars of debt. Within six months we split up, and he still hasn't paid me back.
>
> I think there's something in me that purposely keeps away men who have their financial thing together, financially solvent men. Maybe I'm afraid of not being the one in control—I don't know.

Sometimes a man who is codependent with money will hook up with a partner who demands a high style of living that he tries to provide, even if he secretly has to go into debt to do it. Wayne, the compulsive debtor we met in the last chapter, grew up with a father like this:

My mom demanded a very, very high lifestyle. She grew up in the back of a deli, so she always had a thing about living in a nice house. She had over fifty pairs of shoes, hundreds of outfits, and only took taxis—thousands of dollars in taxis.

Meanwhile, my father's business wasn't doing well at all. He wasn't paying the bills for the store because he was spending it, pretending to my mother that everything was OK. His store slowly became empty of supplies because he wasn't ordering inventory. He started borrowing stock from other stores, and ultimately not paying the mortgage.

I remember vividly my father telling me, "If you get home before Mom does, if there's anything that looks like a bill in the mailbox, take it and hide it so she doesn't get upset." Then he started borrowing money from me, which he never paid back.

Eventually, they lost both the business and the house, so she must have known that the lifestyle she was living wasn't based on anything real. But they still kept up appearances. They rented a luxury house with five bedrooms in a very upper-class area; my mother put thousands of dollars into decorating, artwork, murals. I can't imagine where it came from. Somehow my father kept giving her whatever was necessary to live her fantasy life. Meanwhile, he's in his early sixties, floating from job to job. He must have been borrowing from other relatives at this point—I don't know.

But they never communicated. The myth was that they were living this upper middle-class life and that he was "providing" for her. Total fantasy land.

Gives Inappropriate Gifts

The money codependent is known for her lavish gifts, gifts that often exceed the level of intimacy in the relationship and are given not as a genuine expression of caring but in an attempt to win approval, gratitude, and/or adoration. Barbara Hutton, the Woolworth heiress who spent her entire inheritance of $50 million, gave millions in dowries to each new husband and huge amounts of alimony when the marriages ended. She was also known to give sable coats, diamond rings, and Rolls Royces to total strangers who happened to be nice to her.[2]

Enables Spenders and Debtors

The money codependent often gets stuck in a repetitive dance with a compulsive spender and/or debtor whom she bails out of financial difficulties, unwittingly enabling the pattern to continue. Often, the recipient doesn't even *ask* for the handout; the codependent just automatically provides it.

Larry, a member of Alcoholics Anonymous, recalls that early in his recovery he kept giving another member of AA money to get his car fixed. The friend was supposed to get money from an inheritance but never did. Larry gave him hundreds of dollars for various repairs before finally catching on that he was enabling. But for Larry, who grew up in an addictive household, such endless giving came naturally. "I got all caught up in worrying about his car problems, his debt problems. Meanwhile, I wasn't taking care of my own life." But that's one of the hooks for the codependent giver. As long as I'm focusing on your problems, I don't have to be experiencing my own feelings or taking responsibility for my life.

The dance between a money codependent and a spender/debtor is harmful to both parties. If a parent doesn't set financial limits with a child, for instance, that child never learns to deal with limits. Looking for the bailout may become a lifelong pattern. It's not good for the giver either, who focuses on others at the expense of her own life and inevitably ends up feeling exploited. And the relationship suffers, because this fiscal imbalance breeds not only resentment but subtle demands for control in exchange for the debt. "After all I've done for you" is not a good basis for intimacy.

Sometimes, the codependent starts to get healthier and isn't willing to participate in the dance anymore. This can cause confusion and resentment for the receiver, who has come to expect and rely on the codependent's philanthropy. Suddenly, the rules change. Michelle, a money codependent, lived with Stan for eight years before she got into therapy and self-help and began recovering. The changes she made affected their relationship:

> Over a period of time, I did change the ground rules. Where I had been OK taking care of him financially for a long time, I gradually started to resent that he wasn't pulling his own weight. I think I used money as a control mechanism, but the healthier I got, the less I wanted to *pay* for that questionable advantage. Stan felt confused by the shift in me, and eventually we split up.

Vulnerable to Exploitation

Because the money codependent gives *compulsively*, she doesn't assess the merits of each situation. She tends to lend money to poor risks and never get repaid, or otherwise get exploited, betrayed, taken advantage of, victimized. Diana is a thirty-year-old adult child of an alcoholic with a pattern of attracting men who use her, live off of her, but never give back much in return. Several years ago she met a man who was on an extended visit to the mainland from Hawaii. They quickly became romantically involved and within weeks were talking about their future together. Before he left to return home three months later, she gave him her savings of $5,000 to put toward a house they talked about buying together. She was to join him soon.

A month later, when Diana arrived in Hawaii, she was shocked and devastated when her lover failed to meet her at the airport and then seemed to be dodging her phone calls. It quickly became apparent that he had another girlfriend and had no intention of settling down with Diana. She never got any of her money back.

Men who are codependent with money have a similar pattern of getting ripped off. Lee is in his mid-forties. Several years ago, he got a substantial settlement from a motorcycle accident and kept bragging to his friends about the windfall. Several people hit him up for loans. He gave one person money for a car, which was never repaid, and gave another money to start a business, but that money was actually spent on cocaine. In all, Lee lost half his money. He's beginning to get some insight into this pattern:

> I have such a desire to be part of a family, to be accepted, that I make poor financial decisions. Growing up, I had no relationship with my father whatsoever. He actually turned me in to the police during the sixties when I was dodging the draft, so that shows you what my sense of family is like.
>
> So I try to create this sense of "good family" with the people around me. I want to believe they care about me. My craving to belong gets in the way of my common sense, and I get shafted a lot. Then it's like a self-fulfilling prophecy. I find out these so-called friends don't value me after all.

Freudians would probably argue that both Diana and Lee have a masochistic *need* to be shafted, taken advantage of, mistreated, and unloved. As Edmund Bergler put it long before the term *codependent* came into use, some people have "inner neurotic tendencies to be the prey of a [parasite]." They choose this type of person, he asserts, for the purpose of satisfying their unconscious wish to be kicked around.[3] Very often, the person codependent with money has a personal history of victimization in some kind of dysfunctional family or marriage, so the role feels comfortable, familiar. They compulsively recreate this complex of feelings in an effort to "undo" it and get it right this time. But they only keep getting it wrong.

Feels Uncomfortable Receiving

It's no accident that the money codependent winds up in relationships with takers. She is uncomfortable receiving. As much as she yearns to be taken care of, she still opts to spend whatever money, time, or effort necessary to be the one in control. When the money codependent does receive something, she feels indebted, which, of course, is uncomfortable. She feels compelled to "make it up" to that person, to give an equivalent gift in return, as soon as possible. She can't imagine anyone giving to her without strings attached.

Colleen, the money codependent met earlier, is the child of an alcoholic father who often beat her and her brother when he was drunk. As a child, of course, Colleen felt powerless to avoid this treatment, because her survival depended on him. As an adult, though, she makes sure she's never in such a powerless position again, by always being the provider. Her inability to receive without feeling trapped has had a deleterious effect on her relationships.

> There's a pattern in my life. My lovers cannot take care of themselves, and I'm always helping them out. I think it would be scary to be with someone who had money and could give to *me*, because it would be my father, controlling me and killing my soul. As long as I'm with someone who doesn't have money, he doesn't have power over me. It puts me on even ground.

By hitching up with takers, the money codependent generally avoids having to receive much. That hurts, but it's an acceptable trade-off, given her association of money with control.

At the core of money codependency, behind the need to control and the fear of abandonment, is the devastating belief, "I am not enough." The money codependent doesn't feel deserving to receive just as she is. She believes that anyone who gives to her will surely withdraw once he finds out how inadequate she really is. Therefore, she has to carve out a niche by making herself needed and demanding as little as possible.

Rachel is a forty-four-year-old department store manager and money codependent. She was brutally raped and beaten when she was seventeen, and her self-esteem has never recovered from this and other episodes of abuse. Her only long-term relationship was a disastrous two-year marriage to an alcoholic. Rachel poignantly describes how her self-hatred has fueled her spending on men. She speaks from the vantage point of someone newly recovering:

> I never thought there was anything a man would want from me besides sex or money. So every time I've gone out with a guy, I've tried to buy his love. I once cosigned a loan for this guy because I figured he wouldn't love me if I didn't agree to it. The funny thing was, I didn't love *him*. I just didn't want to be unlovable.
>
> Another time, I remember being put down all weekend by a guy I was dating, then taking *him* out to dinner. I felt he didn't want to be with me because I was so fat and ugly. I thought I had nothing to offer, so I should at least treat him. "Poor Brandon," I said to myself, "he's stuck with me, so I've gotta make it worth his while." I paid for his movie, his dinner.

As a result of this compulsion of mine, whenever
I'm dating someone, I get really in debt, which makes
me miserable. At one point, I actually had to sell my
home because I was so overextended. I was paying my
mortgage with credit cards, then I'd go to a bar with
some guy and buy the whole place drinks, just to show
him how cool I was even though I was fat and ugly.

Needless to say, without a solid sense of self-respect and
self-regard, a person like Rachel cannot achieve a gratifying,
healthy, intimate relationship. She can only try to give a partner a reason not to leave her. Of course, knowing she is buying whatever loyalty she enjoys does little in the long run to
enhance her self-esteem. "I felt like such a shit after I'd spent
all this money on a guy. 'Why am I doing this?' I'd ask myself.
It's not as though I even liked these guys. I just felt I had to
justify my existence, give them a reason to be with me."

Resents the Role

The compulsive giver often resents giving so much, even
though he doesn't know how to stop. Michael owns a nightclub on the West Coast. When his friends come in, he always
feels obligated not to charge them. They protest a little at
Michael's generosity, but they always let him do it. And he resents it, even though he offers:

They know I'm going to offer to pick up the bill.
They say no as a perfunctory thing, but they don't
mean it. And I insist as a perfunctory thing, but I
don't mean it. If I could set boundaries, I know it
would help me, it would probably help them, and
I'm sure it would help our relationship. But I can't
do it. Not yet. It's my role to be the successful one,
the together one, the provider. I resent it, but I also
get some feeling of superiority out of it.

Gains Identity from the Role

Michael, the nightclub owner, also has a history of bailing his brother and sister out of financial crises. Though each time he calls it a loan, he never sees the money again. Michael resents having to do this, just as he resents subsidizing his friends at the nightclub, but at the same time the role of provider makes him feel good. "It's like an identity," he says. "It's hard to give that up. I'd have to give up the cheap, immediate hit I get from inappropriately picking up the tab, the feeling of being the successful one, the savior. If my identity is based on that role, and I give it up, who *am* I? Who am I, if not the savior?"

Gives in Ways that Backfire

Codependent giving often backfires. The receiver—though seduced by the goods—often resents feeling controlled, trapped, and/or infantalized in the role of the one who is financially inept. Often, she can't help but show her resentment or ambivalence about the largess she is receiving. The codependent giver feels doubly burned: here she's given so much of her resources (money, time, energy, love) and the recipient has the nerve to be ungrateful!

Such an exchange once occurred between my mother and me. You'll recall that I was a spender/debtor whom she sometimes bailed out. When I was about twenty-seven, I received a notice from my bank informing me that the remaining $500 balance on my student loan had been paid off. I knew immediately that my mother had done it, thinking she was doing me a favor. But instead of being thrilled, as one might expect, I was enraged—and confused about my own reaction. If we hadn't had a history of money codependency, it might have been received simply as an incredibly generous act and duly appreciated. But because I had always felt like the one who couldn't quite "get it together," I *longed* for a feeling of accomplishment. I was getting some sense of satisfaction from meeting my obligation to the bank and was looking forward to paying it off. When she paid off that last balance, I felt robbed of a chance to be a grown-up. No doubt my anger and lack of appreciation was confusing and disappointing to her.

Gives in Order to Feel in Control

The money codependent has an intense need for control, often because she comes from a dysfunctional family where she had no control over what was happening to her as a child. Now, she seeks control as a way to feel "safe." Kate sees this pattern in her relationship with her husband, Norman:

> Whenever I get uptight about money, I take over our finances. If I'm anxious about bills, I want to control them. Then the balance between us gets off. I get more and more yang, and he gets more and more yin. He says, "Oh, I can't do it, you take over." For a while, I was even balancing his checkbook. He'd say, "You're the smart one; you do it."
>
> A part of me feeds right into that. I like to feel like the one who's got it together, who's in control. In a way, I guess I choose men who act out for me the part of myself I'm most ashamed of: the little kid who's never got it under control. By comparison to him, I get to look good.

The flip side of the codependent's low self-esteem, then, is his grandiosity, the inflated ego with which he tries to make up for his perceived lack of worth. Both Kate and Michael like to see themselves as the person who can take care of everyone else, despite the toll it's taking on them.

Because the person who is codependent with money gives in order to maintain some control rather than out of his fullness, his generosity tends to be selective, directed specifically at those people he is invested in pleasing. He may withhold from other people, like bill collectors. Michael repeatedly bails out his sister and brother, compulsively picks up checks, and gives lavish gifts, but he doesn't pay his bills for months, even when he has the money to do it.

Has Problems with Intimacy

Often, the money codependent has more problems with intimacy than it appears on the surface. As we've already seen, the money codependent tries to control the interaction by doing most of the giving. That's because underneath he is often afraid of the give-and-take required in real intimacy; that equates with being out of control. He is afraid of being hurt or abandoned if he lets go of control.

In a way, giving financially allows him not to give so much emotionally. He *appears* to be intimate and giving but really holds himself back. Eric, the twenty-eight-year-old insurance salesman, frankly acknowledges that his elaborate gifts to girl-friends serve this purpose: "It buys me maneuvering space," he says. "If I give monetarily, I don't feel obligated to give more than I want to emotionally. I have more options."

Some socially isolated money codependents give their money and energy as a way of having contact with others. Ray, a computer technician, fixes computers for any friend or acquaintance who calls him—and doesn't charge them. That would be great if it were a freely made choice, but it isn't. He doesn't charge because he feels uncomfortable asking for money, but he is building up resentment about all the time these free services take. As an underearner, he barely makes ends meet as it is, so he can't afford the luxury of giving services away. But he admits that another reason he does it is for the companionship. It gives him a way to be around people. It reduces his isolation, and he's willing to pay for that.

The money codependent's intimacy problems ultimately stem from the fact that he doesn't feel worth being with unless he's putting out money, energy, or time. He believes that if his partner needs him, she'll be less likely to abandon him. Unfortunately, however, it doesn't work that way. The receiver, over time, resents being controlled and/or infantalized and backs away. Even if they stay together, the codependent doesn't get much satisfaction from buying love. He still feels unlovable, deep down.

Feels Dependent on the Taker

Women who are money codependent, holding their relationships together financially, often feel surprisingly dependent on their partners. It's as if their thinking is distorted and they are unable to see themselves as capable people, even though they handle the finances for both of them. Doris, despite her history of having supported herself very well before getting married, and despite having supported Leo for many years, labors under the illusion that *she* is dependent on *him*. "I haven't been on my own much," she says, when she contemplates leaving him. "I can't imagine making it on my own, without a man."

Comes from a Dysfunctional Family

Most money codependents grew up in some kind of dysfunctional family. Their parents were either addicts, alcoholics, gamblers, or otherwise compulsive. The child learned codependent behavior for eighteen years or so, learned to put other people's needs before his own. Now, he simply continues to do what he was trained to do: take care of others—financially, emotionally, and otherwise. Kate talks about her experience:

> No one ever really took care of me growing up, or at least that's how it felt. My dad was emotionally distant, and my mother was kind of a prima donna, going off to her bridge games and volunteer activities all the time. I took care of *her* children while she

played "lady of leisure," helping create the image that my father was a success, even though he was going bankrupt.

Now I do the same with the men I'm with. I always end up with men I have to take care of. Part of me craves having someone take care of *me* for once— one time—and not have to be the caretaker. I've never had a man take care of me: emotionally, financially, sexually. Never.

RECOVERING FROM MONEY CODEPENDENCE
Start Focusing on Yourself

If you have been a money codependent, focusing so much on other people's needs, it will be important in recovery for you to start focusing on yourself. This can sound like the self-obsessed "me first" rhetoric of the 1970s and 1980s, but it isn't. Self-obsession is what you've *been* doing. The ultimate aim of the codependent, after all, is not altruistic, but self-serving. He wants to covertly control the relationship, elicit approval, and hang on to the hostage. *That* is self-centered. By beginning to shift your attention from taking care of others' needs to taking care of your own, you stop trying to buy approval and pseudointimacy and prepare yourself for the real thing. Remember, you can't truly give of yourself until you have a self to give *of*.

The money codependent often panics at this point. "But she won't be able to manage without my help." "I don't know what he'll do . . ." The money codependent labors under the delusion that without her largess, the other will perish. Jerrold Mundis addresses this need to focus on your recovery first in *How to Get Out of Debt, Stay Out of Debt and Live Prosperously:* "It's true that you can't love someone else if you don't love yourself; it's also true that you can't help anyone else

with money if you can't help yourself. If you're financially responsible for children or others, the single most important
thing you can do for them is create financial soundness for
yourself."[4]

Establish Boundaries, Learn to Set Limits

As we've seen, money codependents often don't have good
boundaries with money or anything else because they grew
up in families where they were trained *not to* be separate but
to meet other people's needs first and ignore their own
inner signals. That's why, in recovery, it's so crucial to become able to say no—to both your own urge to buy love, and
to other people's financial demands.

Michael, the nightclub owner whose pattern is bailing
his siblings out of every financial crisis, practiced saying no
to his brother recently. At first, he lost his resolve, but by not
giving up, he eventually came through for himself.

> My brother Greg came to visit me recently. I knew
> that he was broke, and that the touch was coming.
> Sure enough, he asked me for $300. I was planning
> to say no, but he caught me off guard. We were hav-
> ing a good time together, and I didn't want to be the
> heavy. I told him I'd have it for him the next day.
>
> That night, I couldn't stop thinking about it. I
> knew I would resent it if I gave him the money, that I
> was just doing it to keep up some phony role of "the
> good brother" and to feel needed.
>
> The next morning at breakfast, I took a deep
> breath and said what I'd been wanting to say for a
> long time. I said, "Greg, I don't think it's a good idea
> for me to lend you money anymore. I'd rather con-
> tribute to your life in other ways."
>
> It was really awkward for me, but his reaction wasn't
> as bad as I expected. We ended up having a long talk,
> and that talk enabled me to feel closer to him than I

have in years. I realized that if I can't say no to him, then I have to avoid him, to avoid the hit. Developing limits is helping me get our relationship back.

Only when you are able to say no can you freely choose to say yes when you want to. You can *decide* to give whenever you wish—but you won't *have to,* and that will make it a true gift.

Learning to set boundaries is critical for the money codependent because if she can't set boundaries, she probably won't let herself have much prosperity. If you can't defend yourself against others' demands, then you can't allow yourself to have much, because to *have* makes you vulnerable to your own codependent urges. People *will* ask to borrow it, and some people may even manipulate to get it. If you can't tolerate the discomfort of saying no, of defending your boundaries even if it means disappointing or angering people, you'll give in. The pain of being without good boundaries, of suffering this kind of repeated loss, is so great that many money codependents will opt to stay broke just to avoid it. So if you want a more prosperous life and you suffer from this disorder, it will be essential to build a strong inner resolve to protect your boundaries against violation.

According to Lewis Hyde in *The Gift: Imagination and the Erotic Life of Property,* when a person gives, he establishes or reaffirms a bond with the receiver, which is a large part of the value of a gift. According to Hyde, however, when people treat gifts as commodities, that is, measure them and count them, this bond is undermined or even lost. If we give because we think we should rather than because we want to, the nourishment inherent in the gift—the "erotic bond" as Hyde calls it, is lost. We are giving not as an expression of eros, but to avoid some commodity-based debt we imagine we will incur if we don't give. Hyde cites a Lithuanian folk tale in which riches given to mortals by the fairies turn to paper as soon as they are measured or counted: "The moral is this: the gift is lost in self-consciousness. To count, measure, reckon value, or seek the cause of a thing is to step outside the circle, to cease being 'all of a piece' with the flow of gifts and become, instead, one part of the whole reflecting upon another part."[5]

Colleen, whom we met earlier, is now trying to give from this more genuine motivation. In the past, Colleen would spend herself into debt every Christmas in order to give the kind of gifts she thought her family and friends expected. And each year, the shopping ritual wore her out and depleted her. She shopped without joy. Gift giving in her family, as in many others, was doing nothing to nurture the "erotic bond" between the people involved but had deteriorated into a cold commodity exchange. Colleen was told what to get and then spent hours dutifully tracking it down. Worse, she spent months paying it off, with interest, because she spent more than she could realistically afford. But that's changing:

> Last Christmas, I decided I didn't want to be co-dependent and then resent it later. I just wanted to do what I could sanely do. It was hard when they gave me things that were more expensive than what I gave them. I felt a pang of shame or embarrassment. But then I said to myself, "I am giving my true self, my spirit, my love. I'm being there for them in a more real way than ever before."
>
> I'm just trying to trust that people who can receive my real gifts will, and that those who can't—well, I might as well face the true limitations of those relationships. If I have to give a present of a certain financial value in order to be loved, well, what am I really losing?

Learn to Recognize Imbalance, Trust Your Feelings

If you are money codependent, you are by nature compulsive, driven to meet other people's needs by an inner command. Giving is your second nature. In early recovery, it can be very difficult to know when you are giving compulsively rather than freely. You just automatically *put out* and only later start to become aware of your smoldering resentment and feelings of deprivation.

It is possible, however, to cultivate an awareness of imbalance, to learn to recognize it sooner. Often, as codependent spenders, we will have a nagging inner voice telling us, "Something isn't right here," or "I shouldn't be doing this." In recovery, we can learn to listen to that voice. As Sanaya Roman and Duane Packer write in *Creating Money:*

> Give what is joyful to give; do not give money if you feel obligated or forced to give it. Any heavy feelings are signs that such giving is not for the highest good of that person. Some parents feel obligated to continue helping their children even after they are grown and could be on their own. There may come a time when you need to say no to a request for money; your "no" comes from a place of greater love than any resentful "yes" could.[6]

We know when things are out of balance; we have only to admit it to ourselves. The hard part is trusting that if you listen to that voice and don't, say, lend your life savings to some person you hardly know, you will *survive* it if he gets angry or doesn't like you. Not only will you survive; you will be better off—financially and emotionally. Trusting yourself builds self-esteem. You begin to treat yourself as someone trust*worthy*.

It takes a leap of faith to trust your inner wisdom over your casual, compulsive impulses. A full conversion doesn't happen overnight, but you can begin practicing right now. It's very exciting and empowering to become self-possessed and to respect yourself—perhaps for the first time since early childhood.

Learn to Live with Disapproval

Of course, for a codependent to set limits, she must be willing to accept the consequences. Sometimes, people will be relieved that you're not going to take care of them anymore. But other people may get angry. You have no control over what someone else's response is. (Here comes that need to let go of control again!)

The problem most codependents have is that they think other people's disapproval or anger is going to *devastate* them. They may psychically equate it with death. Pleasing others becomes mistaken for a life-sustaining *need,* like the need for food or water. It's important in recovery to begin to dismantle this belief that others' disapproval will be a catastrophe. The real catastrophe is how you've been living, because *that* robs you of self-respect, healthy relationships, the joy of receiving, and maybe your health—not to mention money. It is better to lose others' approval than to go on suffering all these consequences.

Learn to Receive

The toughest challenge of all for the money codependent may be learning to receive. Yet you can't have prosperity if you feel ambivalent about receiving. How do you feel when someone gives to you? Indebted? Fearful? Shamed? Out of control? Embarrassed? Guilty? In danger? Angry? Follow the clues of your visceral and emotional response to uncover the blocks you have to "letting in" and why you always must be "putting out" instead.

Money codependents are sometimes afraid to receive because they think they will owe the giver something, that they will give up some freedom if they receive. But this is a distortion too. Receiving doesn't mean you owe the other person anything. Healthy adult relationships, in fact, *require* exchange and balance. In a truly intimate relationship, at any one time, you may be the giver or the receiver. Roles are exchanged easily rather than remaining frozen.

Infants accept food, love, cuddling, gifts, attention, without apparent fear or guilt. Indeed, it apparently feels *natural* to them to receive. But somewhere along the way, many of us learn to equate receiving with danger, and self-deprivation with survival. And now this terrible distortion has to be unlearned.

Not allowing other people to give robs them of the opportunity to contribute. It undermines their self-esteem, infantalizes them, and engenders resentment. It's another paradox: rather than owing people something if they give to you, you *give* a great deal to them by being a gracious receiver. You owe them more, I believe, if you are never willing to relinquish control, if you deny them the chance to give. As Roman and Packer write in *Creating Money,* "You empower others by letting them give to you, for they then have the opportunity to demonstrate their abundance. . . . Do not see it as selfish for you to receive; see it as the completion of the circle of energy. The more you open to receive, the more you can give."[7] The most giving thing the money codependent can do is to learn to receive.

Learn to Ask for What You Want (and Risk Refusal)

Money codependents need to learn to ask—clearly—for what they want. Rather than hint indirectly or manipulate covertly, we have to take a deep breath and spit it out: "I would like your help/attention/time/opinion/money." By asking for what we want, we begin to define who we are, separate from others, and open up to the potential of getting our needs met and to the potential for real intimacy.

Of course, the other person doesn't have to give us whatever we ask for. That's something we have no control over. We can only take the action of asking and let go of the result. If someone doesn't choose to meet our need, that doesn't make us wrong for asking, bad for having the need, or too worthless to exist. In fact, it doesn't reflect on us at all. Someone else's no is just that person's expression of *him*self.

We have to take the danger out of asking for what we want. Getting turned down doesn't expose you as the one worthless, undeserving person in the universe, setting you apart from everyone else. Getting turned down *connects* you to all of humanity, makes you one of the club. *No one gets what he wants all the time.* Sure, you can protect yourself from rejection or disappointment by never asking for what you want, but then you'll *definitely* not get it. It's like looking for a job: you can't get a job unless you're willing to interview for it and risk not being hired, risk getting rejected. And you can't get any other needs met either—unless you're willing to risk refusal.

Don't Put Your Money Where Your Brain Isn't Welcome

Money codependents are soft touches for lending money or cosigning loans and often don't adequately weigh the risks or take steps to protect themselves. As a result, they get burned disproportionately often. As part of recovery, it will be important to develop some criteria for financial involvements. This doesn't mean becoming stingy or inappropriately withholding; it simply means operating out of high self-regard rather than just trying to please others and win their approval.

Anita Jones-Lee, in *Women and Money,* suggests a good rule of thumb: "Don't put your money where your brain is not welcome." If someone asks you to cosign or guarantee a loan to help capitalize a business, for instance, she suggests making sure that "you receive an identifiable financial benefit and that you at least share control over the source of income used for repayment."[8] Her advice is addressed to women, but it has application for anyone recovering from money codependence.

Start a Special Account for Giving

Because money codependents tend to give regardless of their resources, it helps to establish some sane and structured way to determine what is available for spending on gifts and other forms of giving. I have found it very helpful to have a special savings account for giving. When a birthday, a wedding, Mother's Day, or Christmas rolls around, I then have a fund to tap without draining money needed for bills and other categories in my spending plan.

Having a special account also provides me with parameters. What's there is *all* I have to spend. If that's not as much as I think I should spend, then I get to practice hanging out with those uncomfortable feelings, instead of spending recklessly in order to appease them. I have discovered that nothing catastrophic occurs when I spend what I *have* instead of what I think I should.

To establish a giving account, estimate reasonable annual expenses for birthday, graduation, wedding, and holiday gift giving. Then, each month, deposit one-twelfth of that amount into a special savings account. Some months you may not spend anything from this account, so the balance will grow. Then when you get to those months that are full of occasions, you won't have to go into debt trying to keep up.

It's a great feeling to start giving what you can comfortably afford rather than what you think others think you should give. It engenders *real* feelings of being in control— of yourself this time, not anybody else.

Get Support

Recovery from money codependency entails much more than these few suggestions. It's really about healing from generic addictive dis-ease, which itself means healing from intense feelings of worthlessness and shame. It's almost impossible, and certainly inadvisable, to try to do this in isolation, by yourself. That's why I strongly suggest cultivating and using a support group of people who understand the shift you are trying to make, who validate and support it.

Along with self-help groups like CoDA, psychotherapy with a competent therapist can be a great gift to yourself. Re-

search and interview potential helpers until you find someone who is highly competent and compassionate *and* appears
to have good boundaries. (Don't settle for someone just because he's cheap or nearby.) You will need someone who can
be a good role model for setting boundaries, even though it
may be uncomfortable for you to interact with her at first.
You'll know you're in the right place if she doesn't take care
of you but creates a healthy, supportive environment where
you can learn to take care of your*self.*

CHAPTER 9

FEAR OF SPENDING
Money Hoarding

One cannot enjoy what one constantly fears to lose.

EDMUND BERGLER
MONEY AND EMOTIONAL CONFLICTS

If a person's attitude toward money is essentially a defense against poverty, then this person may never truly experience wealth. The experience of wealth is, after all, a subjective thing.

THOMAS MOORE
CARE OF THE SOUL

FIFTY-YEAR-OLD CLIFFORD has long operated on the belief that if he didn't guard his money very closely, his wife and children would squander it. Clifford has an executive position with a major corporation and spends money fairly freely on his own hobbies of golf and photography. But he always became irritable, angry, and evasive whenever his wife or kids asked for money—even when it was for legitimate expenses like school clothes. He thought they were being wasteful and careless with his hard-earned cash.

Clifford has a habit of speaking in euphemisms, like "Things are tough right now," "We have to tighten our belts," and "Money doesn't grow on trees." Without giving his family any further explanation, upon his pronouncement of any one of these clichés, they were expected to back off from any request. Family vacations and dinners out were actually painful for him, as he spent much of the time thinking ahead to what the bill would be. It never seemed worth it to him.

He lives in fear that some catastrophe will cut off his income, and the thought of being dependent on the largess of others is utterly terrifying. Clifford grew up in poverty and remembers how it felt having to take handouts and wear hand-me-downs. As a child, he promised himself he would *never* be in that position again, no matter what he had to do to avoid it. Clifford has long been acting out unresolved feelings of not having enough. And now he is paying the price. His wife, weary from years of living with a withholder, recently filed for divorce, and he's estranged from his two grown children.

Ellen is a thirty-eight-year-old woman engaged to be married for the first time. She has never run up a credit card, been in debt, or paid a bill late. So what's the problem? She becomes physically ill whenever she has to spend money—even on necessities. At the checkout counter she becomes literally dizzy and nauseated. As a result, she rarely spends on clothes, vacations, or entertainment, shops only in thrift stores, and returns gifts whenever she can for a cash refund. She ruminates endlessly about every purchase decision, to the point where she can spend hours going from store to store trying to decide on a simple thing like a hairbrush—and still come home empty-handed. What's going on in her mind, she says, is this:

> When I'm shopping for something, as soon as I get close to buying it, I think, "Oh, I'm being taken advantage of . . . I could get it for less somewhere else . . . I'm spending more than I should . . . They're laughing at me because they think I'm a sucker . . .

I'm going to be left with nothing." Those are the thoughts that go through my head, over and over. It's like torture.

Unlike the deprivation addict, Ellen never goes anywhere broke. She always has at least $100 in her wallet—just in case. And despite the fact that she's got over $100,000 saved, she still fears being broke.

I just want to know I won't have to take any hand-outs, that I'll be able to pay for my house and clothes. When I see homeless people on TV, and they say they once had a home and a job, it scares the daylights out of me. I think that's my biggest fear—not being able to pay for basics.

I feel that if I'm not totally careful all the time, whatever I have will disappear. If I let up my vigilance for one minute, I'll just lose it all.

Ellen's money pattern has cost her several relationships. And there's already tension building over money with her fiancé, whom Ellen describes as a spendthrift. He makes a lot, she says, and spends a lot. Recently, he convinced her to take a vacation with him, and they split the cost. Ellen didn't say this to him, but privately she complains that the money she spent on the vacation "wasn't worth it."

Money hoarders like Clifford and Ellen are haunted by irrational fears of not having enough. They become obsessed about every expenditure and hold on to money in a grim, rigid, compulsive way, forgoing pleasures and sabotaging relationships in order to ward off imagined catastrophic poverty. They cannot enjoy their earnings or give freely to others— even those closest to them—because they are so afraid of parting with any of their money supply. It's as if they believe that money is their lifeblood and that with each expenditure, they lose a little of themselves, a little vitality, a little power.

You will note from these examples that the money hoarder is not just someone who practices sound financial planning, because even when he comes into money, through an inheritance or a successful business endeavor, the money hoarder still can't relax and enjoy it. In fact, the more money he gets, the worse he becomes. Like every other form of addiction, this disorder is progressive, and with greater access to the drug, it only intensifies.

The money hoarder makes a virtue of not spending. For him, the uppermost goal in life is to never run out—of money or anything else. He may purport to be saving for certain goals—a big trip, major appliances, renovations on the house. But even when he accumulates enough money to realize this goal, he often cannot bring himself to spend the money. He puts off today's gratification in favor of tomorrow's "security." Of course, a certain amount of planning and delayed gratification is appropriate and healthy, but this person delays gratification permanently.

The compulsive withholder operates in conserve mode not only regarding money but regarding everything else. He tends to hold back his emotions, energy, libido, and time as well as his cash. He is not expansive, but constrictive, controlled. According to psychoanalytic theory, the money hoarder (commonly known as a miser) is anal compulsive, deriving pleasure from holding onto everything. If his parents were overdemanding or punitive in the process of his toilet training, the theory goes, he may have developed a dread of submitting, of giving in to others. As an adult, his pleasure is derived not so much from acquiring money (like wealth addicts), or from expelling it (like compulsive spenders), but from retaining it, *holding on.* Having money makes him feel in control; spending money makes him feel vulnerable and out of control.[1]

As a result of his fixation with holding on, however, there is no flow in the hoarder's life, no circulation. His defensive, constricted approach to life tends to repel people and opportunities, so he ends up with plenty in his passbook or under the mattress (hoarders tend not to trust banks) but little true wealth. He tends not to seek adventure, develop creativity, pursue interests, cultivate relationships and community, or improve himself—because it might cost too much. It's not just money he keeps locked up, but his soul.

Here again, hoarders come in all income brackets. There are poor and middle-class hoarders as well as monied ones, like the legendary W. C. Fields. Suspicious that others were trying to swindle him out of his money, Fields is said to have placed his earnings in some two hundred different banks, each account under a different name. After his death, only forty-five of the accounts were ever found.[2] In another example, the billionaire J. Paul Getty put pay telephones in his mansion, presumably because he feared guests would run up his phone bill.[3] And we've all heard about Howard Hughes, who grew more suspicious and miserly with age and wound up a total recluse. For these wealthy people, money was not something used to enhance their lives, but something clung to *for* dear life—out of fear and insecurity.

Compulsive money hoarding appears to afflict more men than women, although Lieberman and Lindner suggest in *Unbalanced Accounts* that this could be because "men have always had more money to fear losing."[4] It could also be because women are trained to make other people happy, and it's hard to be a withholder and please others at the same time. And the male stereotype of "superprovider" can make some men fear that everyone wants something from them, prompting them to want to hoard and hold back.

Whatever its etiology, a chief negative consequence of money hoarding is its effect on the person's relationships. The money hoarder may manage to hold onto his money, but he often alienates his spouse, children, and friends, who feel overcontrolled by the hoarder's skinflint behavior. By stockpiling money he builds financial security but diminishes his interpersonal security. He's like the legendary King

Midas, who when given one wish asks that everything he touches turn to gold. He gets his wish, but nearly starves to death when his food, water—indeed, everything he touches—turns to gold and can no longer nourish him. There he is, surrounded by riches and impoverished in the most fundamental sense.

Unfortunately, whereas those around the money hoarder often see it as a problem, the subject himself almost never does. Madeline's father was extremely tightfisted when it came to giving money to his wife and children. Whenever they asked him for money they were grilled and made to feel irresponsible or selfish. Having to ask for money became such an ordeal that Madeline simply learned to do without many things that she wanted. As an adult, she has developed a pattern of deprivation addiction, re-creating the familiar condition of being without.

Throughout the ages, many pejorative labels have been heaped on people with this money disorder, including tightwad, miser, stingy person, and cheapskate. But though his behavior is understandably hard on family and friends, it's important to understand that what drives this person's need to hoard and tightly control finances is not really mean-spiritedness, but *fear:* fear of not having enough, fear of ending up poor and dependent, fear of becoming a bag lady, fear of catastrophe, fear of being taken advantage of. Deep within, he doesn't trust that anyone will be there for him, so the prospect of ever having to depend on anyone else is terrifying. His fear of becoming dependent is so great that he'd rather forgo today's pleasures in order to protect against all potential catastrophes of the future. Money to him is like a security blanket. If he has money, he feels secure; if he's spending money, he feels vulnerable.

It's interesting to note that the word *miserable* comes from the same Latin root as *miser,* underscoring the fact that compulsive withholding is a painful condition, more often born of fear than of intentional malice.

INDICATIONS OF MONEY HOARDING

Spends with Difficulty

The compulsive withholder has a lot of trouble parting with money. He rarely spends on luxuries or sheer pleasure, because he considers such expenditures unnecessary, extravagant, and self-indulgent. And when he must spend to pay bills and other necessities, he becomes upset, irritable, and depressed—even when he can afford it. Just talking about money makes him uncomfortable. As with other addicts, his moods are affected by whether or not he's got his fix—in this case a supply of money—to hold onto and hoard.

Some money hoarders become physically sick when they have to spend money, as Ellen describes: "When I have to spend money, it makes me sick. I get terrible anxiety, and sometimes nauseated. I can get the item as far as the checkout counter and then have to take it back to the shelf. I get, like, I can't go through with it. It's really weird."

For a person with this money disorder, deciding to make a purchase can be torturous. Karen, another money hoarder, thirty years old, describes what she went through last year when she bought a car:

> It was a traumatic experience. Even after I started the paperwork for it, I went back to the dealer eight times because I kept changing my mind. I'd cancel the order, then reinstate the order, then cancel it again. Finally the salesman said to me, "Look, we're going to have to raise the price of the car because you've changed your mind so many times." I just couldn't let go of that money.

When she does manage to buy something, Karen says she feels panicky afterward. There have been times when she hasn't been able to sleep for ruminating on whether she's made a mistake.

Even when money is given to her for the express purpose of buying something, Karen has trouble spending it. Last year, her mother gave her $100 to buy a jacket for her birthday. Knowing how Karen holds on, the mother specifically said, "I don't want you to keep the money. I want you to buy a jacket." But a year later, Karen still hasn't done it. She's tried on dozens of jackets, but she can't bring herself to spend the money.

Finds Gift Giving Especially Painful

The compulsive withholder also finds it very painful to buy gifts. Ellen describes what she goes through at holiday time:

> It's very traumatic for me. Last year around Christmas I spent every evening after work shopping, trying to find the right presents and then getting myself to go through with it. It was horrible. I ended up buying everybody the same thing, because it was on sale.
>
> I'm always afraid that when the person opens the gift he's going to think it's cheap, that I didn't spend enough money on it. But I can't bring myself to buy expensive things, so I just obsess and obsess.
>
> Recently my sister said to me, in front of everyone at Thanksgiving, "Ellen, you're so damn neurotic about presents." It was like someone stabbing me. It really hurt. I know I am, but I can't stop it.

Contrary to what people might assume about someone with this pattern, the compulsive withholder often finds it just as difficult to *receive* gifts. The same sister recently bought Ellen a beautiful—and expensive—sweater for her birthday. She likes the sweater but can't stand to think about how much it cost, and is thinking of taking it back to the store to get the cash. "It's not worth spending seventy dollars for a sweater," she says. "I'd rather get a sweater for twenty dollars and put the difference in the bank."

Ellen also hates getting expensive presents, she says, because she's afraid she'll be expected to be that generous in return. "Growing up, there were always strings attached to any gifts my mother gave me. She'd make me pay in some way. She'd say 'Look how good I am to you, and you're so rotten, you're so mean to me.' That's why I'd rather no one give me anything. That way they won't expect anything back."

Evaluates Everything By How Much It Costs

The person with a pronounced fear of spending complains a lot about prices and uses cost as the chief criteria in most decisions. She has a hard time enjoying vacations, recreation, and anything luxurious, because she's calculating in her mind how much it's going to cost. Everything is evaluated by price rather than by the contribution it can make to the quality of life. Whether she likes something doesn't matter as much as how much it costs. This is true even if she has plenty of money.

George and Jane are multimillionaires in their sixties. George's lifelong dream has been to live on the seashore and own a boat. They now have the waterfront dream house, but Jane, a money hoarder, insists on renting out the dock because she can't stand to lose an opportunity for income—even though they have millions. Accumulating and holding onto money is the main goal as Jane sees it. Everything else is subordinated to that.

Because cost is the main criterion the money hoarder applies to consumer decisions, he often jumps at the chance to get anything free or on sale—even if he doesn't care much for the items involved. Richard, a wealthy retired CEO, cuts out all "Buy One, Get One Free" coupons from fast-food joints. Then he stocks up on free burgers, freezes them, and eats them all week long. According to his family, Richard will eat *anything* he doesn't have to pay for: "He won't throw anything away," observes his son. "I've seen him eat spoonfuls of extra ketchup that got poured onto his plate by accident, because he couldn't stand to see it go to waste."

Fears Being a Sucker

The compulsive withholder has a pronounced fear of being taken advantage of. Often when she hesitates to buy something, it's because in the back of her mind she harbors a fear that the seller is trying to get the best of her, that she's making an unwise purchase. Ellen always hears her mother's voice in the back of her head saying, "You can get it for less."

Always Says "I Can't Afford It"

The compulsive withholder always has an excuse for not spending. "I can't afford it" is her favorite refrain, even when she really has plenty of money if she chose to spend it. But "I can't afford it" is an excuse, covering up the real reason for her unnecessarily constricted spending: fear and insecurity.

Follows Withholding with Self-Reproach

Just as other addicts often feel guilty and ashamed after a binge, the money hoarder often feels remorse after a withholding episode. Karen gave a lawn party and asked a friend's band to play at it. Although they did a great job, she couldn't bear to pay out any money, so she passed the hat and asked party guests to chip in for the music. Afterward, she was flooded with embarrassment and shame for being so cheap. But at the time, like other addicts, she couldn't help herself. She had to do it.

Never Gets What He's Saving For

The money hoarder often claims to be saving for some specific purpose: a new car, a major vacation, a house, a rainy day, retirement. But even after he's accrued enough money for the purported goal, he still can't spend it. When the time comes, he finds another excuse not to do it "yet." As authors Herb Goldberg and Robert Lewis put it, "The person who unnecessarily hoards money for a rainy day at the age of thirty is usually still waiting for the rain at seventy, only now the hoarding is done more rigidly."[5]

James, a successful businessman, always told his wife, Sharon, that they couldn't afford to go on vacations, because they had to sock away every penny for retirement and also pay for expensive life insurance plans. James was more concerned with what would happen after he died, quips Sharon, than with the quality of his present life. Finally, after years of bickering about their different priorities, the pair received a windfall and wound up with an extra $2,000 in the bank. Sharon hoped that now they could take a special vacation. But again, James insisted that they sock it in the bank.

Sharon was exasperated. "Fine," she said. "Put the $2,000 in the bank, and when you drop dead from overwork I'm going to spend it on the most expensive black dress I can find. And it will be a *sensational* black dress!" With that, James relented, and the couple took a vacation—which is not to say he enjoyed it. Most of the time he spent calculating how much they were spending for everything they did.

Fascinated with Money Itself

We have all seen pictures of the miser poring over his gold and silver pieces, delighting in the shimmer and shine of the metals, the feel of such weight in his hands, and the delightful "chink" sound of coins hitting together. The miser, in these common images, appears fascinated with his money, literally spellbound by it.

Today's miser looks a bit different. Because we don't tend to keep our fortunes in coins anymore, money hoarders must now be content to pore over bank statements, stock certificates, passbooks, possessions, and other symbols of wealth. Still, some money hoarders don't trust banks or stock exchanges and keep their money in cash stashed around the house—only now it's in bills instead of coins.

Margaret, sixty-five years old and a wealthy widow, keeps her money in jars buried all around her yard. Each one contains several thousand dollars. Periodically she digs one up and moves it around. Once she found a jar had broken, and the money in it was muddy. She washed and dried it before putting it in a new jar. Her daughter, Rene, was visiting at the time. "You can't imagine this scene," Rene recalls, still incredulous. "There I was, visiting with my new baby, totally broke, and she asks me to go get the money out of the dryer. Did you ever see $7,000 bouncing around in a dryer? It was like torture to me."

Perhaps it was this same kind of fascination with the "real coin" that drove Nelson Bunker Hunt and William Herbert Hunt to try and corner the market on silver back in the 1970s. Together with some wealthy Saudi princes, the Hunt brothers bought futures contracts on $14 billion worth of silver. If the silver nominated in those contracts had been purchased (it wasn't, and the Hunts lost $1.75 billion), they would have owned 80 percent of all the silver mined in 1979. Piled up, their silver would have reached some fifteen miles into the sky.[6] Now *that's* a pile that would please a money hoarder.

Pays Bills with Compulsive Promptness

Though he often has trouble parting with money, the security-conscious hoarder may well pay his bills on time. Often, in fact, he prides himself on never having a past due bill, paying a late fee, bouncing a check, or getting a single dunning phone call. He may even pay with compulsive promptness, the moment a bill comes in. Fearing authority figures, he does whatever is necessary to stay in good graces. Thus, his punctilious spending for bills serves the same purpose as his withholding does in most other instances: it shores up his sense of security and defends against his fear of poverty. Rachel explains:

I've always had this fear that something would happen to jeopardize my credit, my house, my ability to
survive. So I pay my bills related to those things the
day they come in. I have friends who think nothing
of paying a telephone or utility bill late. I would
never do that. The worst thing in the world to me
would be having something turned off. As far as I'm
concerned, the next stop would be "bag lady."

Paranoid About Getting Swindled

Typically, the money hoarder is somewhat secretive about
how much money she has, because she fears being ripped off
or taken advantage of. She fears that people may want to borrow it or steal it or that salespeople and service providers will
overcharge her if they know she's got money. Or she worries
that her partner or children will spend it carelessly. Whatever
the anxiety, she plays her cards close to her chest. She may
even keep a secret stash of money that no one knows about.

Ironically, the money paranoid person often *does* get
ripped off, so her fear becomes a self-fulfilling prophecy. She
seems to attract the very people who will play out that role in
her script. As Annette Lieberman and Vicki Lindner suggest
in *Unbalanced Accounts,* a person who grew up in an unstable
home will often choose partners who give her reason to
maintain the same defenses that helped her survive as a
child.[7] If not trusting was an adaptive behavior when she was
growing up, she may now choose partners who give her good
reason not to trust them, thus becoming a victim of the very
thing she fears—exploitation, betrayal, loss. She fears she
will be deprived of her money, and she is.

This is exactly what happened to Lynn. At thirty-five,
Lynn moved to the Southwest with her young daughter following a divorce largely precipitated by money differences
with her former husband. Lynn is admittedly tight with her

money, spending as little as she possibly can. She lives close to the bone, bargains with merchants for rock-bottom prices, and prides herself on her financial savvy. She expects people to take advantage of her, and she isn't having any of it. Ironically, the same money attitudes that drive her to hoard also make her vulnerable to scams. If someone is claiming to help her save a buck, she is inexorably drawn in, leaving behind her better judgment.

That's what happened when she took in a border several years ago to bring in some extra money (even though she had $50,000 in the bank). Matt, a twenty-five-year-old drifter who, it turned out, had a pattern of exploiting older, single women, answered her ad and moved in. He quickly made himself valuable on Lynn's farm, fixing things, building things, and generally being handy. She and Matt also became lovers. When he offered to give Lynn $10,000 to finish paying off her mortgage, she jumped at the chance. This, she told her friends, would allow her to extricate herself from "the system." She wouldn't owe the bank a penny anymore. Her overwhelming drive to (a) get money, (b) secure her home, and (c) beat "the system" canceled out any reservations she might have had about why he was making such an offer. Within six months after she got this "free" money, the pair split up and Matt moved out and initiated the first palimony suit in that state. He won, and Lynn was ordered to give him his own $10,000 back *and* an additional $10,000 for services rendered on the farm.

Lynn, who was nearly paranoid about others (including "the system") wanting her money, and always on guard against exploitation, walked headfirst into the trap of a scam artist. (He has since filed suit against the next woman he dated, with whom he also ingratiated himself.) Her addiction to money made her especially vulnerable to his scam, but in her eyes, this experience only proves that people really are out to rip her off.

Joyless Relationships

Because the compulsive withholder has trouble sharing and exchanging, his relationships often lack the richness that comes from give-and-take. He is distrustful, suspicious, and defended against anyone wanting too much, so it's hard to get close to him. Then too, his withholding of money, emotions, and time fosters resentment among those he comes in contact with, creating even more distance.

When Anita was about thirteen years old, her new stepmother, Shirley, put locks on the kitchen cupboards and refrigerator, supposedly to keep Anita and her sister from consuming too many groceries. Needless to say, this profoundly withholding act did little to endear the new stepmother to Anita and her sister. The ill will the children then felt toward the stepmother undoubtedly reinforced her suspicion that "these kids were out to take advantage of her." Living with a person with a withholding compulsion this severe had profound effects on Anita, who re-creates those early feelings of deprivation through her own self-defeating money pattern today.

Has Experienced Traumatic Deprivation in the Past

The hoarder's immense longing for "security" usually makes sense, given his previous life experiences, which may well have included some sort of deprivation or exploitation. If he lived through the Great Depression of the 1930s, he may have been humiliated when his family had to accept charity and vowed never to put himself in the position to have to take handouts again. Or perhaps he grew up in an alcoholic family and never felt he could count on anyone to take care of him. Or maybe he had relatives who survived the Holocaust by fleeing Europe, who later taught him that only with enough money could one be safe. Whatever the case, he has somehow gotten the message that he must never be vulnerable again to forces outside his control, and the impression that money is the savior to depend on.

Sometimes the deprivation experienced by a money hoarder was of an emotional nature. Ellen was considered a tomboy as a little girl because she liked to play baseball and climb trees. She was also an avid rock collector. Though her mother disapproved of this hobby, Ellen searched out special rocks and pored over books to learn about them. One day when the family was packing to move to a new house, Ellen went to find her beloved rock collection and learned that her mother had thrown it out. "It was horrible," Ellen recalls. "I got the clear message that who I was didn't matter to them. They didn't want me to be that person." Now, as an adult, Ellen has trouble letting *herself* be who she is and giving *herself* the things she values. She is an avid bicyclist but hasn't been able to buy herself a decent bike—even though she could easily afford one.

Other money hoarders may have grown up feeling vulnerable and powerless in the hands of abusive or addicted parents and now seek to have as much control as possible over their lives. Making sure you never run out of money and have to rely on others is one way of trying to maintain control. Money becomes protection against a hostile and unpredictable world. Money becomes a "higher power."

Fears Being Unable to Generate More

Many money hoarders harbor an irrational fear that once they spend money, they'll never be able to replace it. They don't have confidence in their ability to generate more money, even if they always have in the past. There is no sense of a renewable flow of prosperity. To them, it seems only a precious little trickle that they've somehow managed to tap into but can't count on.

Covers Up Feelings of Dependency

Behind the money withholder's facade of self-sufficiency, he is often quite dependent on a spouse or someone else; he just hides it well. According to the psychoanalyst Edmund Bergler, the "tightwad" is usually a passive and dependent person—but covers it up with a "pseudo-aggressive defense," by withholding money from others. He appears to be the tough one, the one in control, while really he may be quite emotionally insecure, haunted by fears of abandonment. As Bergler notes, "Some husbands hold on to their purse strings to disguise their holding on to their wives' apron strings."[8]

Fears Losing Control

Karen insists that if she weren't so controlled and cautious about money, she would probably overspend. "If I let myself go, I would just spend wildly. That's why I don't go shopping. If I let down my guard, I'd go crazy." When Karen says she'd go crazy, she means, of course, crazy spending. But her choice of words may point to the underlying fear of many money hoarders: a fear that if she lets down her guard and lets everything "flow," she might just spin out of control— not only of her spending, but of her feelings. Feelings like fear, vulnerability, anger, even rage, might start flowing as well. And her fear is that if she lets herself feel, she won't be able to regain control. She'll go crazy.

RECOVERY FROM MONEY HOARDING

People with a fear of spending often have a hard time getting into recovery, for several reasons. First, they usually don't think they have a problem. They have few debts, generally have healthy savings accounts, and pay their bills on time. In some ways, they *have* what many other people are striving for. And what they don't have is harder to quantify: the true wealth engendered by being in the flow of life, giving and receiving, developing creatively, pursuing leisure and self-knowledge, building community.

Second, even when compulsive withholders do acknowledge a problem, they are sometimes reluctant to spend money for psychotherapy and other healing aids to address it. Ellen tried going to therapy once, but never got past writing out that first check:

> I remember crying all the way home from that first and last session—not because of any emotional realizations, but because I'd just thrown sixty dollars away. I was telling myself, "You should have just taken sixty dollars and thrown it in the garbage. It was the same thing." I couldn't stop berating myself. I think the therapist was pretty good, too, but I just never went back.

There is a way around this barrier, however: self-help groups are free. And though Debtors Anonymous sounds like the wrong place for a person without debt, it has been helpful to people with a wide variety of money disorders—including the fear of spending. Here are some other recovery suggestions:

Expand Your Definitions of Wealth and Security

The person who holds on to money for dear life needs to learn that he's clutching the wrong thing. Money is just a *symbol* of security; it's not the real item. By clutching, withholding, and accumulating in a rigid, constrained, and obsessed manner, the person with a pathological fear of spending *undermines* the very thing he claims to want—security. Without a loving connection to others in his community and family, he is rendered far more vulnerable to the vicissitudes of life than he would be just from lack of money. Ironically, by remaining in a rigid, withholding posture, the "life force" or libido that he fears losing with each dollar spent is actually *less* available to him than it would be if he loosened up.

If the money hoarder is to heal, he will need to learn that he can take care of himself in ways *other* than saving and holding on. He can treat himself lovingly, buy the things he needs, take vacations, participate in the dance of life. He can cultivate an "affluence of satisfaction," as Lewis Hyde calls it.[9]

Stop Catastrophizing

The money hoarder's irrational fears about being broke create his own psychic impoverishment. Controlled by fear, he is neither free nor rich. He "catastrophizes," in Albert Ellis's words, that going on a vacation will lead to becoming homeless.

Ellis, in his approach to therapeutic change known as Rational Emotive Therapy, has developed ways to identify and counter the irrational fears and beliefs that often drive people. In a book with Patricia Hunter, *Why Am I Always Broke?* Ellis applies RET to what the authors call underspending. They describe a sixty-year-old patient who—despite having half a million dollars in the bank—panicked whenever she had to spend money. Her spending was so inhibited that even though she very much wanted a cat, she felt she couldn't afford the money for cat food, so she denied herself the pet. She had lived through the Great Depression and World War II, and though she hadn't suffered particularly in either, she was still haunted by fear of what such events might bring. "You just never know," she always said.

In a dialogue with the patient, Ellis pointed out that in order to live a full and interesting life, she would have to give up the idea of having to be totally in control of all events around her before she relaxed and spent any money. Here is the persuasive case Ellis made:

Unfortunately, you never can be completely sure of anything! There is always some possibility that dreadful things could happen sometime. So one other attitude change you can make is this: that even if some very unfortunate event did occur, you could cope with it, and you would have the resources to help yourself survive and be happy. And that if you don't survive, then at the worst you would die. That would be highly unfortunate, but we all die, anyway. . . .

. . . certainly we all would prefer to live as long as possible. Life is enjoyable in many ways. . . . But your irrational fears of dying in poverty won't let you live long and happily! When you let fear, rather than enjoyment, dictate your actions, you may continue to *exist* but hardly to really *live*.[10]

Live As If You Have Enough—Today

For the person recovering from hoarding, spending money on himself and others can be a way to affirm prosperity. By loosening his grip and allowing money to circulate more freely, he sends a message to his psyche that there *is* enough. Because energy follows thought, thinking and acting as if there is enough creates the *condition* of enough. Likewise, thinking and acting as if there's not enough creates the *condition* of lack.

Harold, for example, earned an average income from his job as a store manager and had modest savings. Objectively speaking, he had enough to live comfortably and securely. But because he was ultrafearful of what the future held, Harold deprived himself of hobbies, vacations, entertainment, and other pleasures. He kept telling himself that "someday" he would have all those things, after he saved enough money. Ironically, by so fearing poverty, he created the *daily experience* of poverty. He rarely went anywhere, socialized much, or enjoyed many pleasures. Year after year went by, and Harold never felt he had enough yet to start enjoying himself.

Regina, by contrast, had roughly the same amount of income and savings. But with it she bought the used piano she wanted, went frequently to plays and concerts, and gave gifts she knew would please the people she cared about. By living as if she had enough, she created the *daily experience* of prosperity. Both people had the same amount of money to work with, but Regina didn't feel she had to wait until she had all the money she wanted before creating the kind of *life* she wanted. Too often we mistake money as the goal, when money itself is nothing more than green paper. It's what we *do* with money that determines to an astounding degree whether we're rich or poor.

Of course, creating the life you want—whatever your income—means giving up the victim role. You can't live as Regina lives and continue to prove to your family how miserably they failed. You can't give yourself what you want and still enlist sympathy for your impoverished condition. You can't enjoy plenty and still enjoy making five dollars stretch all week. To live prosperously, you have to give up the secondary payoffs of living so close to the bone. You have to accept responsibility for really living.

Let It Flow

As noted earlier, withholders often harbor fears that if they let go of their vigilant grip on money, they will be swindled and exploited. And because they associate money with their very "life force" or libido, each outgo of money is experienced as a loss of power, energy, self. But this fear of losing libido is based on a false premise, so they worry needlessly. Letting money flow (in a healthy, self-caring way, not compulsively) doesn't *decrease* one's power or libido, it *increases* it.

Money is like blood or energy—it needs to *circulate* in order to keep the whole organism (the person and the community) healthy. If the circulation gets blocked, as it does with the money hoarder, the result is a deadening, a petrification, of that part of the whole. Nutrients stop flowing there because the circulation is cut off. The circulating blood in your body keeps you healthy; the circulating money in your life keeps you wealthy—in the true sense of the word. Unless blood flows *out* of a part of your body, fresh blood cannot flow in, carrying nutrients and oxygen to each cell. It is just as true that when you allow money to circulate, you increase opportunities for it to flow back to you, carrying with it more wealth-nutrients, such as community, creativity, goodwill, and self-esteem.

Lewis Hyde notes in *The Gift* that, according to Welsh traditional belief, when fairies give bread to the poor, the loaves must be eaten on the same day they are given—or they turn to toadstools. Gifts—anything bestowed on you, be it talent, material prosperity, or love—must be consumed, in other words, not hoarded. "Scarcity appears when wealth cannot flow," writes Hyde. "When someone tries to dam up the river, one of two things will happen: either it will stagnate or it will fill the person up until he bursts."[11]

It is ironic that the very thing the hoarder is trying to do—assure that he has plenty—is undermined by his grasping. Only by relaxing his grip and allowing what he has to be used up, to be "eaten," so to speak, can he assure his own survival. Otherwise, what he has received turns to toadstools and fails to nourish him. "If I hoard my treasure," observes Philip Zaleski in *Parabola* magazine, "content to bask in the gleam of gold, I nourish only my ego. If, on the other hand, I circulate my money, I cultivate its living power. . . . To participate in sacred exchange, money *must* circulate."[12]

What better or truer security is there than being part of a community of people—family, friends, or some other group—who look after each other? When crisis strikes, a savings account or insurance policy provides one kind of security, but it is one's relationship to others and access to mutually given support that really determines whether or not one will thrive. While trying to amass what he thinks of as security (based on dysfunctional beliefs promulgated by our culture), the money hoarder often neglects his store of true wealth, thus undermining his *true* security.

As noted, gift giving is especially painful for people who hoard money. They worry about how much money they're spending, but they also worry about being considered too cheap. And if they receive a gift, they worry that they will be obligated to reciprocate. For the person with so much anxiety about gift giving, recovery is learning to lighten up about it. Again, the key is to get into the flow, and keep your resources in motion.

In this regard, we have much to learn from "Indian givers." Again, Lewis Hyde illuminates the subject by citing other cultural traditions. Apparently, among some Native American and other tribal peoples, when a person receives a gift, he is expected to pass it—or something of like value— along to someone else. To profit by hoarding a gift for your personal advantage is to behave immorally, putting yourself in the debt of the original donors. So if a man receives a goat, rather than considering it part of his permanent wealth, he throws a big party and feeds everyone. In fact, notes Hyde, whenever people have begun using tribal gifts as capital (selling tribal artifacts to outsiders for profit, for example), the social fabric of the group has been destroyed.

The Puritan colonists, upon observing this Native American tradition of moving gifts on, thought it was a very strange and even offensive practice. They were more accustomed to a capitalist view of property, wherein the gift is assumed to become part of one's own assets. Thus, the pejorative use of "Indian giver" in our culture generally refers to someone who gives and then rudely asks for his gift back. But Hyde claims that tribal people who refrained from hoarding gifts actually "understood a cardinal property of the gift":

> Whatever we have been given is supposed to be given away again, not kept. Or, if it is kept, something of similar value should move on in its stead. . . . As it is passed along, the gift may be given back to the original donor, but this is not essential. In fact, it is better if the gift is not returned but is given instead to some new, third party. The only essential is this: *the gift must always move.* There are other forms of property that stand still, that mark a boundary or resist momentum, but the gift keeps going.[13]

Each of us—and not only the money hoarder—has much to learn from this notion that wealth must circulate if it is to nourish us. Perhaps because our gifts don't move, our entire nation is failing to thrive. Even the richest among us often feel poor. Maybe there is another way to organize our personal and national economies that recognizes not only the morality of giving but the wisdom and (yes) even the expediency of it. For as Hyde puts it, "In the world of gift . . . you not only can have your cake and eat it too, you can't have your cake *unless* you eat it." Perhaps we need to start eating our cake, consuming true wealth rather than just hoarding money.

CHAPTER 10

LIVING ON THE EDGE
Addiction to Deprivation

The counterpart of the admirer of money is the despiser of that commodity. Both are neurotics. . . . The despiser of money has his unconscious reasons too.

EDMUND BERGLER
MONEY AND EMOTIONAL CONFLICTS

It is madness to do everything for money, but it is equally mad to do everything for nothing, or next to nothing.

ARLENE MODICA MATTHEWS
YOUR MONEY, YOUR SELF

THE DEPRIVATION ADDICT is the person who compulsively lives on the edge, despite her ability to do otherwise, as if deprivation had some appeal in and of itself. She is often a compulsive underearner with a marked discrepancy between her ability to earn and her actual financial achievements. In addition to avoiding income, she also deprives herself of other things she wants, like decent housing, new clothes, medical care, vacations, and other pleasures. In this way, she is her own biggest creditor. She goes into debt to *herself* by not meeting her obligations to take care of her own needs.

Because her commitment to self-deprivation is not conscious, it is also not subject to conscious control. In fact, the person who is addicted to deprivation may be steadfastly *trying* to achieve financial stability and unable to understand why she isn't succeeding.

People who find themselves always living on the edge can come from any income group. Some sons and daughters of the wealthy are as likely to be addicted to deprivation as those who grew up in lower-income families.

This is *not* the person dogged by poverty beyond her control. It is the person who compulsively keeps herself broke for reasons that have less to do with finances and more to do with psychic struggles being played out through the symbol of money. She has what is often called a "poverty mentality." Her impoverishment is a *metaphor* that bespeaks painful inner feelings of worthlessness, shame, and deprivation. She compulsively seeks the experience of deprivation, creating in the material world the impoverishment she feels inside.

This is also not the person who consciously chooses a simple, nonmaterialistic lifestyle—and enjoys it. The person addicted to deprivation is *not* at peace with his financial status, yet seems unable to break the cycle of struggle and hardship. The person who seeks a simple, voluntary poverty cultivates detachment as a spiritual state; the person addicted to deprivation is as attached to *not having* money as the wealth addict is to *acquiring* it.

The negative consequences of this money disorder are obvious: shame, humiliation, struggle, debt, and resulting depression strain the immune system and often render this person vulnerable to stress illness. His ability to tolerate gratification in relationships is also limited, so he may avoid or sabotage them, leading to loneliness and isolation.

Despite many offers of work in her field, thirty-one-year-old Anita labors at low-paying clerical jobs that she despises. She has trouble speaking up for herself and negotiating raises because, she says, she feels "less than." She is always short of money and has never taken a real vacation. Recently, she sold some treasured heirlooms left to her by her deceased mother to pay for car repairs and other expenses. She steals toilet paper and paper towels from public places and routinely searches under vending machines for dropped coins.

Anita, as you may recall, grew up with an alcoholic father. Her mother died when she was eleven, and shortly afterward, her father began sexually molesting her. Being totally dependent on him for her material survival, the young Anita experienced herself as trapped. "I couldn't do anything about the abuse growing up because I had to depend on my father for food, money, bus fare, school clothes. So having money meant the complete loss of my soul, no control over what happened to me." Not surprisingly, Anita came to associate material security with being trapped. In her psyche, having nothing felt safest.

In recent years, Anita has begun to suffer chronic bronchitis and asthma, which finally compelled her to seek medical help, and that led to a referral for psychotherapy. Anita talks about what she has realized about her money pattern:

> By the time I was an adult, even though my father wasn't attached to the money anymore, internally the association was made: I didn't want anything to do with it. My walls were up; nothing was getting in. I believed that to be true to my self, I'd have to be poor. I'm trying to change that now, because I don't want to do this to myself anymore.

Ray dresses in worn, shabby clothes and drives a beat-up car. He associates having money with being a total creep, because his parents had money and were "right-wing reactionaries." Ray rejected their values, and money along with it: "Money always represented this gloating, arrogant, callous way of life that I hated," he says. "Money was the enemy. So I really don't care about it that much. Basically, I believe that money corrupts the soul, although it probably won't corrupt me, because I'll never get enough of it."

Ray's work skills are in an area of technology that usually pays well. But because of his commitment to deprivation, he's never made the kind of money available in his field. He calls his current job "deadening," with poor wages, no benefits, and low morale among co-workers. He'd love to quit, he says, but doesn't know what else to do.

Friends and acquaintances often call Ray for help when they're having trouble with their computers or need help with anything electronic. Ray can't bring himself to charge anyone who asks for his help, even people he doesn't know. In his mind, it would be politically incorrect, "ruthless," to charge. At the same time, he resents the time it takes. "I clearly recognize that there's a self-esteem problem here," he says, "and that the political stance is a way I cover up the fact that I feel unworthy to charge." Still, he can't seem to change his pattern.

Ray's father was a rage-aholic who beat both him and his younger brother—the latter severely. Ray managed to avoid the worst beatings by keeping a "low profile":

> I remember him reaching around in the car once and boxing my ears real hard for fooling around and laughing too much. After that, I learned to keep a very low profile, never to upset him. I don't ever remember acting like a kid after about the age of five. I wouldn't dare make noise.
>
> I think this stayed with me as an adult too. I basically try not to rock any boats or upset anyone. And that affects the jobs I take, my income level, and my ability to negotiate. I associate having money with being too visible, having too high a profile—and that feels dangerous. In my mind, you're either the victim or the ruthless one. I guess I'd rather be the victim.

Ray's fear of being ruthless serves a good purpose, in his psyche at least. It helps him keep a low profile, which keeps him safe, or so he deeply believes. If he were to make more money, he'd risk becoming more visible and powerful, perhaps letting his *own* anger out—and getting smacked back down.

INDICATIONS OF ADDICTION TO DEPRIVATION

Underearns

Getting a promotion, professional recognition, or financial success all cast a person further into the adult arena, and for the person addicted to deprivation, this can be frightening. Though she generally works hard, she never feels like a "real adult." If an opportunity arises for recognition, promotion, or money, it is liable to stir up feelings that she is out of her league, a fraud masquerading as a grown-up.

Melissa is a thirty-eight-year-old landscape designer who's been running her own company for ten years but still feels like a kid:

> I don't charge as much as I should, because when I give someone a bill I'm always afraid they're going to look at it and say, "Who do you think you are? I'm not going to pay this!" I've been told I'm really good at what I do, but I feel so small, not like a real grown-up. The only reason I know I'm a grown-up is that my friends are now teachers and lawyers and have kids.

People who are addicted to deprivation often have a hard time allowing themselves to make money doing what they most enjoy. To avoid guilt and others' envy or criticism, they would rather work at a job they hate or do what they want but struggle at it.

The deprivation addict also tends to *overwork* at her low-paying job, putting in long hours and taking work home. Jerry, who was emotionally abused by his father throughout childhood, has been in money recovery for a couple of years now, and drug recovery for five. He recognizes this pattern:

> I had one boss who was the spitting image of my father, only I never put it together. He was angry, demanding, and cheap. Every day I would break my back for this guy, and every day he would put me down—and he didn't pay a lot. But I couldn't ask him for more, because I was afraid he'd say, "You're not worth it." Pay is something so measurable; I couldn't bear to hear someone say, "You're not worth that much." I'd rather not ask for it.
>
> And I stayed at this job for five years. There's no question that I was drawn to that situation. It fit with my feelings about myself at the time: "I'm not worth much."

Because she feels so undeserving, the deprivation addict would rather not have people expect much of her. If given a promotion, she may become anxious, fearful that she's not going to measure up, and will try to find a way out of it. In the 1970s, I was rapidly promoted at the drug treatment program where I worked from counselor to assistant director and then to director. Each promotion came as a surprise to me, because I had no idea I was doing a particularly good job and felt lucky that anyone would even let me work for them. The final promotion to director proved more than I could tolerate. I became quite anxious and depressed—and asked to be demoted. A puzzled executive director complied, and that was the end of my upward mobility. Too grown-up for me!

Sometimes, the underearner doesn't flatly decline a promotion but sabotages it by flubbing an important project, picking a fight with the boss, or procrastinating. Reggie, a writer, dreamed of being able to bring poetry readings into a large state prison system. After applying and qualifying for a state grant to implement the project, he had only to complete the final paperwork in order to get started—and get paid. But he never followed through. "I just blocked it out, never did it," Reggie recalls.

Such procrastination is common among those addicted to deprivation. They wait for things to happen *to* them, rather than making things happen. Then, when nothing does, they blame others or "the system." Meanwhile, procrastination serves as a convenient tool to ensure not going anywhere. That's why just learning to "show up" is a major part of recovery.

Content to Dream

Some people who are addicted to deprivation become compulsive dreamers, always hatching schemes to get money but never quite getting them off the ground. He *appears* to want money, but the reality is that he repeatedly fails to get any—and remains broke or dependent on others. He's always preoccupied with *plans* for getting money but never actually gets it. He stays in a perpetual state of fantasy.

Because this person is psychologically stuck re-creating deprivation, his dreaming probably provides some relief, for by identifying himself in fantasy as someone who's going to strike it rich, he escapes the painful reality that he is—on another level—bent on being deprived. Usually his failure in various money-making ventures is practically assured by the fact that he doesn't acquire the knowledge, experience, or resources necessary for the field he has chosen or just doesn't take the necessary steps to make it happen.

Paul, for example, opened a travel agency with no knowledge of that field, sunk everything he had into it, and went under in a year. Then he borrowed money to invest in a rock band, and later a personnel agency. Each time, his enthusiasm and show of confidence was not grounded in any rational consideration of what would be needed. He was overoptimistic. Positive thinking is a very useful tool, but what looks like positive thinking in the dreamer is really just a way he sets himself up to fail.

Kareem is a multitalented musician and dancer who fits this profile. Whenever he gets money, he sinks it into some unrealistic venture that never goes anywhere. After dancing with one small company for just a year, he decided to start his own company. When people and organizations were reluctant to fund it, he rationalized that it was "all political." Determined to show people he could do it, he borrowed $10,000 to stage his first performance and wound up that much in debt.

Deciding instead to become a record producer, Kareem rounded up enough money to make several demo records with promising new artists, sure that he could get a deal with a major record company. But when one company did show interest, he sabotaged it by repeatedly rescheduling meetings early in the negotiations. They eventually lost interest. Kareem has no conscious awareness of the part he played in nixing the deal, however. "They reneged on me," he says.

Next, Kareem decided to invest in a friend's new public relations firm. First, the friend asked Kareem for $2,500, then said for $5,000 he could be a full partner. Kareem liked that idea, because he felt it would give him legitimacy in the business world. "I thought as an officer, doors would open for me. I'd have respectability; people would lend me money; I could get a mortgage." Eventually, Kareem sent his friend $13,000, much of it borrowed. His friend, it turns out, blew much of the money on cocaine, and the company was shut down by the IRS for failure to pay taxes.

Kareem still has a list of other ideas he feels confident will succeed. Right now, he's thinking about opening a nightclub. "I'm very optimistic that it's going to happen," he says. "I'll be rich; it's just a matter of time." Trouble is, he's having difficulty getting anyone to bankroll him anymore. And right now, he's quite broke. But maybe that's the whole idea.

Loses Things of Value

I used to set myself up to lose anything of value that I had. The examples are painfully numerous: I left my apartment unlocked (in a high-crime area) until someone finally "broke in" and stole my stereo and jewelry, left a new ten-speed bike on the front porch until someone took it, left an expensive leather jacket on the seat of my unlocked car until it was taken. I even gave my car keys to a known drug addict so he could do some work on it; the vehicle was never seen again. I promptly lost any jewelry that was given to me, particularly if it had any monetary or sentimental value.

Needless to say, this experience of frequent loss is an extremely painful feature of addiction to deprivation, but it's one that fits with the compulsive need to be bereft. And because it *is* compulsive, it feels out of your control. You're not consciously aware of the part you're playing in it.

Engages in Self-sabotage

Some people who are addicted to deprivation allow themselves to accumulate a certain amount of money and success and then do something to sabotage it. If they manage to make or win a lot of money, they may lend it to a poor risk, gamble, invest it in some risky venture, or otherwise squander it. The key to understanding this as a compulsive pattern (and not just bad luck or poor judgment) is that it happens over and over again.

Usually, the self-saboteur has a sense of relief once he's broke again, as Dean did. By age forty, Dean had acquired half a million dollars in assets by buying and selling real estate. But, he says, something just didn't feel right. Being successful made him very anxious. Then Dean made a series of bad decisions—lending large sums to a friend who was a compulsive gambler, and entering into several poor investments. Dean's now broke again, but oddly enough, he says, it feels right. "Worthless people don't have good stuff," he says, reflecting on how he feels about himself and why he thinks he did it. Dean is now recovering in Debtors Anonymous and is at least aware when he is undermining himself.

Tony, the video director we met earlier, has noticed a similar pattern. Whenever he gets close to the kind of opportunity he longs for, something "happens" to interfere with it. He was hired to direct a network special, then promptly broke his leg and had to give up the opportunity. And during rehearsals for another important production, he was hospitalized with asthmatic pneumonia and had to be replaced. In fact, Tony believes his long-standing battle with asthma is a metaphor, a physical manifestation of his fear of living, breathing, expanding—being.

Deprives Herself in General

It's not only money that the deprivation addict avoids but other kinds of gratification as well. She may run from gratifying relationships and stay in unsatisfying ones; she may deprive herself of relaxation, vacations, and entertainment. She may dress shabbily, denying herself the pleasure of looking good, and may even go without decent food and health care. Again, she experiences all this deprivation as something that's happening *to* her and usually doesn't see how she is contributing to it.

Certainly one aspect of this disorder is a feeling of not deserving more. Anita, the young woman whose stepmother locked the refrigerator and cupboards and who was also sexually abused, relates that "I felt I didn't deserve to live the way other people did. So let me not take up any space or receive anything from anyone. Excuse me for living." As she became an adult, Anita started depriving *herself*.

A disproportionate number of people who are addicted to deprivation come from families in which there was alcoholism, drug abuse, or compulsive gambling. For the person from a dysfunctional family, struggle, deprivation, and lack of recognition feels normal. Having enough feels like too much. Rosalyn, a bright, attractive woman from an alcoholic family, said it never occurred to her that she was underearning. She is only half-joking when she says, "I thought it was OK to make $800 a month when my living expenses were $1,200. The feeling of crisis, struggle, and shame that resulted felt normal to me." She explains:

> When you grow up in an alcoholic or any dysfunctional household with parents who are entirely stressed out, the kids get out of touch with their own needs. You get used to having to work really hard for love. You come to believe that you can't get anything unless you struggle hard for it, drive hard for it. What you want is hard to get. There's no comfort. So it's like separation from yourself, and addiction to discomfort, struggle.

A person from a dysfunctional family may also have an irrational feeling of guilt about having survived better than other members of the family. Frittering money away and staying broke becomes a way she keeps her power in check so she doesn't become "too together" and pose a threat to others in the dysfunctional family. She always lets the others know how much she is struggling.

Money Illiterate

The person addicted to deprivation usually doesn't know much about finances and doesn't *want* to know. When the subject comes up, she spaces out. To her, money is an incomprehensible subject that only other people understand. She doesn't keep good financial records and frequently loses money through errors, oversights, late fees, and bounced checks. If she tries to read the business section of a newspaper, she gets anxious and glazes over. The language of finance is foreign to her, and this money illiteracy serves the purpose of keeping her on the outside of the financial world—right where she wants to be.

Sometimes the person addicted to deprivation suffered some shaming incident as a child from which she drew the conclusion, "I'm not capable of dealing with money/commerce/the world." When Deborah was five or six years old, her mother took her to a circus. While they were sitting in the bleachers waiting for the show to begin, Deborah spotted a clown selling balloons and asked her mother for money to buy one, which she received. Deborah recalls excitedly dashing down the bleacher steps and approaching the clown. What she didn't realize was that the balloons this clown was "selling" were all half-deflated, pathetic-looking balloons. It was meant to be a joke.

As five-year-old Deborah naively tried to buy a balloon, unwittingly playing the "straight man" in the clown's comedy routine, he hammed it up, and pretty soon he had the people on the bleachers laughing. The more earnestly she tried to buy a balloon, Deborah says, the more the crowd roared. She doesn't recall when she caught on to the joke. All she remembers is being flooded with shame as she made her way back up the bleachers to her seat. "I felt so foolish," she says. "The conclusion I must have drawn, in whatever way five-year-olds draw conclusions, is that money matters were something *I* should stay away from. I don't know what I'm doing and will end up being humiliated."

Contempt for Money

Some people who are addicted to deprivation, like Ray, whom we met earlier, believe that having prosperity will make them bad, politically incorrect, spiritually bankrupt.

Applying black-and-white thinking, they make it a sin to have plenty and a virtue to be broke. "Money is evil, and those who have it are greedy and corrupt. If I become prosperous, I won't be a good person anymore." With this belief, of course, he tries hard to maintain his status as a have-not.

Sometimes, the person with contempt for money experienced his parents as preoccupied with financial success, uncaring and inattentive. He may have concluded that people with money are all stressed-out, busy, corrupt, and greedy—and decided that money was bad. Others saw a family member defeated by financial forces and squared off against money then. When Reggie, the writer, was a teenager, his father's shoe store was put out of business by a multinational chain. He remembers how it affected him:

> My father's store represented goodness to me. He carried only quality things. To me, my father had integrity, honesty, generosity, humility, a nongrandiose lifestyle. When his store was put out of business by the big chains, it was the end of his life. He tried to open another store, but it went bankrupt. It was very painful to watch. I was at the auction where his final stock was sold off, and my heart ached. I couldn't handle watching him be broken like that. I think I made up my mind that day that money was the enemy. People with money to me were arrogant, gloating, and greedy—not like my father.

The problem with putting all rich people down and keeping yourself poor is that by making things so black-and-white, you often deny your *own* money shadow and project your greed, your cravings for power, your selfishness, onto "those others" and never own it. Judgmental attitudes toward people with money also can cover up painful feelings of inadequacy and impotency in the money-generating department. If you can't admit these feelings to yourself, you may cover them up with an intellectual defense: "I don't have money because I *choose* not to. I am more principled than other people."

Sees the Choice as Struggle or Guilt

Many people with this money disorder seem to believe that if they have prosperity, they will be hurting others; therefore, it is better to be deprived so as not to feel guilty. That is the choice, as they see it. They have to keep struggling or feel guilty. If the deprivation addict tries to go on vacation, she usually sets herself up to pay for it in some way—by getting sick or running out of money. Whenever Deborah takes a vacation, she always assures people beforehand that it's going to be a "low-budget trip." She explains that she'll be staying in cheap hotels or camping—really roughing it. Her life should be hard, and she doesn't want people to suspect that it isn't. So she hides whatever prosperity she has.

Part of the fear is that if people think things come easy to her, they might stop helping her. Often, the deprivation addict was brought up to be passive and dependent, and she's doing her best to live out the script.

Fears Loss of Autonomy

Other deprivation addicts reject money not so much on political grounds but for reasons related to lifestyle. This person believes that to have money he would have to become a workaholic, not have any fun, and be a slave to the system. Of course, believing that, he stays broke. His fear is not totally unfounded; we have all seen people lose themselves in the process of chasing big bucks. But for the person addicted to deprivation, the fear of losing freedom itself becomes enslaving.

Sometimes, the person with a "poverty is freedom" association gets an adrenaline kick out of living on the edge. He prides himself on being able to get by without earning or spending much and looks down at people who buy into the system. But to reject money because your parents were enslaved by it is not a decision based on choice. It's a *reaction;* it's being "not your parents." And not being able to pay your bills and having to worry about money all the time is just as enslaving as being attached to accumulating money. Addiction to deprivation is not freedom, but just another attachment—an attachment to struggle.

People who fear losing their freedom if they get money are often afraid of commitments and responsibilities of all kinds. They avoid close emotional involvements for the same reason: the fear of being tied down, of losing total control. In reality, they may be staving off unacknowledged feelings of dependency by remaining fiercely independent.

Fears Envy

The person addicted to deprivation is especially fearful of envy and would rather keep herself in an unenviable position than risk it. Whatever she does have, she makes sure she works very hard for so no one can envy her. She believes, deep down in her unconscious, that "if things come too easily to me, others will hate and resent me—and want to hurt me."

Psychoanalytic theorists might say that such a fear is actually a projection, that this person actually envies and resents *others* and would like to hurt *them*, but among the people I interviewed, the intense fear of others' envy usually had a real basis in the person's history. For instance, Pam, the writer we met in earlier chapters, experienced intense envy coming from her mother, as illustrated in this memory:

> I remember once my aunt bought me a beautiful blouse, and my mother actually said it was too expensive for me and made me give it back. The message whenever something good happened to me was

"Who do you think you are?" It seemed as though she didn't want me to have anything. If I did anything better than she did, or was given anything nicer than what she had, there would be a major chill.

On some level I internalized the belief that I was not supposed to have anything nice—unless I stole it or struggled for it. Prosperity would never flow to me; it would always be a struggle. To stay safe I should never *look* too prosperous. Keep a low profile. No one will take potshots at you if you don't look too happy.

For some people, having money feels so unsafe as to be the psychic equivalent of death. This was the case for Jerry. Jerry's father told him repeatedly when he was a child that he would never amount to anything. Being extremely bright and skilled as an architect, Jerry grew up to make money relatively easily. But he also lost or squandered it as quickly as he got it. "There is a certain sense of control that I get out of staying on empty," he says. "It really feels like I would die if I were successful."

Remains "Loyal" to the Group

People with this money disorder often associate success with isolation. The fear is that if they rise out of their present condition, they'll be abandoned and won't belong anywhere. This is especially true for people from lower-income backgrounds, who fear being rejected by their family and friends if they get "too big for their britches." Deborah remembers, "My father's favorite song when I was growing up was 'Sixteen Tons.' He was always singing it: 'Sixteen tons, and what do you get? Another day older and deeper in debt.' Somehow I got the feeling that our family was the underdog, and I took that as my identity."

This fear of rejection from the group is somewhat justified. People who climb out of deprivation often *do* experience others' envy, jealousy, and resentment. When Cathy, a high-achiever from a working-class family, had a possible scholarship to Harvard, her mother warned her against going there. "You'll stop caring about your family if you go to a place like that," she said. "You'll forget about us." So Cathy went instead to a state school and eventually went on to pile up debts throughout her twenties and thirties.

> With my other debtor friends, it was fun to be poor and think ourselves superior to the rest of society. We saw ourselves as outlaws; it was sort of romantic. It was consistent with my identity. But when I eventually started to make it in my career, I found myself trying to play it down around them because I was so afraid they'd think I was too good for them now and reject me. But that wasn't healthy either, for me to have to "hide my gold." Now I'm just going to be me, and if anyone has trouble with that, so be it. That's their problem. I'm not going to hang onto membership in a dysfunctional club anymore.

Fears Loss

Some deprivation addicts harbor a fear that anything they get of value will be lost or taken away from them. Because they generally have poor boundaries, they feel powerless to stop anyone from taking from them. Rather than go through the grief of loss, they'd just as soon stay deprived.

People who have been sexually abused are especially vulnerable to feeling this way. A person whose boundaries were repeatedly violated is likely to draw the conclusion that "I can't keep anything. Whatever I have of value will be taken away. Therefore it's safest not to have anything." She keeps a low profile, fearing that she will be violated in some way if she is too visible. Not having feels safest. It might also be a natural impulse to avoid violation by just keeping *everything* out—including money. Anita relates to this:

Whenever I get any abundance, it brings up my incest issues. The basic problem is in receiving. I have trouble receiving, being open, being receptive. Because my father was both the one who gave me money and the one abusing me, I felt very much trapped. Money was associated with complete loss of control. So as an adult, not having anything gave me the illusion of safety. The high for me became *not* having anything, getting by on as little as possible. It was how I got a sense of peace, a release from anxiety.

But in truth, I've been endangering myself all over again, starving my soul of pleasure. I'm discovering now, with the help of a support group, that I can have abundance *and* be safe. I'm not the helpless little girl I was then. I have boundaries now, and I can defend them.

It's not only women whose incest experiences have affected their relationship to money. Dean was sexually abused by an uncle. Though for years he blocked the memories, he acted it out in his life through compulsive deprivation, until he went into therapy and started uncovering the intense shame that drove him.

The message I internalized from that abuse was that I was bad. Otherwise, nobody would do this to me. Then I acted out these feelings by running out of money and making myself feel bad. I set myself up to be a victim over and over—without blinking an eye. I also didn't take care of my body. I didn't go to the doctor. I'd physically exert myself way beyond what is healthy. I'd do all this because I felt I wasn't worth much.

The fear that if you have money, people will want it is not entirely unfounded. People with money often *are* besieged with requests for loans, grants, and investments. I got a glimpse of this the first time I tooted my financial horn. I was attending a self-help group for people wanting to transform their relationship to money. One evening, I shared my pleasure about my growing income with the group. Because I'd always kept any outward signs of prosperity to a minimum for all the reasons cited, this was a real departure for me. Sure enough, exactly what I feared occurred. The next night another member of the group called and asked me for a "grant" to help him pay his debts. I was floored, and managed to say no, retreating into my underdog identity by assuring him that I really didn't have *that* much money. I realized from this incident how critical it is for the deprivation addict to establish healthy boundaries.

Sends a Message Home

The person addicted to deprivation often has unresolved anger at his parents. He thinks as long as he stays deprived, he can prove how badly he was treated. It's a way of saying, "Look what you've done to me; I never got enough." He thinks that to become prosperous would be to give up his claim on a lousy childhood. Other people, like Jill, spend their whole lives in struggle in order to punish a parent who stressed money-making:

All my mother ever talked about was money. She was very demanding, critical, and controlling. She wanted the social status that came with money, and clothes and jewelry were very important to her. If her kids succeeded, she felt that reflected on her. So I made a decision *not* to produce and therefore *not* to satisfy her. I would deprive her of what she wanted from me. I delighted in proving to her that I couldn't care less about money. I dressed in hippie clothes, which drove her crazy. It was like I was saying to her, "See, mother, *you're wrong.*"

Then I found out, as I grew older, that I really have all the same fears she had: she never felt good enough as she was and tried to get it through money. I've had all those feelings too; I just expressed it differently. We think we're doing the opposite of our parents, and so often it's just the other side of the same coin.

Feels Financially Impotent

Deprivation addicts often describe experiencing profound powerlessness and inertia in the financial arena, what I call "financial impotence." Bright, educated people say things like, "I don't feel capable of generating money," "I don't know how to do it," "I can't take care of myself," and "I feel I'm powerless and can't make any decisions." Sometimes it seems to be an inherited sense of powerlessness, as Kara, an African-American musician, explains:

I feel I inherited a sense of powerlessness from my parents. I think they were pretty overwhelmed by the world and communicated to me that we were not people who made money; that's only for other folks. This belief has played itself out in my career. It's as though I have this glass ceiling over me that I don't let myself go past. I even have had nightmares about trying to get out of a cellar and I don't have any strength to open the door. My arms just turn to rubber.

It's a mystery to me how people take care of themselves. Nobody told me how to do it; I didn't get to see anybody's process. I just thought it was something that happened to you one day, the way girls get their periods, spring flowers come up, someday you just *know* how to deal with money. I'm still waiting for this know-how to hit me. In the meantime, I'm totally at a loss.

Sometimes, the person addicted to deprivation has identified with a financially impotent parent. Karen, whom we met in the last chapter, has always been a low earner. Recently, when she was struggling to make ends meet, her mother remarked, "Oh, you're just like your father." That's when it hit her: she's been acting out the role of "failure, just like her father."

When I was a kid, my mother always told me that my father didn't know how to make money. She came from a richer family, and she never felt that my father was as good as her brothers. She'd say, "Your uncles are wealthy, and your father doesn't have anything."

I remember feeling angry at my mother for saying bad things about my father. I felt, "I'm going to love my father regardless of what you say." My way of being loyal to him was to become like him.

Sometimes, competition between father and son for the role of dominant male gets played out financially. If the son's earning potential threatens the father's sense of superiority, there may be an effort to cut the son off from the financial flow in the family, to render him financially impotent. Ken, the son of a successful entrepreneur, remembers as a young boy being the "crown prince." He had everything he wanted and was constantly told he would someday take over the business. Then, suddenly, when Ken was eighteen, his father informed him that the business was being sold. Ken still remembers the shock: "It was as though the world I'd grown up in suddenly ceased to exist. Here I had been groomed for eighteen years to take over a successful business, and all of a sudden I had nothing. I was out on my rear, in a world I hadn't been prepared to make my way in."

For the next twenty years, Ken limped from one unsuccessful venture to the next. Whenever he tried to launch a business, his father refused to help him.

> It was very confusing. When I would ask him to back me in a business venture, he would always beat around the bush and ultimately say no. I didn't understand. I interpreted it as I must not be good enough, I must be wrong, I'm no good at business. Because he would always shoot holes in it. He'd say, "What do you know? You don't know anything."
>
> What I didn't realize then was that my father was actually in competition with me. He always had to be right. "I'm a self-made rich man, and you'll never be as good as I am." He never said it in so many words, but that's what came across.
>
> So more and more, I tried to compete with him in the worlds where I felt he *couldn't* beat me: I got really good in art, with women, and with drugs. Those were the three arenas where I knew how to operate. I just could not compete with him in the financial realm, where he could judge what I was doing and cut me down.

RECOVERY FROM ADDICTION TO DEPRIVATION

Goethe once wrote, "Nothing is more difficult to endure than a series of pleasant days."[1] He could easily have been writing about the deprivation addict, as this is his core issue—learning to tolerate pleasure, ease, and abundance. Still, with a commitment to recovery and with the support of others, it *is* possible to heal from this painful money disorder. And as with other money addictions, the ramifications of recovery from compulsive deprivation go far beyond the balance sheet. With recovery, we begin to allow ourselves more fulfillment, not just financially, but in love, pleasure, health, and other areas as well. As our money disorder heals, so does our ability to receive and *take in*—in general. Try the following pathways to recovery.

No Deprivation—Just for Today

When I realized some eight years ago that the core issue for me was addiction to deprivation, I thought, "This problem is so pervasive and insidious. How can I abstain from something so vague? At least with alcoholism, it's clear what the person has to do to recover—not drink, one day at a time. What can I *do* to recover from compulsive deprivation?" Then it hit me. I have to do the same thing: I have to avoid "drinking from the cup of deprivation" one day at a time. It helped me to concretize my recovery goal. I began to hope for the strength to forgo the "drink of deprivation" each day.

I also began to understand what deprivation is—and isn't. I began to see myself perpetuating my identity as a have-not, apologizing to people for vacations and other pleasures, and assuring them that I really wasn't having a good time. I began to know when a relationship was a dry well and to suspect that I deserved more. It's a continuing challenge to recognize deprivation when it occurs. Sometimes I slip into struggle for a while. But now I catch it sooner, and correct it.

Stop Romanticizing Deprivation

For those of us with a history of attachment to struggle, it is necessary to stop indulging in black-and-white thinking. Making money bad because some people have used it for destructive purposes is like making water bad because it has caused floods. Water is just as capable of quenching thirst and watering gardens as causing destruction. Likewise, money is just as capable of feeding people as exploiting them, of cleaning up a toxic dump site as creating one. It all depends on the values and motives of the person in control of the resources. If those of us who are striving to live by life-affirming values make money bad and divorce ourselves from it, we will be abdicating our responsibility to use resources for good. To make money bad is to forfeit our stewardship.

Keeping ourselves in struggle is hardly the answer to the world's problems. When we are preoccupied with our own survival—worried about an impending eviction or trying to raise the money to get our car fixed—we are less likely to devote our money and energy to important causes. When are we most able to share with others—when we have nothing ourselves, or when we have plenty? Being another broke person doesn't help the planet or anyone on it.

Devotees of different spiritual disciplines have sometimes taken vows of poverty in order to avoid becoming attached to, distracted by, or seduced by riches. And some people who are addicted to deprivation rationalize their rejection of money by pointing out the suffering in the world that greed has caused. But the Indian yogi Sri Aurobindo suggested this is an error, that rather than shrink from money, people might better put money to work "for the Divine."

> Most spiritual disciplines insist on a complete self-control, detachment and renunciation of all bondage to wealth and of all personal and egoistic desire for its possession. Some even put a ban on money and riches and proclaim poverty and bareness of life as the only spiritual condition. But this is an error; it leaves the power in the hands of the hostile forces. To reconquer it for the Divine to whom it belongs and use it divinely for the divine life is the supramental way for the Sadhaka [seeker].[2]

We must accept the responsibility that is placed in us as trustees of the earth's resources.

Develop a Prosperity Consciousness

Because struggle feels normal to the deprivation addict, in recovery he has to cultivate a sense that *prosperity is normal.* This takes time and awareness, but it is possible to make the shift. For me, the very word *money* had negative associations. I connected it with struggle, anxiety, loss, fear—other people, not me. Now, I associate money with things like stability, comfort, pleasure, self-esteem, safety, relaxation, giving, creating, responsibility, empowerment, being grown-up—*me.* Just by writing these words I can feel the shift that has taken place in my identity.

It is important to realize that prosperity doesn't come from opposing what you *don't* want. Prosperity manifests by having clear images and speaking the truth about what you *do* want.

If you still have strong convictions that receiving will be dangerous, or that you are not deserving of much, you will probably continue to sabotage any progress. Therefore, a crucial aspect of developing a prosperity consciousness is *preparing yourself to receive.* It is necessary to become able to see yourself prospering in your mind's eye—without rejecting the image. The images we hold are very powerful. If you can't picture yourself relaxing in a hammock in the sun (or completing the book, or playing in the band, or living in a nice place, or leading the workshop, or being well loved), chances are you won't take the steps necessary for it to happen.

Visualization is not just some New Age gimmick amounting to wishful thinking but a truly effective and powerful tool. It is also a spiritual discipline that requires alignment with a higher power. It's not about "I want, I want" in the willful, egoistic, self-indulgent sense. It's about uncovering your heart's desires, for that, I believe, *is* your inner wisdom guiding you in the direction of your life purpose. It's about seeing that image in your mind's eye—and then surrendering it to that which is highest and best. There are many books on creative visualization available to aid you in this process. One that I have found most helpful is Shakti Gawain's *Creative Visualization*.[3]

To create prosperity, it is also necessary to declare it, to become able to say it out loud. Affirmations are a powerful antidote to fear and other barriers. For the person addicted to deprivation, it can help to use an affirmation such as, "I am prosperous and I haven't changed my values." "I am prosperous and I am innocent." "I am safe. Jealousy and envy cannot hurt me." "Others rejoice and celebrate my success." "It is safe for me to prosper." Write your own affirmations, those that speak *your* truth.

Work on Developing Boundaries

As we've seen, some people who are addicted to deprivation avoid having much because they believe it will be taken away from them—borrowed, begged, stolen, or lost—and they don't think they can bear the resulting feelings of loss and grief. That's why it is crucial in recovery to develop boundaries. Until I could say no, I could not let myself have any prosperity. I only sabotaged and avoided it. As long as I was defenseless, I wouldn't put myself in the position to have anything. Without a containing vessel, you can't hold abundance, any more than you can carry water without a jug. Now I know I can take care of myself; I can say no (or yes) whenever I choose to. Whatever happens, I know I am not going to abandon *myself*. I don't have to compulsively lose anymore.

Start Showing Up

With procrastination one of the major tools of self-deprivation, it's important in recovery to start showing up: show up for the job interview, show up for the meeting, show up for the talk, show up for the concert, show up at your desk, show up for the date, show up to ask for a raise. Show up, take the action—and let go of the results.

Because a fear of being judged inadequate has fueled our procrastination in the past, we now have to accept our imperfection. There is absolutely no way we're going to be perfect, and to even try is to fight a losing battle. It's hopeless. When we really *accept* this, something shifts. We can give that workshop and not worry so much about screwing up, play in that concert and not worry so much about hitting the wrong notes—because we already accept our humanity and fallibility. Success for the person addicted to deprivation means feeling the fear of failure—and showing up anyway. It means daring to be visible, to be known, to feel stupid, to not understand something, to ask questions, to be envied, to feel foolish, to be turned down—to be seen as imperfect, flawed. Success is just showing up.

Give Up Suffering

Perhaps you haven't wanted to give up the suffering role because you thought it was the only way to validate your experience of childhood abuse. "If I'm not suffering, does this mean 'person X' never abused me? Am I letting him or her off the hook and making myself wrong? If I don't feel victimized, am I in denial?" No, no, and no. Giving up your suffering role is not the same as being in denial. It's a shift from powerless to empowered, from passivity to action. You can still know what you know, trust your perceptions—and simply not be willing to suffer any longer. Staying a victim actually proves nothing; it just keeps you stuck.

Moving beyond being stuck means opening to deeper levels of feeling. To admit to ourselves that we want something is to admit that we don't have it or didn't get it, and that can hurt. That's why when we start taking better care of ourselves in recovery, we may reawaken feelings of loss and deprivation that have long been repressed while we acted them out. This reawakening is painful, but necessary. In some ways, staying deprived has been a defense against *feeling* deprived. To move out of that state is to awaken feelings of loss, rage, and shame. It requires a lot of support to move through these feelings.

In recovery, it helps to devise some symbolic way of declaring your new commitment to self-fulfillment. By symbolically and officially renouncing your commitment to struggle, you send a psychic message to every cell in your body that a shift is taking place. The goal is no longer to suffer and struggle; the goal is to live as gratifyingly and pleasantly as possible.

When you change your founding principles, it has profound ramifications for your life. It's akin to a corporate restructuring, wherein a new CEO changes the way the company is run, or even a revolution, wherein a repressive dictator is overthrown by a compassionate visionary. This revolution, however, is from within.

Take a Money Mentor

A deprivation addict cannot recover as long as she continues to surround herself with other people committed to struggle, any more than an alcoholic can recover while hanging out in bars all day. That's why in recovery, it is important to find some prosperity mentors, people who have abundance and whose values and lifestyle you also respect—people who give generously but also have boundaries, people who have healthy money habits, people who have true wealth.

That doesn't mean you have to cut off all contact with friends or relatives who reinforce your poverty mentality. But it will be important to minimize their input and effect on you, to protect yourself while you are healing from dis-ease. You need to be around people who rejoice in your prosperity and don't begrudge it, people who want to create not destroy, people who are on their own path to gratification and not trying to keep you enrolled in the Ain't It Awful Club.

Make Friends with Money

I was one of those people who looked upon money—and anyone who had money—as wrong, evil, bad. Naturally, while I held money in such contempt not much of it came my way. I realized in recovery that I had to make friends with money.

As I might with an actual person I was in a dispute with, I decided to call a meeting with money. I went into a meditative state and asked money's representative to join me for this dialogue in my imagination. What followed was a real healing session. I told money why I'd been carrying such a grudge against it, lodged all my complaints about it, and explored the consequences of my position. Money told me about its true nature, introduced me to the notion of money empowerment, and discussed our potential truce and partnership. The dialogue evolved slowly and organically.

Nothing changed instantly in my bank account or wallet as a result of this exercise, but I can honestly say that things were never quite the same either. Some change occurred on the psychological level, where recovery from this money disorder begins. The dismantling of a major barrier to my prosperity began with that dialogue.

This may or may not be a tool that you want to use, but the point is to find some way—through writing, meditation, ritual, fantasy, dialogue—to make friends with money.

Keep At It

There's no quick fix from money disorders, including addiction to deprivation. Nine years after starting my recovery, I still have to lovingly encourage myself sometimes to take care of business: to balance my checkbook, keep the tally, pay my bills. Confusion, denial, anxiety, and discouragement still wash in and bog me down sometimes. One day recently, I misplaced both my bills and my checkbook. Losing things like this and getting mired in chaos and confusion was all part of my old pattern.

For a little while after I misplaced these items, I fell into another aspect of my old pattern: I didn't even look for them; I just tried to ignore the whole problem, while a free-floating anxiety and sense of discouragement washed over me. But what's different now is that I have the ability to see when I am doing this and have some tools to counter the paralysis. So gently, slowly, I brought myself back to the task at hand. I stopped what I was doing, took my time, looked for—and found—the missing items. I *took care of business,* which is all part of recovery for the person addicted to deprivation.

CHAPTER 11

WHEN YOU CAN'T GET ENOUGH
Money Hunger

> *I love money. I love money more than I love the things it can buy. Does that surprise you? Money: it don't care whether I'm good or not; it don't care whether I snore or not; it don't care which God I pray to. . . . There's only one thing I like better: other people's money.*
>
> CORPORATE RAIDER LAWRENCE GARFIELD
> (PLAYED BY DANNY DEVITO) IN THE FILM
> *OTHER PEOPLE'S MONEY*, ADAPTED FROM THE
> PLAY BY JERRY STERNER

> *It's not that she doesn't love me, because she really does. It's that she loves money more.*
>
> DORIS, A YOUNG WOMAN TALKING ABOUT
> HER MOTHER

THE *TAO-TE CHING* TEACHES that striving to do one thing more and more stridently causes its polar opposite to appear. An exaggerated striving to be rich makes a person poor in spirit, which is to say, in his experience of life. That's what this chapter is about: how overstriving to be rich can make a person poor. When you are compulsively driven to acquire more money and material things despite the negative effects on your relationships, health, and other interests; when you suspend your better judgment, abandon your principles, and even risk arrest in order to acquire more; when no amount of money is ever enough, because the more you get, the more you want—you are in the throes of a money hunger known widely as greed.

Unlike compulsive spenders, whose high is expelling, or hoarders, whose high is keeping, the money hungry get their high from getting. It's not the money per se, or even the things it can buy that they crave so much as the *act of getting* and especially of *getting more than other people.* And whatever they get—bonuses, cars, a dream house, new companies—fails to satisfy for long. Having achieved it, they become restless and bored and go in search of a new deal, new excitement—a new conquest. Once again, Donald Trump, in *Surviving at the Top,* unwittingly described this symptom: "The same assets that excite me in the chase often, once they are acquired, leave me bored. . . . For me, you see, the important thing is the getting . . . not the having."[1]

The stereotype that all rich people are driven by greed, however, is false; the majority are not. Money hunger is evenly distributed throughout the socioeconomic classes. There are plenty of middle-class people driven by it. And everyone who seeks to make a good living or even dreams of becoming wealthy is not greedy. The difference is this: the nonaddict uses money to expand and enhance his life, to give himself more experiences, enrichment. But the money hungry person relates to money as if getting material wealth were the end in and of itself. He focuses more and more on getting money, but his *life* becomes more and more narrow, restricted, and impoverished.

Being money hungry doesn't necessarily help a person to become wealthy, either. Though some people become rich because of this disorder, more are destined to remain poor or middle-class because of it, because greed makes people particularly vulnerable to scams and get-rich-quick schemes. If a con artist can make the money hungry person believe that *he* has stumbled upon the world's most lucrative money-making opportunity, the latter will often hand over his money. The lure of easy money is so seductive to this person that he quickly suspends his better judgment.

Gluttony is out of fashion in our times because it's at odds with having a perfectly slender body. But greed has taken its place, and it is a similar compulsion in many ways: gluttony is an obsession with food; greed is an obsession with money. The glutton can never get enough to eat; the greedy person can never get enough money to be satiated. When we see someone acting as a glutton, we are repelled by the naked neediness revealed. But throughout the 1980s, wealth addicts were considered not only normal but role models that we all could emulate. When Ivan Boesky gave the commencement speech at the University of California's business school in 1985, he told the graduates, "Greed is all right, greed is healthy. You can be greedy and still feel good about yourself." The audience burst into applause.[2]

In many ways, greed for money in the eighties was like lust for sex in the sixties. During the "greed liberation" movement, the idea was to throw off the shackles of guilt and send yourself into oblivion on the high of money. Like the stereotypical sixties hippie who wanted to "ball every chick in sight," the greed addict of the eighties wanted to make every buck, and "fuck it if you can't buy it," as Dennis Levine once said.[3]

But also like the earlier "free love" movement, the "greed is good" movement led not to more freedom but to greater enslavement. Just as sexual lust—without some emotional relatedness—often leaves the seeker empty, unsatisfied, and compulsively searching for more, so too money lust, at the expense of emotional and spiritual relatedness, fails to satisfy for long. Both the free love seeker and the money addict miss the point. Both are engaged in adolescent-like behavior that unwittingly reveals how *un*free and dependent they actually are.

Thinking of greed as a *money disorder* akin to other compulsive behaviors, rather than simply a selfish approach to material goods, can help not only those who are enslaved by this insatiable hunger for more, but our larger society as well. As Jay B. Rohrlich wrote in a *New York Times* article about Wall Street's "money junkies," it places the problem in a clinical rather than a moral framework.

> We must make value judgments about conduct that breaks laws and hurts others, but a clinical attitude keeps the focus on the humanity of offenders. Defining alcoholism as a disease rather than a sign of moral decadence has led to successful treatment strategies. If money addicts were seen in this light, personal and organizational tragedies could be prevented.[4]

Loretta is not a wealthy woman, but she is driven by money lust. All she likes to talk about are her holdings. Dinner conversations with her husband and daughters revolve around money. Once she lent her elderly mother several hundred dollars and charged her interest. "How can you do this?" Loretta's brother asked. "It's business," Loretta replied. She prided herself on her business savvy.

One of the investments she was proudest of was $100,000 she placed in a highly touted real estate partnership that promised to triple her money in five years. Loretta was very impressed with the developer, who took her and her husband out on his yacht and to dine at an exclusive country club afterward. The developer himself was just moving into a new thirty-room mansion—further proof to Loretta of his Midas touch.

At first, Loretta invested $25,000 in the partnership, then she gradually increased it to $100,000—most of her nest egg. A few of her friends expressed concern, given how unrealistically high the promised return was. But Loretta so craved the increase that she suspended her own critical thinking.

Then things started to sour. First, she heard that the developer wasn't returning phone calls, that he had suddenly left town and his whereabouts were unknown. Next she learned that his thirty-room mansion had been put up for sale. Then came the newspaper headlines: The development company was a scam. The partners had been living a lavish lifestyle off of investors' money, falsifying records of the company's holdings. Loretta was plunged into a severe anxiety-depression, unable to sleep or eat.

Fifty-five-year-old David grew up in a family of modest means but always knew he wanted to succeed. His parents put all their money into sending him to a private boys' school, where he met and mingled with the sons of the wealthy. He felt cheated because he didn't have a sleek sports car like some of them did, didn't summer in exotic places. He longed for the day when he himself would be really rich.

Five years later, David's father died and left no fortune for his mother or him, just a nice home and a few small investments. It was then that David determined to create his own "inheritance." By forty-five, he was CEO of a large corporation—and his life was revolving around money. He spent a lot of time counting in his head, comparing his salary and stock options to those of other executives. Each year, the numbers he wanted to reach went up geometrically. Where once he had thought making a million dollars would be the ultimate achievement, now he thought in terms of tens of millions.

At first, his growing wealth seemed to serve him well. He felt more in control of his life, more secure, more powerful, more attractive to women. Along the way, he married and had a child, but his primary focus remained on his career. Most days, he left home at 5:00 A.M. and returned at 8:00 or 9:00 P.M. Whenever he arrived at a financial goal, the goal jumped ahead. He was never satisfied, never felt he could just relax and enjoy it.

Then came the stock market crash of 1987; David lost a good deal, on paper at least. Compulsively driven to make it up, he started thinking about how he could make a fortune fast and get back to where he was. He started engaging in secret, illegal activities that eventually defrauded his company of more than $3 million. With each new injection of cash into his private coffers, he was driven to acquire more, even though he was jeopardizing his career, reputation, and family, and even his freedom. Ironically, he never really enjoyed the money he had. Now he's serving five years in prison, and his wife is suing for divorce.

INDICATIONS OF MONEY HUNGER

Fiercely Competitive

If a T-shirt were designed for this group of money disorders, it might say "Eat Your Heart Out," for the wealth addict enjoys making others envious. He's always in competition to have the most, the first, the biggest, and the best. In *Wealth Addiction,* Philip Slater noted that things have value for this person only to the extent that other people want or need them. That's probably why, Slater conjectures, there was a surge in sales of large, gas-guzzling cars during the energy crisis of 1973–74. Some people wanted to demonstrate that *they* could afford to keep gas in big cars, even if others couldn't.[5]

You don't have to be a psychoanalyst to figure out that what drives this person to compete so ferociously is probably not great confidence but a nagging suspicion that he is inferior. The back of his "Eat Your Heart Out" T-shirt, in fact, could say "Without Money, I Am Nothing," because this conviction is what drives him from deep inside. Like the schoolyard bully who gives the weakling a hard time because he sees his own weakness and vulnerability in him and can't stand it, the wealth addict harbors contempt for those he deems less successful, largely because he is so judgmental toward any signs of what he would deem failure in himself.

Overwork

In the effort to acquire ever more money, the wealth addict often overworks. Whether involved in legal or illegal activities to gain his fortune, he'll work around the clock, ignoring his needs for rest, exercise, and proper nutrition. Almost no time—evenings, weekends, or vacations—is off limits for business-related phone calls and work. To him, the old saw "Time is money" is a great truth.

This view of time as a currency that he can trade for money inevitably erodes his family life. His spouse learns not to expect much of him in terms of time or emotional involvement and settles into an armored distance of her own. His children come to crave attention and may act out to get it. Eighteen-year-old Ian, son of a corporate manager, describes how his dad's view of time affected him:

> He used to say it a lot, "Time is money." And I got the definite sense that I was wasting his time if I asked for attention. It was like time was another of his *possessions,* and he wouldn't give me any of it. Most evenings and weekends he'd be on the phone or at the office. He'd give me money so he could get out of giving me time.

The wealth addict's withdrawal from relationships and his singular focus on money-making activities leads to growing tension at home, which only reinforces his focus on career and material rewards; the more he feels like a failure at home, the more intent he becomes on being a financial success. He tells himself that he is sacrificing in order to give his family the best things in life and bemoans their lack of appreciation. But in reality, he is withholding much of himself from them.

Emotionally Cold

Because they value money above all else, wealth addicts can seem quite emotionally cold. Monica, whose father is a wealth addict, reached out and contacted him recently after ten years of estrangement. When he called her back, he had his secretary place the call and then spent most of their conversation bringing her up-to-date on how his various investments were doing.

Wealth addicts are often cynical, in fact, about emotions, considering them so much "touchy-feely bullshit." Carl, the former drug dealer, explains:

> When a girlfriend or someone else would say something to me about some emotional thing, or express a value for something other than money, I would say, "Hey, save that crap for someone else. Everyone's out to make a buck, don't kid me. Anybody who says money isn't the bottom line is lying."
>
> When you're addicted to money, you can't have a real, intimate relationship at all. You can't be driven to make money and at the same time have a calm, loving relationship with a woman. You can't. It can't be done. Money is inside of you, more than anything else, and you're inside the money. It's in your mind, it permeates every part of you. It *is* your primary relationship.

People, like Carl, who are involved in illegal money-making schemes, often substitute for real intimacy the intense bond of co-conspirators, the connection they feel to others involved in the same activity. These ties can be very powerful, especially for someone who has had trouble forming meaningful bonds in life. They allow him to feel connected but without the demands of real intimacy. Ilan Reich, an attorney and one of those convicted in a Wall Street scandal, when first confronted with the truth by his law partners, began to sob. Among the reasons he'd done it, he said, was for friendship, because he was lonely. He hadn't, in fact, even taken the money he was paid.[6]

Seeks Diversion

Part of the seduction of the money-making game is also the constant action, excitement, anxiety, and challenge. The constant busyness required to make a fortune—fielding a hundred phone calls in a single morning—can be a great diversion from any unwanted feelings and moods lurking within, and from the pressures and strains of intimacy. Stuart, a successful entrepreneur, put it this way: "I'm programmed to get money—period. If I analyzed myself, I'd say the purpose is diversion. I make money instead of having a life."

Wants Only What He Doesn't Yet Have

Most wealth addicts feel constantly deprived, irrespective of their actual incomes or possessions. An upper-class stockbroker may feel deprived if he can't buy a yacht the size of his colleague's, losing sight of his own affluence. The insider trader tells himself he's going to stop when he gets $20 million, but once he does, he pushes the goal ahead to $30 million, then $40 million. He only wants what he doesn't yet have.

As a result, people with this money disorder develop astounding distortions about what constitutes poor. Like an anorexic with psychotic-level distortions about her body who feels too fat at eighty pounds, the greed-driven person can feel too poor with millions. Michael Milken, when he received $700 million one year as a bonus pool for his Beverly Hills division of Drexel Burnham Lambert, complained angrily to his New York boss that it wasn't enough. He kept $550 million for himself and divided $150 million among his colleagues in the department.[7]

Hungers for Power and Control

The wealth addict usually has major issues around power and control. Part of what attracts him to acquiring money is the feeling of power and control it gives him, which he uses to avoid underlying feelings of insecurity and vulnerability. He finds the illusion of power provided by money intoxicating and irresistible, as Jason, the recovering stock market junkie, describes: "It wasn't really the money I wanted so much as the power I felt when I was making it. I cared more about being in the game than about how much I made. Feeling that sense of power was what I craved."

Under the sway of such power intoxication, wealth addicts often think they can do anything, pull off any deal, make any amount. They convince themselves that the rules that govern other people's behavior don't necessarily apply to them. And because money lust is so widespread in our society, the belief that "everybody's doing it" feeds this denial.

Wealth addicts are prone to use money to exert power and control *over others* too. If someone dares to frustrate his chances of making money, the wealth addict will scheme a way to defeat this enemy. A parent who is a wealth addict may threaten to withhold money from an adult child—or alternatively promise to give him money—contingent on some behavior as a way of maintaining control over him.

The wealth addict's work compulsion derives in part from this need for control too. He fears deep down that if he stops the constant maneuvering and deal-making, the whole house of cards will collapse. Walter, a writer who became a money-hungry entrepreneur, describes the feelings behind his drivenness: "I work in my business somewhere between ten and fifteen hours a day and many weekends. I think I have some kind of fear that if I relax and do something fun for just a moment, if I let up control, it'll all go away."

According to Edmund Bergler, what he calls "exaggerated ambition" is an unconscious defense mechanism against repressed passivity, sometimes stemming from depression.[8] A person who suffers from this repressed passivity fears being incapacitated by it if he gives in to it. Apparently, so long as his defense of constant action and deal-making holds up, he doesn't have to acknowledge or address his depression, passivity, and feelings of powerlessness. His defense against such feelings has been to strive for omnipotence so as never to be vulnerable. His driving belief is, "If I am powerful enough, I will always be able to get what I want—to *stay in control.*"

COMPULSIVE TAKERS

A subgroup of people driven by greed acquire what they want specifically by living off of *other* people's financial wealth. They're what I call "compulsive takers" and others have called "gold diggers." They fail to contribute much to either their family or their community but latch on to some way to be taken care of financially by mooching off of parents, relatives, "the system," serial insurance claims, and other sources of support. The compulsive taker is *not* the homemaker who helps create a nurturing household while a partner brings in the material income but someone who only *drains* a household or community and contributes little materially or otherwise.

Compulsive takers have many of the same qualities as wealth addicts, only they do their acquiring indirectly and passively. They may even oppose the system in which their benefactor gets his money, but this is less a thoughtful political analysis than a cover-up for feelings of inadequacy. They don't think they *can* make it in the world of career and finances, so they pretend not to want to.

Like the wealth addict, the compulsive taker is never satisfied. No matter how much others do for him, help him, or take care of him, he always manages to turn things around and feel poorly treated. This can be extremely frustrating and confusing to anyone closely involved with him, because you never seem to be able to win. Edmund Bergler notes that this is because the "parasite," as he calls him, is a psychic masochist. "Unconsciously, he wants to be refused. . . . If they don't get, they feel unjustly treated. If they do get, they again feel unjustly treated—because they didn't get enough."[9]

Lela, an aspiring children's book writer and an adult child of an alcoholic, fell into this pattern for a while, living on public assistance, borrowing from relatives, and showing up at friends' homes at dinner time. "I wanted to live off the fat system, skim the fat off the land," she recalls. "I told myself that if society didn't appreciate my talents, why should I work hard at anything? At the same time, I felt inferior. I didn't think I *could* make it."

Randy, a forty-one-year-old compulsive taker who has worked only two of the past twenty years, has been living on insurance settlements, relatives, and friends. After dropping out of college, he fraudulently won his first insurance claim by lying about the facts of the case, which involved an auto accident. Then he organized a rent strike in his building. (Though most rent strikes are undoubtedly valid, Randy admits he organized this one so that he could live rent-free for a while.) Then he went to work for a short time, sued his employer for a minor injury, and lived off of those proceeds for a while. While he was flush, he obtained credit cards, charged an expensive stereo system and other equipment, and then never made the payments. To escape his creditors, he left for Europe, and when his funds ran out, he wrote friends back home to send money. Their donations lasted him another three years. Then he filed an insurance claim for lost equipment. After that settlement money was exhausted, he came back to the United States and moved in with his ailing father. In Randy's own words, he then "engineered Dad's getting rid of his money so he could get on Medicaid." When Randy's father died, Randy came into an inheritance that carried him another five years or so. Finally, for the last three years he's been living rent-free in various friends' homes. Recently, he wrote his extended family for money and is getting ready to do a mailing to all the people he met at a political conference, asking them to send money to support his "activism."

Yet, by his own admission, Randy is far from an ascetic when it comes to material luxuries. He buys only the best. When he got into drinking raw juices last year, he bought the most expensive commercial juicer on the market for $1,700. He has top-notch professional recording equipment because he occasionally plays the electric guitar. Randy is also gaining some awareness of his pattern and is candid in his reflections: "For a nonmaterialistic person, I'm very attached to things. I only like the best, and I spend a lot for the things I buy. What I've failed to do is make the money to pay for them."

Randy alludes to one underlying dynamic of the compulsive taker: he feels inadequate to make it on his own, overwhelmed by his own passivity, and powerless to change: "I'm in an old pattern. I'm going to have to get a job soon, and I don't trust that I'm going to do it. I've been terrible at that in the past." His inertia may well be contributed to by depression.

According to Edmund Bergler in *Money and Emotional Conflicts*, most takers harbor resentment toward a parent who they felt coldly rejected them. If a taker grew up in a family where the primary emotions expressed were in relation to money, he may unconsciously try to take people's money away, as if to say, "I shall take away what you love most: money."[10] He feels entitled to be taken care of by others now because he feels he was inadequately cared for in the past. Randy, for instance, admits that living in friends' homes without paying rent makes him feel loved.

Olivia, another compulsive taker, says she only wants boyfriends who can buy her lots of expensive things. Her current boyfriend is keeping up with her demands by running up his credit cards. "That's his problem," says Olivia coldly. "If he wants me, he's going to have to work for it." Notably, as she talks about her past, she describes how cold her father was and how he failed to provide for her in any way. Now she's going to get what she deserves.

But like the bargain hunter, the compulsive taker is the one who loses in the long run. Throughout his life, he's intent on getting *something for nothing*, when in reality he robs himself of the sense of self-worth that comes from contributing and taking responsibility: by remaining dependent on lawsuits, the system, and other people, he never takes charge of himself—and perpetuates his own deprivation.

RECOVERY FROM MONEY HUNGER

One might think that the solution to money lust is to reject money, to live a stripped-down, ascetic life. But this is not so. To recover from money lust, one has to commit to giving oneself the *best life possible*. The point is not to reject the prospect of improving your financial condition but to refocus on improving your *life*. The first step is to acknowledge that your approach to money is depleting you—physically, emotionally, and spiritually. Once you've admitted that it has had negative consequences, then you can start getting rich in the true sense.

People, Places, and Things

The wealth addict has to break off with those people who are associated in his mind with access to deals, big money, fast money, in order to recover. For Jeremy, that meant avoiding the people he used to share insider stock information with. He found that in order to stop participating in the illegal activity, he had to quit his job at a large investment house and break off all relationships with other brokers and people in the business. He did this all at once—cold turkey—and recalls how extremely difficult it was:

> It was very, very hard. Because I was still getting phone calls from these guys and they were saying, "It's a good time to invest in this or that; we're going to make a killing." I tell you, dropping out of the game was harder than anything I've ever done. To make $500,000 just like that is the most tempting thing. "Am I doing the right thing?" I would ask myself, over and over. "I'm giving up all this money." Then I'd have this vision of getting arrested and somehow knew I had to get out. Cold turkey was the only way I could do it. And I have no regrets about breaking off with those people.

Focus on Your Nonfinancial Assets

The first time I came across the concept of "nonfinancial assets" was in Paul Hwoschinsky's book, *True Wealth*. That some nonfinancial aspects of our lives, such as health, education, creativity, self-esteem, beautiful surroundings, family, and community, can be *assets* every bit as valuable as any limited partnership or 401K struck me as a profound truth. Yet most of us discount this aspect of our wealth. We have been so blinded by the illusion that all that matters is money, that we no longer even *see* how rich we are. We think nothing else matters if we don't have the bucks. We deny our true wealth by disregarding it.

For the person trying to heal from the depleting futility of money hunger, learning to recognize true wealth when we see it and feel it is the cornerstone of recovery. Here's a partial list of nonfinancial assets, adapted and expanded from Hwoschinsky's, from which to ponder your own "portfolio":

- Education
- Health
- Intelligence
- Knowledge
- Sexual pleasure
- Relaxation
- Memories
- Time
- Adventure
- Intuition
- Discipline

- Children
- Community
- Personal growth
- Self-esteem
- Love
- Integrity
- Service
- Vitality
- Inner power
- Wisdom
- Hope

- Talents/Skills
- Creativity
- Spiritual faith
- Self-awareness
- Beautiful surroundings
- Supportive relationships
- Communication skills
- Commitment to oneself
- Gratifying work
- Safety

With this new way of looking at assets, the term *invest-ment* takes on new meaning. Money spent on effective psychotherapy can be a great investment, for instance, if it yields dividends in self-esteem. It's not just how many stocks we own that reflects how wise our investment strategy has been. And when we acknowledge our nonfinancial assets, their actual value increases, because now we can fully use and enjoy them instead of discounting them.

Nonfinancial assets are quite different from what we've been accustomed to thinking of as assets. For one thing, they're much more accessible. You don't have to be from a rich and powerful family to have the wealth of a beautiful garden outside your door, or to cultivate rich friendships, or to enjoy the freedom of self-acceptance. Some nonfinancial assets—like a strong spiritual connection, self-knowledge, creativity, wisdom, intuition—may even be *fostered* by coming through trials in life.

But the best thing about nonfinancial assets is that they are sustainable. We don't have to bulldoze rain forests, damage the ozone, or exploit anyone to become rich in relationships, community, and creativity. Just the opposite: the development of our nonfinancial assets actually *contributes* to others. The more we pursue nonfinancial assets, the greater our supply becomes, and the more we can benefit others. By contrast, the addictive pursuit of money inhibits the growth of our nonfinancial assets. It sends us into a "true wealth" recession.

In *Webster's* dictionary, one of the definitions given for the word *wealth* is "well-being," though a notation reminds the reader that this meaning is obsolete. Perhaps we need to revive this obsolete meaning and start using money as one resource with which to cultivate well-being rather than as a fetish to substitute for it. If we can learn to cultivate well-being first—with or without lots of money—and let material wealth grow out of that, we will be in a position to enjoy our money and be prospered by it.

Build Community

When you look back on your life someday, what do you think you will remember? The salary you made in 1990? The day you got the new microwave? The third car? The fourth TV? That special time at the mall? The project you stayed late to work on every night? As important as these can seem at the time, none is going to seem so important in retrospect.

What will probably matter most in hindsight are the relationships you've had: the memories, adventures, laughs, shared crises, mutual support. Stella, a sixty-five-year-old teacher, has not accumulated a lot of money but has cultivated very rich and satisfying relationships with her family and friends. She reflects with humor on the path she took: "Whatever happens to other people's fortunes, I will always have wonderful memories. Of course, if I get Alzheimer's, that would be the ultimate reversal of fortunes, because memories are what I've invested my whole life in."

Investing in relationships is a good move, even from the most utilitarian point of view. Strong relationships are more likely to provide comfort and assistance in infirmity and old age than all the insurance coverage you can work late to pay for. As the business consultant and author Michael Phillips has noted, there is liable to be a lot of social upheaval in the years ahead, and having strong relationships will be an important form of personal security.[11]

Stop Idealizing Material Wealth

Part of recovery is learning to look realistically at what acquiring more money and possessions can do for us—and what it can't. Acquiring surplus wealth means a reduction in some kinds of stress: less worry about bills, less doing without. But realistically, it also means an increase in other kinds of stress. Tune into the hardships of the relentless drive to acquire money and possessions: the long commutes, long work days, lost free time, stress illnesses, the burden of so many things to maintain, the astronomically high debt payments that in turn limit your options. And money, being a very potent substance, can be challenging to handle without self-destructing. Lewis Lapham studied fifty wealthy families and found that with few exceptions, "the lives of the heirs were marked by alcoholism, suicide, drug-addiction, insanity and despair."[12]

So money doesn't solve all problems; it only solves *some* money problems. This is not to make money wrong or bad. But don't assume that acquiring more of it necessarily equates with living happily ever after. Instead of striving to be rich, strive to cultivate *well-being*. Let the money flow out of that condition.

CHAPTER 12

IF YOU LOVE A MONEY ADDICT

I kept thinking that if I could just explain things to him more clearly, he would finally "get it" that we can't keep spending money. Sometimes I thought I was getting through, and then—the next day, he'd come home and tell me what he just bought on the Visa card.

TRACY, WIFE OF A COMPULSIVE SPENDER
AND DEBTOR

JUST AS THE PEOPLE who live and work with an alcoholic are inevitably affected by the alcoholism, so too the close friends and family of people who are compulsive with money often suffer some negative effects. It's hard to live with a compulsive debtor and not be affected by the unpaid bills, dunning phone calls, and enormous tension. And living with a compulsive earner who's out bingeing on deals every night is bound to evoke feelings of loss and resentment, as will any close involvement with a hoarder or an underearner. Life can get pretty unmanageable if you're involved with a money-compulsive person, and you may experience some of the following:

Fear that creditors will harass you, that you will go bankrupt, that he'll do something illegal and get arrested, that you/he will be ruined financially, that you/he will be embarrassed in the community, that there won't be enough, that your/his health will suffer from the stress.

Loss. The money-compulsive person's attention and energy may be increasingly focused on money—getting it, dealing with creditors, shopping. Money overshadows everything else, including your relationship. You may feel you don't count for much anymore.

Victimization. You may feel victimized and helpless, as if some role is being imposed on you that you hadn't bargained for. This feeling may be all too familiar, reminiscent of the role you've played with others in the past.

Feeling set up. The money addict's behavior may bring out responses in you that you don't like much. You may feel set up to be the critical parent, the nag, or the money police. When Tracy suggested to her compulsive spender husband that they not use their credit cards anymore, Art complained that she was being unreasonable. "Are you saying if the car breaks down, we can't fix it, we can't get to work?" he shouted indignantly. You may feel you've been set up to play this part, then criticized for it. Your relationship may be deteriorating as you and your friend or partner get stuck in these polarized roles.

Frustration. You've probably tried many approaches at "fixing" this person, among them being reasonable and logical, explaining things, pleading, arguing, ignoring the problem and hoping it will go away, playing detective, scheming, taking over, trying to figure it out, making excuses, trying to hold things together, covering up, and threatening. All this has been very draining, exhausting—and it hasn't worked. Once in a while, he promises to change, but it only lasts a short time.

Meanwhile, your life has been increasingly consumed by these efforts to cure him and protect yourself from the effects of his addiction. You keep thinking you can do it if you just try harder and find the right approach. But just as he is losing more and more control over money, you feel you're losing more and more control over him.

Confusion. His excuses for the spending, chronic debt, overwork, underearning, or chronic losses are so convincing that you get confused and think maybe it really *is* your problem, that you're just overreacting. Sometimes you see his money behavior as a plus: "He knows how to have a good time." Sometimes, you see it as a problem: "He's ruining our credit." Mostly, you're confused.

Enabling. When he asks you to cover up, make a phone call for him, lend him money, or otherwise bail him out, it's really hard for you to say no. To do so would seem cold and uncaring, and you can't bring yourself to do it. Besides, you don't want to see him go to jail, be humiliated, or have to declare bankruptcy. Each time you "help out," you tell yourself it's the last time. Until the next time.

Silenced. You feel obligated to keep the secret about his money problems, to help maintain the illusion that "everything's fine," because he's putting on a face for the outside world. You may also feel you can't complain because he spends money on *you,* or because everyone else thinks he's so terrific.

Wayne, whom we met in earlier chapters, grew up feeling responsible for his parents' financial problems. At his father's request, he would hide bills from his mother and run interference with creditors' phone calls. His father, a compulsive debtor and codependent, always promised to get it together, but he never did. Instead, he kept trying to provide the illusion of upper-class status to his wife.

As a teenager, Wayne was often asked to lend money to his father, which was never paid back. And he worried about the house being repossessed, about his father losing his small business, about his mother finding out about the bills, about his father's health, about his parents' financial burden someday falling to him.

Like many children of alcoholics, Wayne was "parenti-fied," made to take care of his parents—emotionally and otherwise—when he was still a child. Instead of worrying about drunk driving and cirrhosis of the liver, Wayne worried about bankruptcy and eviction. The secrecy surrounding the family's money problems created further feelings of shame and isolation. The toll all this took was considerable. Wayne himself became a compulsive spender and debtor and has already lost one marriage in part because of his own dysfunctional money pattern.

Forty-five-year-old Tracy has been married for seventeen years to Art, a compulsive spender and debtor. She's always been the "squirreler," she says, and he the "spender." Last month, Art was laid off from his job as a computer programmer, and she learned just how much of a spender he had been. She was shocked to find they have $45,000 in uncollateralized debt, when she thought the figure was about $7,000. How could she have been in the dark about such a critical issue? Tracy always let Art handle the couple's finances, despite his history of bankruptcies and his reckless spending, even though she, as an accounting instructor, is quite capable herself. She knew he was spending beyond their means, she says, but hadn't let herself think about how he was pulling it off.

Tracy herself is the child of parents who were chronically in debt and grew up feeling that she should be able to fix their problems. Because that never worked, she did what many of us do—she married somebody with the same problem her parents had and spent seventeen years hoping *he* would change.

Tracy admits she knew from the beginning that Art had a spending habit. She remembers on their first date, he left his car double-parked and ran into a corner store for a pack of cigarettes. "He came out five minutes later with $200 worth of stuff: pipes, gourmet foods. I said to myself, 'I think there's a problem here.'" But Tracy admits she didn't really want to see it. Her previous husband had been a gambler, and she didn't want Art to have money problems too, so she just blocked it from her mind. She told herself he was just fun-loving.

Shortly after marriage, when Art suggested that they pool their money, she went along with it, thinking maybe he would exercise more restraint with joint funds. But the bigger the pool got, the more he spent. The next year, when Art suggested that he take over paying the bills, she went along with that too—even though he'd been bankrupt once before, and despite her reservations about his spending. As time went on, she never reviewed bank statements, so she didn't realize he was driving the credit line up—in her name—to $20,000. "Every once in a while, he would say, 'Could you just write a check for $3,000 so I can pay off these other accounts?' What I didn't know was that after they got paid off, he ran them back *up* again. He got the statements. I never even looked at them."

Art, meanwhile, is the kind of guy everyone loves: he buys great presents, picks up the tab, volunteers everywhere. "He likes to be the nice guy," Tracy says, "the guy people adore." Friends who know them have no idea, she says, that they're in serious financial trouble. Art always acts as if he's rich. Meanwhile, he doesn't see himself as compulsive at all. "Who me?" Tracy says, imitating him, "I'm just generous!" Oddly enough, it was this very trait, Art's "generosity" that initially attracted Tracy to him. With her more tightfisted approach, she thought it would be a good balance. "His spending is the best part of him and the worst part of him," she says.

Early on in their marriage, Tracy picked up on the fact that "the way to Art's heart" was to go along with his buying sprees. Whenever she did, he acted affectionate toward her. When she complained about his purchases, he told her she was just "too tightfisted." She figured maybe he was right, that she was the one with the problem. Besides, she didn't feel she could complain about his spending because he

spent a lot on her and on her children from a previous marriage. Now and then, she would try to explain to him about
income and outgo, credit ratings, and things like that. "He
would seem like he was getting it, like we were having a
breakthrough. He'd promise not to charge anymore and to
pay off the debts. But then as soon as the toaster broke, he'd
be out putting a new one on the credit card. Everything was
an 'emergency' to him. He always had an excuse to spend
money."

To help support this marathon spending spree, Tracy
left her job in academia and took a demanding, high-pow-
ered corporate accounting job that she hated but that paid
very well. After several years of fast-paced working and living,
she was exhausted and wanted to quit but found it difficult
to get off the merry-go-round. "Once you've bought into
that lifestyle," she says, "everything depends on your big
salary—your big mortgage, your status car, your high-pow-
ered social life, the whole thing." Unable to extricate herself
from a lifestyle that was burning her out, Tracy did what lots
of people do at that point—she got sick. Having a chronic illness then gave her an excuse to slow down and insist they
move to the country and, in her words, "cash out." Tracy still
didn't specify that she wanted Art to stop spending so much,
but she admits this was her silent hope.

About a year ago, Tracy started seeing a therapist for
help with depression and codependent behavior. With growing confidence, she is starting to set limits on the behavior
she will accept in her marriage—and to stick to them. "It's
taken me fifteen years to be able to risk this," she says. "But
now I know I'm worthy of love. If he doesn't love me now
that I'm drawing the line, it will hurt, but I will survive and I
will go on. Not so much is riding on whether he approves of
me now; I am freer to say what I really feel." Art, for his part,
is making a concerted effort to change his pattern. For now,
he's stopped charging and hasn't bought any big-ticket items
for a while.

But this is not the first time Art has pledged to stop creating new debt. Once, last year, he tried to get a handle on it. He drew up a detailed budget on the computer, and that was the end of it. "Obviously it didn't work," says Tracy. "He continued to spend. He always thought he was going to get ahead, 'a couple of months from now.' Then at the end of last year, some emergency home repairs cost us over $1,000—and that set off a downward spiral; he started really spending. The worse things are, the more he spends. I guess that's because he feels hopeless or something, and that makes him spend even more."

COPING SUGGESTIONS

Dealing with a money addict really is like dealing with any other kind of compulsive person. The same principles apply.[1]

DON'T:

Belittle. Piling on the shame has never helped any addict to recover, and it does nothing for you either.

Police. Don't search for, hide, or throw out charge cards, gambling paraphernalia, or any other things related to his money behavior.

Rescue. Addicts seek help and change only when the pain of their present pattern becomes more than they can bear. Therefore don't cover up for him anymore, make excuses, bail him out, cosign loans, pay his bills, or lend him money.

Use guilt. Guilt doesn't work on compulsive people. "If you really loved me, you'd stop (borrowing, withholding, shopping, underearning)" only adds to the person's guilt and shame, driving him further into secrecy and fueling the cycle of self-destructive behavior.

Anticipate problems or dwell on the past. Either course drains energy from dealing effectively with the challenges of today.

DO:

Take steps to protect yourself, to minimize the effect his self-destructive money pattern has on your own finances. This can mean asking for a "financial separation," establishing separate accounts, splitting responsibility for joint bills, and so on.

For ten years, Barbara's husband, Allan, drifted from one low-paying job to the next while Barbara paid the bulk of the family's expenses. As Barbara grew more and more exhausted, stressed-out, depressed, and resentful, she was forced to seek help for herself. A therapist suggested Debtors Anonymous, because she obviously had her own money issues. With help from that group, Barbara was able to ask Allan for a "financial separation," precipitating a temporary crisis in their marriage. But much to Barbara's surprise, setting this firm limit also prompted Allan to seriously pursue income for the first time in his life.

Give up on fixing him. The most crucial step in your own healing will be accepting the fact that you are—as they say in Al-Anon—*powerless* over the addict. You cannot fix him, reform him, or change him. That is *not* something within your power to do. Continuing to try makes you a codependent. He's overfocused on money, but you're overfocused on *him.*

To give up on fixing him doesn't mean you stop caring. To "detach with love," as the recovery slogan goes, is not selfish; it is real giving. It is giving the addict what he needs most: the chance to be responsible for *himself.* Only when he accepts responsibility for himself can he possibly recover. He's probably going to have to experience the negative consequences of what he's doing before he gets motivated to seek any kind of help, so the kindest thing you can do is stop blocking the path.

If you are a codependent, detaching from an addict is not easy. When you stop focusing on him, you'll have to feel your own feelings and face your own problems—something you may have been avoiding. It may help to read the chapter on money codependency for further support.

Learn about addictive disorders. Consult a professional, read, go to self-help groups, whatever you prefer, but *learn* about addictive disorders and recovery. This will help eliminate some of your confusion about why he doesn't just stop.

Set limits, and be consistent in enforcing them. *You* decide how you will live and what your boundaries will be. "I will not lend or give you money" is an appropriate limit to set with a compulsive debtor. "I will not live with you after January if you are not carrying your own weight financially" may be a reasonable limit to set with a compulsive underearner.

Of course, setting limits means you have to be willing to risk angering or even losing the other person. And you will have to give up being *needed* as your main role in the relationship. If you're actively codependent, these can be major stumbling blocks, in which case you'll probably need to do some work on yourself through therapy or self-help groups before you can take this step.

Tracy, for instance, told Art that she is not willing to incur any more debt in her name. She recognizes she cannot control whether he opens a new credit line or charge account in *his* name, but she is not willing to have any new debts incurred in her name, nor to have any of her income go to pay off such debts. "It's taken me fifteen years to be able to say this," says Tracy. "It wasn't until I made progress with my own self-esteem that I could say 'No, this is not OK. I'm not going to live like this anymore.' But now I know I'm worthy of love. If he doesn't choose to love me as I am, with these boundaries, it will hurt, but I will survive and I will go on."

Get support. Don't remain isolated in your concern about the money problems or in your focus on the addict. Debt-Anon, a self-help group specifically for those affected by someone else's money pattern, is available in some cities through Debtors Anonymous. CoDA (Codependents Anonymous), a Twelve-Step self-help group for codependents, may also be helpful, and these meetings are increasingly available.

Focus on your own life. Learn to put the bulk of your attention and energy back into your own life. Rather than focus on what's going to happen to your partner's finances and future, focus on creating a satisfying life of your own, one that includes recreation, hobbies, and just plain fun. You're the only person you can change, so you might as well put your efforts there.

People who choose to have active addicts in their lives often are (unconsciously) afraid to face their own issues and feelings. Focusing on the problems caused by the compulsive behavior provides a distraction. In recovery, focusing on what *you* want can stir up anxiety. At these times, you may be especially vulnerable to relapse, to falling back into your old roles as worrier, rescuer, and money police. Doris, the wife of a compulsive spender and debtor, explains: "As long as I could focus on *his* spending, *his* debts, and him in general, I didn't have to feel my own feelings. His obsession became my distraction."

As you start to focus more on your own life, your money-dysfunctional friend may do something to try and hook you again. He won't like it that you're withdrawing your attention from him and may unconsciously try to reengage you in his problems. Be vigilant and try not to fall into this trap. If you do, extricate yourself as soon as you realize it. Don't give yourself a hard time; just get back to your new perspective, and detach again.

Remember that you are not to blame for the other person's problems or compulsive behavior. You didn't cause it, you can't control it, and you can't cure it. Assuming responsibility for someone else's problem takes away *his* right to be responsible for it and enables the dysfunctional pattern to continue. The truth is, his behavior is *not* under your control. Only your behavior is.

Speak your truth. Tell the person how his behavior is affecting you, if it is. Do this in a supportive way, and not in haste or in the heat of crisis and tension. Remember, the purpose of speaking your truth is not to try and change him but simply to affirm *for yourself* that you are not willing to live in fantasy or denial anymore. Such realistic feedback is also the kindest thing you can do for him.

When you express yourself, however, don't expect him to see it your way. Just state it, and then let go of whether he gets it or not. This is *your* truth we're talking about here, not his.

Forgive yourself. Even if you have made some mistakes in the past in how you dealt with this money issue, it doesn't mean you are dumb or bad. It just means you didn't have the knowledge and/or self-esteem to handle it differently. Have compassion for yourself.

If the Money-Compulsive Person Enters Recovery

Some final notes for the person whose loved one does enter a self-help group, therapy, or other healing approach:

Don't expect an instant cure. Recovery from money disorders, as from all addictions, is a process, not an event. There may be many ups and downs over the course of years.

Don't try to control his recovery, pry into counseling sessions, or call his sponsor.

Do offer your support and love if you can genuinely do so, acknowledging progress.

Don't expect it to solve all the problems in the relationship. If you've been intimately involved with a person with a compulsive money problem, you may be under the illusion that once this is addressed, the two of you will ride off into a glorious sunset—never to fight again. In fact, some other issues—which have until now been ignored or played out through the money issue—may surface. Look at recovery as an opportunity to address some *new* issues in the relationship, rather than expecting to be the perfect couple or the perfect family. The good news is that though you may not live happily ever after, you will, with recovery, gain the opportunity to deepen and enrich both your own life and your relationship.

CHAPTER **13**

MAKING PEACE WITH MONEY

He who knows he has enough is rich.

LAO-TZU
TAO-TE CHING

THIS IS AN EXCITING—if challenging—time to be alive.
The recession of the 1990s, bone-aching weariness from
overwork, and a growing awareness of consumerism's heavy
toll on us are all helping to break through our collective denial about money dysfunction. There is a growing awareness
that the way we've been managing our resources—individu-
ally and collectively—is leading us not toward enrichment
but impoverishment, even for the materially well off. As we
reassess our priorities and develop healthier attitudes, we
move toward what I call Right Use of Money.

What *is* Right Use of Money, or "healthy money"? How
does one achieve it? First of all, it doesn't have anything to
do with actual dollar amounts. You can have few resources
but utilize them in healthy ways and feel prosperous, just as
you can have plenty of money and still be dysfunctional with
it. What matters is not how much you have, but how you use
it, and how you experience it.

Of course, none of us can become *perfectly* healthy with
money, because recovery is an ongoing process, but we can

head in the right general direction. Some guidelines for recovery have been introduced in the preceding chapters. Basically, the healthier and sounder you become in managing your resources, the more likely you will be to do the following:

- Use money as a *means* to a life well lived.
- Communicate clearly about money matters.
- Take assertive action on your own behalf when necessary.
- Ask for what you want.
- Save without hoarding, and out of self-care rather than fear.
- Spend in ways that enhance your life, without undue anxiety, fear, or guilt.
- Accept realistic limits on spending; spend less than you bring in.
- Eliminate expenses that do not serve your true interests.
- Avoid unwise debt obligations.
- Play fair in matters of money; practice integrity in all your affairs.
- Expect just compensation for your work.
- Reject work that requires the sacrifice of your health, relationships, or peace of mind.
- Acknowledge the "shadow side" of your money habits, without self-rejection.
- Accept without crippling envy that some people have more than you do.
- Accept without crippling guilt that you have more than some people.
- Share resources with others, passing the gifts along.
- Maintain clear boundaries, warding off exploitative demands on your resources.
- Experience "enough."
- Express gratitude.

SOME CLOSING THOUGHTS ON MONEY RECOVERY

Give Up

To recover from any compulsive behavior, it is necessary to go beyond admitting intellectually that there's a problem to accepting it on a deep emotional level. In this case it means accepting that (1) I have a compulsive pattern with money, (2) this pattern has had negative consequences for me, and (3) I am powerless to change the pattern using willpower alone. Out of this admission comes the openness required to begin recovery.

Admitting powerlessness is a psychic hurdle for every compulsive or addicted person. You've been using a substance (in this case, money) in order to feel more powerful, in control, and secure, and now you're supposed to admit that you're powerless? To give up hope of controlling your pattern runs counter to your way of operating in the world. You're used to trying to control *everything!* Not being in control feels humiliating.

But there is a paradox in addiction recovery. Each of us *does* have a lot of power, but only if we first acknowledge our limitations, become receptive, and ask for help. That's where the power lies. Admitting I am not in control of my behavior gives me access to the power I *do* have. It's the power that comes from *telling the truth and facing reality.* Pouring attention and energy into maintaining an illusion of control saps your power. The minute you say, "I have a problem that I can't handle myself," you reclaim your power.

To take this first step, you must let go of the addiction-generating belief that you *should* be perfect and all-powerful. When the compulsive person finally understands that to be limited is not shameful but human, her humiliation can be transformed into humility. "I am just like everybody else. I am human, I have limitations." Honesty and humility are two important antidotes to addiction. By humbly and honestly admitting powerlessness over your addiction, you tap into your true power.[1]

Throw Away Those IOUs

Because so many of our compulsive money patterns have to do with old baggage, with past emotional debts we're still carrying on our psychic books, it's important to come to terms now with those unresolved issues in order to move on. However valid our feelings of not having gotten enough—attention, love, guidance, money, whatever it was—by continuing to feel that other people still owe us something, we keep ourselves stuck. We either stay broke to prove how deprived we were, or conversely, we try to prove how worthy we really are by amassing possessions. In either case, it's as though we're standing around waving our IOUs, waiting to collect, while life passes us by.

Think about it: if a business put all its resources into collecting past-due accounts and nothing into production and development, it would eventually fail to thrive. That's what a lot of us have done. We've been so fixed on collecting old IOUs from our parents, siblings, ex-spouses, and children that we've failed to do the work necessary to create new "income" in the form of true prosperity. By not letting go of past emotional debts, we perpetuate a sort of psychic impoverishment. We're stuck in the role of creditor.

If you have experienced past injustice, it's important to feel it, grieve it—and then *write it off as a loss*. You have to give up the idea of proving anything to "them," getting anything from them, outdoing them, or making sure you *don't* outdo them. There's plenty of hope for getting what you want today but only if you stop focusing on yesterday. Undertake whatever psychotherapeutic work you have to do to leave the past behind.

Go Forward into the Fear

Of course, you may be reluctant to give up your IOUs, because as long as you stay focused on collecting, you never have to actually *feel the feelings*. Once you let go of your creditor stance, you have to actually experience and work through any past issues of deprivation and disappointment. And once you've written off past debts, there is nothing holding you back anymore. You have to move into the present and take responsibility for getting your needs met today. You have to change.

When you do start to take the actions to change your money pattern, you may also come up against a barrage of old fears about what you can and cannot do. "Forget it, *you* can't manage money, you're a spendthrift!" "Don't spend that money, you'll end up a bag lady!" "You can't prosper like this; they'll all hate you." "Forget relaxing, man, you're supposed to be the provider." "You can't refuse to lend him money; why else would he like you?" Going forward into your fear is probably the most difficult aspect of money recovery.

Doing something foreign to your pattern—whether it's earning more, not borrowing, spending less—will feel strange and awkward at first. Deborah, a recovering deprivation addict, took a course in investing, something that always seemed entirely out of her realm. She didn't have anything to invest yet but wanted to shift her identity from being someone who "doesn't know about these things" to someone who is informed and makes choices. Taking that course activated all her old beliefs about herself:

> The minute I walked in there, I started to sweat. I felt like a fraud. The old tapes were running: "Who are *you* to talk about stocks and bonds? Who are you kidding? You're out of your league, sweetheart." Over the next three hours, I kept spacing out. But each

time, I would bring myself back and pay attention for a while. Then I'd mentally slip away again. Still, when the course was over, I felt great—just for having faced my fear and survived it. It's like holding a yoga position. You have to stretch and hold, stretch and hold.

Be There for Yourself

Learn to trust yourself. By this, I don't mean trust the compulsive urge to run up your credit card, or your workaholic thoughts about canceling your vacation. That would be trusting your dis-ease. I mean trust your *true* self, your higher self, your heart's desires. Trust your feelings and what they are telling you, rather than suppressing and denying them.

If you develop a sense that you can depend on and trust yourself, you won't be so vulnerable to the illusions of security that appear to be available through money, food, drugs, or other people. You will develop a sense of *personal potency* that is another antidote to addictive tendencies. Personal potency is not about power over others or *will*power. Personal potency is having a sense of confidence (from the Latin *confidere,* "with trust") in yourself and a spiritual source. Anita, the young woman who has struggled with addiction to deprivation, talks about the self-trust she's developing and how it's aiding her recovery:

In the past, I saw the world as a very hostile place against which I couldn't defend myself. I felt I needed to withdraw and isolate in order to protect myself. For me, that meant not doing anything, not having anything.

Now I'm learning that I can participate fully in life as long as I'm committed to being there for myself. The key is trusting my feelings, allowing them to just be. Because if I don't listen to them, then I don't know when something is hurting me, so I'm really endangering myself. Not listening to your own feelings is like being anesthetized. You can touch a hot stove and not know it's burning and not know to take your hand away.

But learning to trust my feelings is going to be a long process, I think. It's not a one-shot event. I've successfully masked my feelings for so long that it's going to take a while for me to thaw out. But that's OK. It'll take as long as it takes.

Make Amends

Eventually, make amends to those people—including yourself—that you hurt or harmed with your compulsive use of money. This suggestion borrows from the eighth and ninth Steps in Alcoholics Anonymous: "Made a list of all persons we had harmed, and became willing to make amends to them all," and "Made direct amends to such people wherever possible, except when to do so would injure them or others."[2]

When Deborah was in her twenties, she took a kickback, an illegal payoff, for helping someone collect more money than he was entitled to from a city agency. As she progressed in her money recovery, she wanted to "get right with the universe" by making amends to those she had harmed. She sent a money order for that amount to the agency with an anonymous note. "I didn't use my real name," she says, "because I didn't want to harm myself. I just wanted to return the funds." After that, Deborah saved up enough to send another anonymous money order to the department store where she used to shoplift. Deborah has also begun making amends to herself, by taking better care in all aspects of her life.

Declare Money Innocent

As we've seen in our examination of various money disorders, many people with money dysfunction hold a polarized view of money. We either have contempt for money, or we worship it. It's easy to see how we came to view money in such black-and-white terms. The New Testament of the Bible contains numerous references to money, most of which present earthly affluence in a polarized framework, for example, "Ye cannot serve God and mammon" (Matthew 6:24), and "It is easier for a camel to go through the eye of a needle than for a rich man to enter the kingdom of God" (Mark 10:25). It seems either-or: either you serve God, work hard, and forgo material pleasures, or you will have hell to pay.

But perhaps it is time to declare money innocent. As many of us are realizing, our responsibility as both spiritual and material beings is neither to worship *nor* to reject wealth but to use it in ways that bring both aspects of our being together. Without a rich spiritual life, we can never truly possess and enjoy our material riches. And without manifesting our spirit in the outer world (in part through Right Use of Money), our spiritual values can never be made manifest.

Money in and of itself is neutral. The source of money addiction does not lie with money itself but with us, in our perversion of money's role in our lives, in our attempt to use it as a substitute for self-acceptance, community, and inner power. It has been my observation that the more alienated we are from ourselves, from our own power and from a sense of community, the more vulnerable we are to addictions of all kinds. Conversely, the more conscious and tolerant we become of our true selves, and the more authentic connection we feel to others, the more resistant we grow to the compulsive use of money or anything else.

Money, in itself, is neither evil nor a magic potion. If we try to use it for what it cannot deliver—to substitute for self-esteem, win love, protect us from abandonment, and so on—we are bound to be losers. But when we stop using money as a mood-changer and deal with the underlying issues in our lives, heal the addictive dis-ease within that makes us grasp outside of ourselves for something (anything) to make us feel better, *then* we are free to enjoy money for what it is—a facilitator of dreams, not a substitute for them.

Become a Trustee

Because *having* is the basis upon which people are judged in our culture, we tend to think that whatever comes to us is *our* possession. In recovery, it is helpful to think of what comes our way as a gift from the universe, for which we then become the trustee. As Sri Aurobindo, an Indian yogi, wrote, "All wealth belongs to the Divine and those who hold it are trustees, not possessors. It is with them today, tomorrow it may be elsewhere."[3] Thinking of myself as a trustee helps me bring that much more care and respect to my money tasks.

For advice on money, I am learning to turn to people with relevant, demonstrated expertise. Too often those of us who are dysfunctional with money take advice from anyone who offers it to us—a neighbor, a buddy, a relative—without regard for how wisely that person handles his *own* financial affairs. Or, we do the opposite and are overimpressed with someone just *because* she's a broker, lawyer, banker, or accountant. In money recovery, it's important not to turn over all responsibility for your money management to anyone else. That would be like a recovering alcoholic making it someone else's job to keep him out of bars. Use your consultations with advisers as opportunities to learn, but remember that *you* are still responsible for your resources.

Know That You Have Enough

Kelly decided at the age of twenty-five that she wanted to make a million dollars and set out to do that. She told herself that once she made that million, she could pursue her creative interest in writing, settle into a committed relationship, move to the country, and kick back and relax. So for the next twenty years, she worked at an entrepreneurial job that she didn't enjoy. She worked some twelve hours a day and many weekends. She rarely did any writing and pushed relationships away because they interfered too much with making money. Week after week, month after month went by. Before she knew it, Kelly was middle-aged, living in a nice Park Avenue co-op in Manhattan, but lacking much fulfillment in her life. She was amassing money, but little wealth. The mid-1990s find her reevaluating her priorities:

> I'm starting to realize that I can't wait until I have a certain dollar amount in the bank before I do the things I want to do. That's old thinking. It's a fallacy to think that if I make lots of money I'll have more time to enjoy life. I have to create an enjoyable life today. And amassing money isn't going to do that. If anything, it interferes with it. All those things I thought money would give me—creativity, time, relaxation, leisure—I have to give myself—now.

Because a sense of deprivation, emotional and spiritual, is at the core of most money disorders, it's imperative to consciously build gratification into our lives as part of recovery. Money is just a convenience. It can help us get where we want to go, but it can't provide the gratification. I can pay for an elaborate all-day beauty treatment and still not feel beautiful; I can buy an adventure vacation and not experience a moment's adventure; I can pay for courses in spiritual development or inner joy—and achieve neither. More money is not the key to enrichment, any more than more sex is the key to sexual fulfillment or more church attendance is the ticket to spiritual enlightenment.

As Lao-tzu wrote, "He who knows he has enough is rich."[4] It's the *knowing* that is key. If you have enough but don't *know* it, you're not rich. It's as simple as that. We have enough when we know we do. This doesn't mean that you should never take steps to increase your income, make sound investments, or otherwise enhance your access to resources. It simply means that an inner state of satisfaction can exist independent of outer conditions. Prosperity, it turns out, is not a dollar amount to be arrived at but a state of mind and an approach to resources that can be cultivated.

Most of us reading this book are, objectively speaking, wealthy compared to the rest of the world. Another aspect of money recovery is to begin to see ourselves in a larger, even global, context. Knowing that I'm one of just 8 percent of people in the world who own a car can help me not feel deprived if *my* car happens to be an older, "no frills" model.[5] With this broader perspective, perhaps I won't be compelled to take an extra job—sacrificing some of my daily enjoyment of life, some of my true wealth—just to get a newer, flashier model.

This work of becoming conscious of how we use money and other resources, of learning to join the spiritual and the material worlds, to live with ambiguity instead of insisting on clear answers, is probably the greatest challenge of our lifetimes. As E. F. Schumacher wrote in *Small Is Beautiful,*

> The true problems of living—in politics, economics, education, marriage, etc.—are always problems of overcoming or reconciling opposites. They are divergent problems and have no solution in the ordinary sense of the word. They demand of man not merely the employment of his reasoning powers but the commitment of his whole personality.[6]

Welcome to long-term money recovery. It's not a quick fix but a continuing process of transformation and discovery.

And Let It Circulate

We would also do well in money recovery to learn to circulate our own wealth more, to support the work being done to improve our communities and the planet, to manifest our spiritual values in the material world. When we share with others, we tacitly affirm our own abundance and acknowledge our interdependence on everyone else. We acknowledge that we are connected to an inexhaustible (divine) supply and affirm that we don't have to cling in fear to that which passes through our hands. By being in the flow, giving and receiving like the intake and outflow of breath, we help forge a sense of community. By giving, I affirm that my well-being depends on your well-being, that as you prosper, so do I. This is so different from the way many of us are used to thinking: "If you prosper, there will be less for me; therefore, I am against you, in competition with you, and must guard my supply from you."

What's needed if we are to recover from collective money dysfunction is perhaps a less patriarchal approach to money. By that I mean less emphasis on hierarchal comparisons, competition, and linear, concrete measures of wealth and more emphasis on its less definable, more subjective aspects; less use of wealth to compete against and beat each other and more frequent use of resources in ways that nurture ourselves, our families, and our communities; more circulation of wealth and less stockpiling of it.

As noted earlier, some so-called primitive cultures pass wealth around in a circular fashion. With this model, if I come into possession of some form of wealth—cattle, a decorative bracelet—I keep it for a while, derive the benefit, then pass it (or something equivalent) along to someone else. The wealth is always moving, circulating like blood or breath. In this model, no one loses wealth when they give it away, because they are still in the circle and will receive more wealth as it circulates. One of the greatest challenges of our time is to foster this awareness of our interdependency and to build community—without sacrificing individual choice and personal boundaries. Again, it comes down to being able to live with a sense of paradox.

If there is a silver lining in the financial and ecological crisis in which we find ourselves as we approach the twenty-first century, it is this: as more and more of us reject a polar-ized, old-world view of money and other resources, we create a healthier, richer society. As more of us begin to nourish and truly *experience* the true wealth in our lives, we enrich not only ourselves, but those around us. Money recovery can be a revolution in the way we value ourselves, and each other. With this new perspective, money is no longer a drug we use to substitute for living but just one of the resources we use to cultivate true wealth.

NOTES

Chapter 1: Money Madness

1. Anita Jones-Lee, *Women and Money* (Hauppauge, NY: Barron's, 1991), p. 30; Lawrence Malkin, *The National Debt* (New York: Holt, 1987), p. 49; Philip Mattera, *Prosperity Lost* (New York: Addison-Wesley, 1990), p. 21; Jason DeParle, "Poor Find Going Broke Is Too Costly," *New York Times,* December 11, 1991; Lewis Lapham, *Money and Class in America* (New York: Weidenfeld & Nicolson, 1988), p. 61; Tony Hom and Edward Claflin, *Smart, Successful and Broke* (New York: Dell, 1991), p. 5.
2. Lapham, *Money and Class in America,* p. 38; Albert Ellis and Patricia Hunter, *Why Am I Always Broke?* (Secaucus, NJ: Carol Publishing Group, 1991), p. 11.
3. Jacob Needleman, *Money and the Meaning of Life* (New York: Doubleday, 1992), p. 41.
4. James B. Stewart, *Den of Thieves* (New York: Simon & Schuster, 1991), p. 208.
5. Aristotle, *Politics,* in *The Works of Aristotle,* translated into English under the editorship of W. D. Ross, vol. 10 (Oxford: Clarendon Press, 1921), book II, 7, 1267a.
6. Russell A. Lockhart, "Coins and Psychological Change," an essay in the anthology *Soul and Money* (Dallas, TX: Spring Publications, 1982), p. 21.
7. Jonathan Freedman, *Happy People* (New York: Harcourt Brace Jovanovich, 1978), p. 136.
8. Paul Wachtel, *The Poverty of Affluence* (Philadelphia: New Society Publishers, 1989), p. 2.

Chapter 2: Money as a Mirror

1. James Hillman, "A Contribution to Soul and Money," in *Soul and Money,* p. 39.
2. Adolf Guggenbuhl-Craig, "Projections: Soul and Money," in *Soul and Money,* p. 84.

3. Lockhart, "Coins and Psychological Change," in *Soul and Money*, pp. 18–19; Jones-Lee, *Women and Money*, p. xiii.

4. Thomas Buckley, "The One Who Flies All Around the World," in *Parabola*, Spring 1991, p. 9; Joe Cribb, *Money* (New York: Alfred A. Knopf, 1990), pp. 24–25; William H. Desmonde, *Magic, Myth and Money* (New York: Free Press of Glencoe, 1962), pp. 38, 121–27; William H. Desmonde, "The Origin of Money in the Animal Sacrifice," an essay in Ernest Borneman's anthology *The Psychoanalysis of Money*, pp. 121–23.

5. Otto Fenichel, "The Drive to Amass Wealth," in Hanna Fenichel and David Rapaport, eds., *The Collected Papers of Otto Fenichel* (New York: W. W. Norton, 1953), p. 96.

6. Elements of this anecdotal composite originally appeared in Arnold Washton and Donna Boundy's *Willpower's Not Enough* (New York: HarperCollins, 1989), pp. 36, 65.

7. Herb Goldberg and Robert Lewis, *Money Madness* (New York: William Morrow, 1978), pp. 52, 78; Melanie Klein, *Envy and Gratitude* (London: Hogarth Press, 1975), pp. 64, 179.

8. Goldberg and Lewis, *Money Madness*, p. 91; Fenichel, "Drive to Amass Wealth," pp. 95–96.

9. Desmonde, *Magic, Myth and Money*, pp. vii, 20–21, 110; Desmonde, "Origin of Money," p. 124.

10. Desmonde, *Magic, Myth and Money*, pp. 15, 110, 127; Max Shapiro, *The Penniless Billionaires* (New York: Times Books, 1980), pp. 7–9; Desmonde, "Origin of Money," p. 124.

11. Ken Wells and Tony Horwitz, "Drowning Man," *Wall Street Journal*, December 19, 1991.

12. Lapham, *Money and Class in America*, p. 185.

13. "Male Potency and the Dow Jones Average," *New York*, October 20, 1975, pp. 10–12.

14. Donald Trump, *Surviving at the Top* (New York: Random House, 1990), pp. 31–32.

15. Lapham, *Money and Class in America*, p. 47.

16. Philip Slater, *Wealth Addiction* (New York: E. P. Dutton, 1980), p. 14.

17. Hillman, "Contribution to Soul and Money," p. 41.

18. Donald Trump, *The Art of the Deal* (New York: Random House, 1987), p. 49.

19. Lapham, *Money and Class in America*, pp. 112–13.

20. Joseph Kulin, "Your Money or Your Life," *Parabola*, Spring 1991.

21. David Carpenter, "Money" entry in Mircea Eliade, *The Encyclopedia of Religion* (New York: Macmillan, 1987), vol. 10, p. 52.

22. Goldberg and Lewis, *Money Madness*, pp. 48–50.

23. Desmonde, *Magic, Myth and Money*, p. 125.

24. W. H. Auden, quoted in Lapham, *Money and Class in America*, p. 215.

Chapter 3: Can Money Really Be an Addiction?

1. Slater, *Wealth Addiction*, p. 185.
2. Terence T. Gorski, *Denial Patterns* (Harvey, IL: Ingalls Memorial Hospital, 1976), pp. 5–6.
3. Teri Agins and Jeffrey A. Trachtenberg, "Designer Troubles," *Wall Street Journal*, November 22, 1991.
4. Bill Powell and Peter McKillop, "Citizen Trump," *Newsweek*, September 28, 1987, p. 53.
5. Dennis Levine, *Inside Out* (New York: Putnam, 1991), p. 18.
6. Adam Smith, *The Roaring '80s* (New York: Penguin, 1988), p. 213.
7. J. Paul Getty, in Slater, *Wealth Addiction*, p. 71.
8. Kurt Eichenwald, "Drexel Suit to Recover Bonus Pay," *New York Times*, February 12, 1992.
9. Ronald Sullivan, "Lawyer Convicted of Theft from Clients," *New York Times*, December 10, 1991.
10. Larry Martz, *Ministry of Greed* (New York: Newsweek, 1988), p. 63.
11. William Glaberson, "Helmsley Gets 4-Year Term for Tax Fraud," *New York Times*, December 13, 1989.
12. Elements of this anecdotal composite originally appeared in Arnold Washton and Donna Boundy, *Willpower's Not Enough* (New York: HarperCollins, 1989), p. 39.
13. Editorial "Come Clean on the House Bank," *New York Times*, March 11, 1992.
14. Todd S. Purdum, "Dinkins Denounces Ex-Treasurer as Inquiries on Campaign Widen," *New York Times*, February 15, 1992.
15. Stewart, *Den of Thieves*, p. 429.
16. Jerrold Mundis, *How to Get Out of Debt, Stay Out of Debt and Live Prosperously* (New York: Bantam, 1988), p. 79.
17. Ken Wells and Tony Horwitz, "Drowning Man," *Wall Street Journal*, December 19, 1991.

Chapter 4: A Money-Addicted Culture

1. Juliet Schor (New York: Basic Books, 1991), pp. 3, 107; David E. Rosenbaum, "The Paralysis of No-Pain Politics," *New York Times*, April 19, 1992; Hom and Claflin, *Smart, Successful and Broke*, pp. 4–5; Hendrik Hertzberg, "The Short Happy Life of the American Yuppie," in Nicolaus Mills, ed., *Culture in an Age of Money* (Chicago: Elephant, 1990), p. 77; Michael Crichton, op-ed piece, *New York Times*, August 10, 1992; Malkin, *The National Debt*, p. 49; Alan Durn-

ing, "Asking How Much Is Enough," *State of the World 1991* (New York: Norton, 1991), p. 154.

2. Schor, *Overworked American*, p. 115.
3. Wachtel, *Poverty of Affluence*, p. 17.
4. Schor, *Overworked American*, p. 3; *World Development Report* (Washington, DC: World Bank); Phillips, *Politics of Rich and Poor*, p. 163; "Harper's Index," *Harper's*, February 1992, p. 11.
5. *Ladies' Home Journal*, December 1988, p. 55.
6. Alan Durning, "Asking How Much Is Enough?" *State of the World*, p. 163.
7. Slater, *Wealth Addiction*, p. 3.
8. Laurence Shames, *Hunger for More* (New York: Times Books, 1989), p. 173.
9. E. F. Schumacher, *Small Is Beautiful* (New York: Viking Penguin, 1973), p. 50.
10. Schumacher, *Small Is Beautiful*, p. 26; Eknath Easwaran, "The Lesson of the Hummingbird," *In Context*, Summer 1990, p. 30.
11. Kevin Phillips, *Politics of Rich and Poor*, p. 7.
12. John Kenneth Galbraith: *Money: Whence It Came, Where It Went* (Boston: Houghton Mifflin, 1975), pp. 283–84.
13. Malkin, *National Debt*, p. 15.
14. Alfred L. Malabre, Jr., *Beyond Our Means* (New York: Random House, 1987), p. 33; Malkin, *National Debt*, pp. 15–16; Smith, *Roaring 80's*, p. 17.
15. Malkin, *National Debt*, p. 5; Alfred L. Malabre, *Within Our Means* (New York: Random House, 1991), pp. 3–4.
16. Malabre, *Beyond Our Means*, pp. 38–39.
17. Malabre, *Within Our Means*, p. 7.
18. Michael Phillips and Salli Rasberry, *The Seven Laws of Money* (Menlo Park, CA: Word Wheel and Random House, 1974), p. 77; Goldberg and Lewis, *Money Madness*, p. 13.
19. Sylvia Nasar, "Fed Gives New Evidence of 80's Gains by Richest," *New York Times*, April 21, 1992; Sylvia Nasar, "However You Slice the Data, the Richest Did Get Richer," *New York Times*, May 11, 1992; Sylvia Nasar, "Those Born Wealthy or Poor Usually Stay So, Studies Say," May 18, 1992; Sylvia Nasar, "Even Among the Well-Off, the Richest Get Richer," *New York Times*, March 5, 1992; Smith, *Roaring 80's*, p. 16; Jason DeParle, "Fueled by Social Trends, Welfare Cases Are Rising," *New York Times*, January 10, 1992; Susan Dentzer, "The Maypo Culture," *Business Month*, November 1989, p. 32.
20. Phillips, *Politics of Rich and Poor*, pp. 80–83; Vance Packard, *The Ultra Rich* (Boston: Little, Brown, 1989), pp. 11–12.
21. Schor, *Overworked American*, pp. 29–31; Schor, "The Overworked American," *New Age*, November/December 1991, p. 35.

22. Jason DeParle, "Young Families Poorer, Study Finds," *New York Times,* April 15, 1992; Kevin Phillips, *Politics of Rich and Poor,* p. 202.

23. Smith, *Roaring 80's,* p. 201.

24. Malkin, *National Debt,* pp. 54–55.

25. Malabre, *Within Our Means,* p. 61; Richard W. Stevenson, "Suit Seeks to Recoup Losses from Executive Life Failure," *New York Times,* February 28, 1992.

26. Smith, *Roaring 80's,* p. 271.

27. John Rothchild, *Going for Broke* (New York: Simon & Schuster, 1991), pp. 13–14.

28. Robert B. Reich, "A Culture of Paper Tigers," in Mills, ed., *Culture in an Age of Money,* p. 98.

29. Sylvia Nasar, "Even Among the Well-Off"; Steve Lohr, "Amid Layoffs and the Recession, Executives Pay Is Under Scrutiny," *New York Times,* January 10, 1992; Malabre, *Within Our Means,* p. 44.

30. Roger Cohen, "Steve Ross Defends His Paycheck," *New York Times Magazine,* March 22, 1992, p. 30.

31. Lapham, *Money and Class in America,* pp. 87–88.

32. Shames, *Hunger for More,* p. 195.

33. "Harper's Index," *Harper's,* July 1991, p. 9.

34. Charles W. McMillion, "Facing the Economy's Grim Reality," *New York Times,* February 23, 1992.

35. Thomas Moore, *Care of the Soul* (New York: HarperCollins, 1992), p. 195.

Chapter 5: The Family Inheritance

1. Victoria Felton-Collins with Suzanne Blair Brown, *Couples and Money* (New York: Bantam, 1990), inside jacket copy.

2. Philip Blumstein and Pepper Schwartz, *American Couples: Money, Work, Sex* (New York: William Morrow, 1983), p. 67.

3. Trump, *Art of the Deal,* pp. 45–49.

4. Robert Lenzner, *The Great Getty* (New York: Crown, 1976), pp. 3–4.

5. Malkin, *National Debt,* p. 22.

6. Joel Covitz, "Myth and Money," in *Soul and Money,* pp. 65–66.

7. John Sedgwick, *Rich Kids* (New York: William Morrow, 1985), p. 329.

Chapter 6: Money to Burn

1. Dr. Thomas O'Guinn and Dr. Ronald Faber, "A Phenomenological Case Study of Compulsive Buying," *Journal of Consumer Research,* Volume 16, Issue 2, September 1989, pp. 147–57.

2. Ellis and Hunter, *Why Am I Always Broke?* p. 30.

3. Ernest Borneman, *The Psychoanalysis of Money* (New York: Urizen Books, 1976), pp. 41–42.

4. Stewart, *Den of Thieves*, p. 82.

5. David Margolick, "Till Debt Do Us Part," *New York Times Magazine*, December 15, 1991, pp. 46–48, 73.

6. Edmund Bergler, *Money and Emotional Conflicts* (International Univ. Press, 1959, 1970, 1985), p. 228.

7. Slater, *Wealth Addiction*, p. 40.

8. Betsy Morris, "Big Spenders," *Wall Street Journal*, July 30, 1987.

9. Bergler, *Money and Emotional Conflicts*, p. 229.

10. Ellis and Hunter, *Why Am I Always Broke?* pp. 47, 62.

11. George S. Clason, *The Richest Man in Babylon* (New York: Hawthorn, 1955), p. 41.

12. Lewis C. Henry, ed., *5,000 Quotations* (Garden City, NY: Doubleday, 1945), p. 301.

13. Rousseau, in George Seldes, ed., *The Great Thoughts* (New York: Ballantine, 1985), p. 358.

Chapter 7: Beyond Their Means

1. Malkin, *National Debt*, p. 49; *Conquer Your Debt*, p. xix.

2. Hom and Claflin, *Smart, Successful and Broke*, p. 5.

3. "When You're Too Far in Debt," *Reader's Digest*, September 1987, p. 50.

4. *New York Times*, December 15, 1991; Arlene Modica Matthews, *Your Money, Your Self* (New York: Fireside, 1993), p. 123.

5. Jason DeParle, "Poor Find Going Broke Is Too Costly," *New York Times*, December 11, 1991.

6. Clifford J. Levy, "Persuading People to Pay Their Bills During Hard Times," *New York Times*, December 15, 1991.

7. Mundis, *How to Get Out of Debt*, p. 21.

8. Michael Quint, "Banks Uneasy at Focus on Credit Cards," *New York Times*, November 19, 1991.

9. Peter Pae, "Credit Junkies," *Wall Street Journal*, December 26, 1991.

10. "Facts out of Context," *In Context*, Summer 1990, p. 5.

11. *Banker's Secret Bulletin*, Box 78, Elizaville, New York 12523.

12. Elements of this anecdotal composite originally appeared in Arnold Washton and Donna Boundy, *Willpower's Not Enough* (New York: HarperCollins, 1989), pp. 112–13.

13. Charles Dickens, *David Copperfield* (New York: Heritage Press, 1937), p. 157.

14. Mundis, *How to Get Out of Debt*, pp. 26–27.

15. Ray Hodgson and Peter Miller, *Self-Watching* (New York: Facts on File, 1982), p. 207.

16. Mundis, *How to Get Out of Debt*, p. 144.
17. Mundis, *How to Get Out of Debt*, p. 88.
18. Mundis, *How to Get Out of Debt*, pp. 88–89.
19. Mundis, *How to Get Out of Debt*, p. 79.
20. Justice Oliver Wendell Holmes, in Eliot Janeway, *Musings on Money* (New York: David McKay, 1976), p. 45.
21. Paul Hwoschinsky, *True Wealth* (Berkeley, CA: Ten Speed Press, 1992), pp. xii, 2.

Chapter 8: Love at Any Cost

1. N. R. Kleinfeld, "Living Poolside, and Wanting More," *New York Times*, June 16, 1992.
2. Packard, *Ultra Rich*, p. 310.
3. Bergler, *Money and Emotional Conflicts*, pp. 102, 105.
4. Mundis, *How to Get Out of Debt*, pp. 53–54.
5. Lewis Hyde, *The Gift* (New York: Vintage Books, 1983), pp. 151–52.
6. Sanaya Roman and Duane Packer, *Creating Money* (Tiburon, CA: H. J. Kramer, 1988), p. 215.
7. Roman and Packer, *Creating Money*, p. 210.
8. Jones-Lee, *Women and Money*, p. 46.

Chapter 9: Fear of Spending

1. Borneman, "Introduction," *Psychoanalysis of Money*, p. 37; Bergler, *Money and Emotional Conflicts*, p. 4.
2. Goldberg and Lewis, *Money Madness*, p. 88.
3. Lenzner, *Great Getty*, p. 3.
4. Annette Lieberman and Vicki Lindner, *Unbalanced Accounts* (New York: Viking Penguin, 1988), p. 178.
5. Goldberg and Lewis, *Money Madness*, p. 39.
6. Stephen Fay, *Beyond Greed* (New York: Viking, 1982), pp. 1–2.
7. Lieberman and Lindner, *Unbalanced Accounts*, p. 188.
8. Bergler, *Money and Emotional Conflicts*, p. 238.
9. Hyde, *Gift*, p. 23.
10. Ellis and Hunter, *Why Am I Always Broke?* pp. 34–36.
11. Hyde, *Gift*, pp. 8, 22.
12. Philip Zaleski, "The Test of Giving," *Parabola*, Spring 1991, p. 18.
13. Hyde, *Gift*, pp. 3–5.

Chapter 10: Living on the Edge

1. Goethe, in Bergler, *Money and Emotional Conflicts*, p. 47.
2. Sri Aurobindo, *The Mother* (Pondicherry, India: Sri Aurobindo Ashram, 1974), p. 15.

3. Shakti Gawain, *Creative Visualization* (Mill Valley, CA: Whatever Publishing, 1983).

Chapter 11: When You Can't Get Enough

1. Trump, *Surviving at the Top,* p. 6.
2. Smith, *Roaring 80's,* p. 209.
3. Stewart, *Den of Thieves,* p. 120.
4. Jay B. Rohrlich, "Wall Street's Money Junkies," *New York Times,* May 7, 1987.
5. Slater, *Wealth Addiction,* p. 23.
6. Stewart, *Den of Thieves,* p. 272.
7. Stewart, *Den of Thieves,* p. 208.
8. Bergler, *Money and Emotional Conflicts,* p. 43.
9. Bergler, *Money and Emotional Conflicts,* p. 105.
10. Bergler, *Money and Emotional Conflicts,* p. 109.
11. Michael Phillips, in Smith, *Roaring 80's,* p. 263.
12. Lapham, in Packard, *Ultra Rich,* p. 315.

Chapter 12: If You Love a Money Addict

1. Some of the principles here are based partly on ideas put forth in Washton and Boundy's *Willpower's Not Enough,* chapter 8, which itself drew inspiration from Arnold Washton's *Cocaine Addiction: Treatment, Recovery and Relapse Prevention,* chapter 10 (New York: W. W. Norton, 1989).

Chapter 13: Making Peace with Money

1. Parts of this section on admitting powerlessness appeared in a similar form in Washton and Boundy's *Willpower's Not Enough.*
2. *Twelve Steps and Twelve Traditions* (New York, Alcoholics Anonymous World Services, 1952).
3. Sri Aurobindo, *The Mother,* p. 16.
4. Lao-tzu, *Tao-te Ching,* translated by Gia-Fu Feng and Jane English (New York: Vintage, 1972), No. 33.
5. Durning, *State of the World 1991,* p. 158.
6. Schumacher, *Small Is Beautiful,* p. 81.

BIBLIOGRAPHY

Adams, Walter, and James Brock. *Dangerous Pursuits*. New York: Pantheon, 1989.

Berg, Adriane G. *How to Stop Fighting About Money and Make Some*. New York: Avon, 1988.

Bergler, Edmund. *Money and Emotional Conflicts*. Garden City, NY: Doubleday, 1951.

Blumstein, Philip, and Pepper Schwartz. *American Couples: Money, Work, Sex*. New York: William Morrow, 1983.

Borneman, Ernest. *The Psychoanalysis of Money*. New York: Urizen Books, 1976.

Chesler, Phyllis, and Emily Jane Goodman. *Women, Money and Power*. New York: Bantam, 1976.

Clason, George S. *The Richest Man in Babylon*. New York: Hawthorn, 1955.

Cribb, Joe. *Money*. New York: Alfred A. Knopf, 1990.

Desmonde, William H. *Magic, Myth and Money*. New York: Free Press of Glencoe, 1962.

Dickens, Charles. *David Copperfield*. New York: Heritage Press, 1937.

Dostoyevsky, Fyodor. *The Gambler*. New York: Penguin, 1966.

Einzig, Paul. *Primitive Money*. New York: Pergamon, 1966.

Eliade, Mircea, ed. *The Encyclopedia of Religion*. Vol. 10. New York: Macmillan, 1987.

Ellis, Albert, and Patricia A. Hunter. *Why Am I Always Broke?* Secaucus, NJ: Carol Publishing Group, 1991.

Fay, Stephen. *Beyond Greed*. New York: Viking, 1982.

Felton-Collins, Victoria, with Suzanne Blair Brown. *Couples and Money*. New York: Bantam, 1990.

Fenichel, Hanna, and David Rapaport. *The Collected Papers of Otto Fenichel*. New York: W. W. Norton, 1953.

Freedman, Jonathan L. *Happy People*. New York: Harcourt Brace Jovanovich, 1978.

Galbraith, John Kenneth. *The Affluent Society*. Boston: Houghton Mifflin, 1958.

———. *Money: Whence It Came, Where It Went*. Boston: Houghton Mifflin, 1975.

———. *The Culture of Contentment*. Boston: Houghton Mifflin, 1992.

Gawain, Shakti. *Creative Visualization*. Mill Valley, CA: Whatever Publishing, 1983.

———. *Living in the Light*. Mill Valley, CA: Whatever Publishing, 1986.

Goldberg, Herb, and Robert T. Lewis. *Money Madness*. New York: William Morrow, 1978.

Hansberry, Lorraine. *A Raisin in the Sun*. New York: Random House, 1958.

Henderson, Hazel. *Creating Alternative Futures*. New York: Berkeley Windhover, 1978.

Hom, Tony, and Edward Claflin. *Smart, Successful and Broke*. New York: Dell, 1991.

Hwoschinsky, Paul. *True Wealth*. Berkeley, CA: Ten Speed Press, 1990.

Hyde, Lewis. *The Gift*. New York: Vintage Books, 1983.

Janeway, Eliot. *Musings on Money*. New York: David McKay, 1976.

Johnson, Edgar. *Charles Dickens*. New York: Simon & Schuster, 1952.

Jones-Lee, Anita. *Women and Money*. Hauppauge, NY: Barron's, 1991.

Krugman, Paul. *The Age of Diminished Expectations*. Cambridge, MA: MIT Press, 1990.

Lapham, Lewis H. *Money and Class in America*. New York: Weidenfeld & Nicolson, 1988.

Laut, Phil. *Money Is My Friend*. Cincinnati, OH: Trinity, 1978.

Leacock, Stephen. *Charles Dickens*. New York: Doubleday, 1933.

Lenzner, Robert. *The Great Getty*. New York: Crown, 1976.

Levine, Dennis B. *Inside Out*. New York: Putnam, 1991.

Lewis, Michael. *Liar's Poker*. New York: Norton, 1989.

Lieberman, Annette, and Vicki Lindner. *Unbalanced Accounts*. New York: Viking Penguin, 1988.

Lockhart, Russell, James Hillman, et al. *Soul and Money*. Dallas, TX: Spring Publications, 1986.

Malabre, Alfred L., Jr. *Beyond Our Means*. New York: Random, 1987.

———. *Within Our Means*. New York: Random, 1991.

Malkin, Lawrence. *The National Debt*. New York: Holt, 1987.

Martz, Larry. *Ministry of Greed*. New York: Newsweek, 1988.

Mattera, Philip. *Prosperity Lost*. New York: Addison-Wesley, 1990.

Matthews, Arlene Modica. *Your Money, Your Self*. New York: Fireside, 1993.

May, Elaine Tyler. *Homeward Bound*. New York: Basic Books, 1988.

Miller, Arthur. *Death of a Salesman*. Scranton, PA: Haddon Craftsmen, 1949.

Mills, Nicolaus, ed. *Culture in an Age of Money*. Chicago: Elephant, 1990.

Molière. "The Miser," in *Comedies of Molière*. New York: The Book League of America, 1946.

Moore, Thomas. *Care of the Soul*. New York: HarperCollins, 1992.

Mundis, Jerrold. *How to Get Out of Debt, Stay Out of Debt and Live Prosperously*. New York: Bantam, 1988.

Needleman, Jacob. *Money and the Meaning of Life*. New York: Doubleday, 1991.

Packard, Vance. *The Ultra Rich*. Boston: Little, Brown, 1989.

Phillips, Kevin. *The Politics of Rich and Poor*. New York: HarperCollins, 1990.

Phillips, Michael, and Salli Rasberry. *The Seven Laws of Money*. Menlo Park, CA: Word Wheel and Random House, 1974.

Roman, Sanaya, and Duane Packer. *Creating Money*. Tiburon, CA: H. J. Kramer, 1988.

Ross, Ruth. *Prospering Woman*. New York: Bantam, 1985.

Schor, Juliet B. *The Overworked American*. New York: Basic Books, 1991.

Schumacher, E. F. *Small Is Beautiful*. New York: Viking Penguin, 1973.

Sedgwick, John. *Rich Kids*. New York: William Morrow, 1985.

Shames, Laurence. *The Hunger for More*. New York: Times Books, 1989.

Shapiro, Max. *The Penniless Billionaires*. New York: Times Books, 1980.

Slater, Philip. *Wealth Addiction*. New York: E. P. Dutton, 1980.

Smith, Adam. *The Money Game*. New York: Vintage, 1976.

———. *The Roaring '80s*. New York: Penguin, 1988.

Spooner, John D. *Sex and Money*. Boston: Houghton Mifflin, 1985.

Stewart, James B. *Den of Thieves*. New York: Simon & Schuster, 1991.

Tocqueville, Alexis de. *Democracy in America*. New York: Collier & Son, 1900.

Trump, Donald J. *The Art of the Deal*. New York: Random House, 1987.

———. *Surviving at the Top*. New York: Random House, 1990.

Wachtel, Paul L. *The Poverty of Affluence*. Santa Cruz, CA: New Society Publishers, 1989.

Washton, Arnold, and Donna Boundy. *Willpower's Not Enough*. New York: HarperCollins, 1989.

West, Mae. *Goodness Had Nothing to Do with It*. Englewood Cliffs, NJ: Prentice Hall, 1959.

Wolfe, Tom. *Bonfire of the Vanities*. New York: Farrar, Straus, Giroux, 1987.

ABOUT THE AUTHOR

Donna Boundy is also coauthor of *Willpower's Not Enough,* a book about recovering from multiple addictions (New York: HarperCollins, 1989). She received her M.S.W. from Hunter College and worked as a counselor and administrator in addiction treatment before going on to become a writer and video producer specializing in recovery topics. She may be reached at P.O. Box 1208, Woodstock, New York 12498.